Conflict Resolution an Needs

This edited volume examines Basic Human Needs theory and interactive problem solving, looking at recent developments in thinking about both and how these might affect peacebuilding in contemporary conflicts of the twenty-first century.

The era in the immediate aftermath of World War II was, paradoxically, a time of great optimism in parts of academia. There was, especially in the United States and much of Europe, a widespread belief in the social sciences that systematic scholarly analysis would enable humanity to understand and do something about the most complex of social processes, and thus about solving persistent human problems: unemployment, delinquency, racism, under-development, and even issues of conflict, war and peace.

This book examines the evolution of Basic Human Needs theory and is divided into two key parts: Basic Human Needs in Theory and Basic Human Needs in Practice. Exploring this theory through a wide range of different lenses, including gender, ethics and power, the volume brings together some of the leading scholars in the field of peace and conflict studies and draws upon research both past and present to forecast where the movement is headed in the future.

This book will be of much interest to students of peace and conflict studies, conflict resolution, psychology, security studies and IR.

Kevin Avruch is the Henry Hart Rice Professor of Conflict Resolution and Professor of Anthropology at the School for Conflict Analysis and Resolution, and Senior Fellow and faculty in the Peace Operations Policy Program, School of Public Policy, at George Mason University. He is author or editor of six books, including *Context and Pretext in Conflict Resolution: Culture, Identity, Power and Practice* (2012), *Culture and Conflict Resolution* (1998) and *Information Campaigns for Peace Operations* (2000).

Christopher Mitchell is currently Emeritus Professor of Conflict Research at George Mason University, Virginia, where he was Director of the Institute for Conflict Analysis and Resolution between 1991 and 1994. Most recently he has published *Gestures of Conciliation* (2000), *A Handbook of Conflict Resolution* (1995) and (with Landon Hancock) *Zones of Peace* (2007).

Routledge Studies in Peace and Conflict Resolution

Series Editors: Tom Woodhouse and Oliver Ramsbotham
University of Bradford

Conflict Resolution and Human Needs

Linking theory and practice

Edited by Kevin Avruch and Christopher Mitchell

Routledge
Taylor & Francis Group

LONDON AND NEW YORK

First published 2013
by Routledge
2 Park Square, Milton Park, Abingdon, Oxfordshire OX14 4RN

Simultaneously published in the USA and Canada
by Routledge
711 Third Avenue, New York, NY 10017

First issued in paperback 2014

Routledge is an imprint of the Taylor & Francis Group, an informa business

British Library Cataloguing in Publication Data
A catalogue record for this book is available from the British Library

Library of Congress Cataloging in Publication Data
Conflict resolution and human needs : linking theory and practice /
edited by Kevin Avruch and Christopher Mitchell
  pages cm. – (Routledge studies in peace and conflict resolution)
  1. Conflict management. 2. Basic needs. I. Avruch, Kevin.
  II. Mitchell, C. R. (Christopher Roger), 1934–
  HM1126.C653 2013
  303.6'9–dc23
                                                         2012042466

ISBN 978-0-415-62990-4 (hbk)
ISBN 978-1-138-84760-6 (pbk)
ISBN 978-0-203-09821-9 (ebk)

Typeset in Baskerville
by Wearset Ltd, Boldon, Tyne and Wear

To John W. Burton, Leonard W. Doob and Herbert C. Kelman, pioneers of interactive problem solving and conflict resolution

Contents

Illustrations

Figures

Tables

Contributors

Mohammed Abu-Nimer is a Full Professor at American University's School of International Service in International Peace and Conflict Resolution in Washington, D.C. He is the Director of the Peacebuilding and Development Institute. Dr. Abu-Nimer is also the Founder and Director of the Salam: Peacebuilding and Justice Institute, and the co-founder and co-editor of the Journal of Peacebuilding and Development. He has written, edited and co-authored many books including *Peace-Building By, Between and Beyond Muslims and Evangelical Christians* (2010), *Reconciliation, Coexistence, and Justice: Theory and Practice* (2001), *Unity in Diversity: Interfaith Dialogue in the Middle East* (2007) and *Peacebuilding and Nonviolence in Islam* (2003).

Kevin Avruch is the Henry Hart Rice Professor of Conflict Resolution and Professor of Anthropology at the School for Conflict Analysis and Resolution, and Senior Fellow and faculty in the Peace Operations Policy Program, School of Public Policy, at George Mason University, and Affiliate Professor of Mediterranean Academy of Diplomatic Studies, University of Malta. He is the author of numerous articles and essays on culture and conflict analysis and resolution, theorizing power in asymmetric conflicts, negotiation, political violence and ethnonationalism, and the author or editor of six books, including *Context and Pretext in Conflict Resolution: Culture, Identity, Power and Practice* (2012), *Culture and Conflict Resolution* (1998) and *Information Campaigns for Peace Operations* (2000). He has lectured widely in the United States and abroad. He was the Joan B. Kroc Peace Scholar at the University of San Diego in 2009, and a Senior Fellow in the Jennings Randolph Program for International Peace at the United States Institute of Peace (1996–1997). In 2011 he was a Fulbright Specialist at the Banaras Hindu University, Varanasi, India.

E. Franklin Dukes is a mediator, teacher and researcher who directs the

He has worked at local, state and federal levels on projects involving environment and land use, community development, education and health. His current work includes consensus building in the Appalachian Coalfields, and he leads an initiative to address the legacy of harm from slavery and segregation at the University of Virginia. He is co-founder and core faculty of the Virginia Natural Resources Leadership Institute. He initiated the "Community-Based Collaboratives Research Consortium" which seeks to assess and understand local collaborative efforts involving natural resources and community development, resulting in the publication of *Community-Based Collaboration: Bridging Socio-Ecological Research and Practice* (2011) and *Collaboration: A Guide for Environmental Advocates* (2001). His book *Resolving Public Conflict: Transforming Community and Governance* (1996) describes how public conflict resolution procedures can assist in vitalizing democracy. He is co-author of *Reaching for Higher Ground* (2000), which describes how diverse groups and communities can create expectations for addressing conflict with integrity, vision and creativity. He is co-author and co-editor for two of the four books that John Burton produced for the St. Martin's Press Conflict series. With Susan Hirsch he is co-author of *Divergent Views of Mining in Appalachia: Reconciling Stakeholders in Environmental Conflict* (forthcoming).

Ronald J. Fisher is Professor of International Relations and Director of the International Peace and Conflict Resolution Program in the School of International Service at American University in Washington, D.C. His primary interest focuses on interactive conflict resolution, which involves informal third-party interventions in protracted and violent ethno-political conflict; relevant publications include *Interactive Conflict Resolution* (1997) and *Paving the Way: Contributions of Interactive Conflict Resolution to Peacemaking* (2005), as well as numerous articles in interdisciplinary journals in the field of peace and conflict resolution. He holds a B.A. (Hon.) and M.A. in Psychology from the University of Saskatchewan, Canada, and a Ph.D. in Social Psychology from the University of Michigan.

Jacquie L. Greiff is the Executive Director of the Center for Peacemaking Practice at Mason's School for Conflict Analysis and Resolution (S-CAR). She received her M.S. from S-CAR and has many years of practical experience working on community building projects in central Bosnia-Herzegovina and Ethiopia. She is the Director of f-r-e-e, e.V. (friendship-respect-education-engagement), an NGO of which she is the co-founder (www.f-r-e-e.eu). Her main research interests are focused on post-conflict reconstruction and development.

Louis Kriesberg is Professor Emeritus of Sociology, Maxwell Professor Emeritus of Social Conflict Studies and founding director of the Program on the Analysis and Resolution of Conflicts (1986–1994), all at Syracuse University. In addition to over 150 book chapters and articles, his published books include *Conflict Transformation and Peacebuild-*

ing: Moving from Violence to Sustainable Peace (co-editor, 2009), *Constructive Conflicts* (1998, 2003, 2007), *International Conflict Resolution* (1992), *Timing the De-Escalation of International Conflicts* (co-editor, 1991), *Intractable Conflicts and Their Transformation* (co-editor, 1989), *Social Conflicts* (1973, 1982), *Social Processes in International Relations* (editor, 1968) and *Research in Social Movements, Conflicts and Change* (editor, Vols. 1–14, 1978–1992). The fourth edition of *Constructive Conflicts* (with Bruce Dayton) appeared in 2012. His current research interests are related to American foreign policy, the Middle East and developments in the field of constructive conflict.

Christopher Mitchell was born and educated in London. He has held academic positions at University College, London, the London School of Economics and the University of Southampton. He was appointed Lecturer in the Department of Systems Science at the City University in 1973 and became Professor of International Relations there in 1983. He joined the academic exodus from Britain in the mid-1980s and is currently Emeritus Professor of Conflict Research at George Mason University, Virginia, where he was Director of the Institute for Conflict Analysis and Resolution between 1991 and 1994. He continues to work on practical and theoretical aspects of peacemaking processes and has recently published articles on the theory of entrapment, on ending asymmetric conflicts and on a multi-role model of mediation. His major works are *The Structure of International Conflict* (1981), *Peacemaking and the Consultants' Role* (1981) and (with Keith Webb) *New Approaches to International Mediation* (1988). Most recently he has published *Gestures of Conciliation* (2000), *A Handbook of Conflict Resolution* (1995) and (with Landon Hancock) *Zones of Peace* (2007) and *Local Peacebuilding and National Peace* (2012).

Susan Allen Nan is a scholar-practitioner trained at George Mason University and now serves at the same institution as Director of the Center for Peacemaking Practice and as Associate Professor of Conflict Analysis and Resolution. Her first engagement in a Burtonian-inspired problem-solving workshop was an Abkhaz-Georgian workshop in 1997. She then completed a dissertation on coordination and complementarity of multiple efforts in the peace processes focused on the conflicts over Abkhazia, South Ossetia and Transdniestria. Her current work focuses on Georgian–South Ossetian peacemaking.

Jamie Price received his Ph.D. from the Divinity School of the University of Chicago. He is the Executive Director of the Sargent Shriver Peace Institute, Research Professor and Founding Director of the Insight Conflict Resolution Program in the School for Conflict Analysis and Resolution at George Mason University, and Affiliate Professor in the Mediterranean Academy of Diplomatic Studies at the University of Malta. His most recent work addresses the problem of developing a foundational methodology in conflict resolution, peacebuilding and leadership for social change, and his touchstone in this effort is the example and achievement of Sargent Shriver. In this connection, he writes articles and essays for a range of scholarly and popular publications, and leads the development and implementation of a number of practical initiatives, including a multi-city project with police departments and community groups to explain and mitigate problems of retaliatory violence in local communities; a joint effort with an international development organization to evaluate the peacebuilding impact of development projects in post-conflict environments; and a cooperative venture with a university to develop a professional graduate studies program in leadership for social change.

Dennis J.D. Sandole is Professor of Conflict Resolution and International Relations at the School for Conflict Analysis and Resolution at George Mason University. A founding member of S-CAR, Sandole received his Ph.D. in politics in 1979 at the University of Strathclyde, Glasgow, UK. He has been a William C. Foster Fellow as Visiting Scholar with the US Arms Control and Disarmament Agency (ACDA), where he worked on the Conventional Armed Forces in Europe (CFE) Negotiations and Negotiations on Confidence- and Security-Building Measures (CSBMs) at the State Department and served on the US Delegation to the CSBMs Negotiations in Vienna, Austria. He has completed Fulbright Scholarships at the Organization for Security and Cooperation in Europe (OSCE), in Vienna, Austria; the Diplomatic Academy in Vienna, Austria; and the MA Program in Conflict Analysis and Resolution at Sabanci University in Istanbul, Turkey. His publications include *Conflict Management and Problem Solving: Interpersonal to International Applications* (co-edited with Ingrid Sandole-Staroste, 1987), *Conflict Resolution Theory and Practice: Integration and Application* (co-edited with Hugo van der Merwe, 1993), *Capturing the Complexity of Conflict: Dealing with Violent Ethnic Conflicts of the Post-War Era* (1999), *Peace and Security in the Postmodern World: The OSCE and Conflict Resolution* (2007), *Handbook of Conflict Analysis and Resolution* (co-edited with Sean Byrne, Ingrid Sandole-Staroste and Jessica Senehi, 2009) and *Peacebuilding: Preventing Violent Conflict in a Complex World* (2010).

Ingrid Sandole-Staroste teaches in the Department of Sociology and Anthropology, and the Women's and Gender Studies Program at George Mason University. She received her Ph.D. from the University of Virginia in Charlottesville, Virginia. She was a Visiting Research Fellow at the International Gender Studies Centre (IGS), in the Department of International Development, Queen Elizabeth House, University of Oxford, UK. Her research reflects an integrative approach connecting the fields of sociology, women's studies, and conflict analysis and resolution, focusing on transitioning societies, including regions of the former Soviet Union. In Central Asia, for example, she has explored the gendered aspects of women's human rights and leadership, development and building sustainable peace. Her publications include *Handbook of Conflict Analysis and Resolution,* co-edited with Dennis J.D. Sandole, Sean Byrne and Jessica Senehi (2009), *Women in Transition: Between Socialism and Capitalism* (2002), *Conflict Management and Problem Solving: Interpersonal to International Applications,* co-edited with Dennis J.D. Sandole (1987), "Women's Social Rights under Communism and Capitalism" in *New Beginning* (Armenia's first feminist journal) (2001) and "Overlapping Radicalisms: Convergence and Divergence between Feminist and Human Needs Theories in Conflict Resolution" in *Conflict and Gender,* co-edited by Anita Taylor and Judi Beinstein Miller (2004).

Solon Simmons is Associate Professor of Conflict Analysis and Resolution and specializes in American politics. He is a sociologist with a Ph.D. from the University of Wisconsin and an undergraduate degree in the History and Philosophy of Science from the University of Chicago. He is the author of *The Eclipse of Equality: Arguing America on Meet the Press* (2013) with Stanford University Press, which explores the nature of dysfunction in American politics, linking it with the collapse of the once dominant conception of social justice that placed economic equality at its center. He has written widely on American political culture and the intellectual roots of escalated political conflict and his work and ideas have been featured in prominent sites in the public sphere, including *The New York Times, The Washington Post, Salon.com, Al Jazeera, Meet the Press, Good Morning America* and many others.

Tarja Väyrynen has theorized conflict and conflict resolution (e.g. *Culture and International Conflict Resolution* (2001) and "A Shared Understanding: Gadamer and International Conflict Resolution," *Journal of Peace Research* (2005)). Her most recent work deals with war, peacebuilding, gender, corporeality, collective trauma and post-conflict silences. She is Academy Research Fellow in the School for Social Sciences and Humanities and the Director of Research Group on Corporeality, Politics and Migration (COMPORE), University of Tampere, Finland. She worked as the Director and Professor in Tampere Peace Research Institute for eight years before taking up the Academy post in 2008.

Acknowledgments

This volume grew out of a conference on the role – past, present and future – of Basic Human Needs in conflict resolution theory and practice, held at the research and retreat center Point of View, on Belmont Bay in Lorton, Virginia. There was a time, coincident with John W. Burton's tenure at the Institute (now School) for Conflict Analysis and Resolution (roughly 1987–1991), when this theory could be said to represent the collective "identity" of many faculty and students at the school – so long as one understood that several of them "identified" mainly in opposition! Since then the collective identity of faculty, students (and now many alumni) has diffused considerably and it is the case that no single "doctrine" or even theoretical orientation can adequately or accurately represent us: as perhaps one can say about the identity of conflict resolution and peace and conflict studies more generally. On the whole this is probably a good thing.

Yet the idea of Basic Human Needs, always thoroughly critiqued and critiqueable, seems somehow protean, and thus always worth revisiting. In addition to the contributors to this volume we would like to acknowledge earlier contributions to our discussions from Johannes (Jannie) Botes and David Dunn. In addition to John Burton (who died in June 2010 and in some ways turned our thoughts back to Basic Human Needs) we acknowledge the powerful presence of two other pioneers in our field connected, in their own way, with the practice Burton introduced, Leonard Doob and Herbert Kelman.

We thank the Dean of the School for Conflict Analysis and Resolution, Professor Andrea Bartoli, for his unfailing support of the range of activities carried out at Point of View, including research, training, teaching and, crucially, practice. Thanks go to the generous donors who gifted to our School this beautiful site on Belmont Bay, the late Edwin and Helen Lynch, and to the Lynch family for their continued support.

Finally, this volume represents our belief that research, theory and practice in conflict resolution and peacebuilding must all each engage in mutual and shared conversation with the others, if our field is to advance in ways that are effective, humane and ethical.

Kevin Avruch and Christopher Mitchell
Arlington, Virginia

Introduction

Basic Human Needs in theory and practice

Kevin Avruch and Christopher Mitchell

The era in the immediate aftermath of World War II was, paradoxically, a time of great optimism in parts of academia. There was, especially in the United States and much of Europe, a widespread belief in the social sciences – during the 1950s and the early 1960s undergoing what was then termed "the behavioral revolution" – that systematic scholarly analysis would enable humanity to understand and do something about the most complex of social processes and thus about solving persistent human problems – unemployment, delinquency, racism, under-development, and even about issues of conflict, war and peace. In this last field, one aspect of this optimism was the growing belief in the power of measurement and quanti- fication, a conviction which grew with the ever increasing capacity to store and analyze large amounts of "hard" data – a trend which had started in the 1940s with Quincy Wright's pioneering studies of war carried out at the Uni- versity of Chicago and subsequently carried on by David Singer at the Uni- versity of Michigan and by Rudolph Rummel at the University of Hawaii.

The birth of interactive problem solving

Another aspect of this optimism was the increased willingness of social sci- entists to be ready to apply the new knowledge directly to solving social problems, initially by accepting that such initiatives needed to be multi- disciplinary – in recognition of the undoubted fact that many of the crucial issues confronting the world in the 1950s and 1960s were scientific, technical, political, economic, psychological, cultural and ethical. Among those seeking to capitalize on this willingness to leave the ivory tower, probably encouraged by the involvement of scholars and academics in policy-making during World War II – were a number of pioneering scholar-practitioners who tentatively began to explore the possibility of applying new knowledge gained from the library and the laboratory to the real world of social, industrial and international conflict in the search for a more peaceful world.

Among this pioneering generation were academics from a variety of disciplines and backgrounds. To a large degree, such innovators were encouraged by the example of scholars from the field of industrial relations and organizational behavior that had begun to introduce their ideas into the real world of industrial and intra-organizational conflict as early as the 1930s and were making an innovative contribution to the creation of relative industrial peace by the 1950s. Many of the ideas went back in time even further – some to the work of individuals such as Mary Parker Follett (1942), who had written about the concept of "mutual gains" from an "integrative" approach to industrial bargaining, and to Kurt Lewin (1948) with his insistence upon the need for "practical theorists." By the late 1950s this marriage between academic theorists, drawing ideas from a number of the social sciences, and practical mediators, conciliators or facilitators had taken hold and become accepted as one road to peaceful relations within and between organizations. Led by such figures as Robert Blake and Jane Mouton (1963), Richard Walton and Robert McKersie (1965), by the 1960s serious works on the new approach were being published by academic presses. If in the world of industrial strife, why not in the world of international or social conflict? In the more purely academic world, meanwhile, the group centered at the University of Michigan launched the *Journal of Conflict Resolution* in 1957.

A period of experiment

Many of the first attempts to introduce new ideas from what had briefly become known as "the behavioral sciences" directly into the process of conflict resolution at an international level were viewed by their innovators as a form of experiment – as a "try-out" of both the underlying ideas themselves and of the process for introducing them into decision-making circles. One of the earliest of these experiments took place in late 1965, when the former Australian diplomat, John Burton, then teaching at University College in London, was challenged to apply some of the new "behavioral" ideas to an ongoing conflict in "the real world." Burton chose to revisit his old region of Southeast Asia and to become engaged in the conflict between Indonesia and Malaysia over the latter's incorporation of large areas of Borneo into its national territory. Accounts of the series of meetings (Mitchell 2005; see also Fisher 1997) reveal just how experimental this initiative actually was, but from the experience emerged the outlines of a facilitative process that made a significant contribution to the subsequent peace settlement and the beginnings of a new vocabulary, which included such terms as workshop, facilitation and problem solving – although Burton (1969) initially employed the term "controlled communication" to label the emerging process. Shortly after Burton's initiative, the Yale psychologist, Leonard Doob, successfully launched what he and his colleague William Folz described as "the Wild Idea" and put together the Fermeda Workshop in Italy, hosting representatives of the rival communities in conflict in the region of the Horn of Africa – Ethiopian,

Kenyan and Somali – for week-long discussions with the aim of altering misleading images and stereotypes and of improving relationships in that explosive region (Doob 1970). This sense of experimentation clearly lasted for a long time, even into the 1980s when the technique was becoming familiar and accepted. Carl Rogers, the counseling psychologist famous for his client-centered approach to therapy and his learning-person-centered approach to learning, conducted a meeting of over 50 participants from Central American countries at the "Rust Workshop" in Austria. Asked about his motives for venturing into the politics of this region, Rogers is said to have replied that he and his colleagues "wanted to demonstrate his technique of how people can learn more about themselves and their feelings" (Rogers 1986: 23).

However strong the feeling of cautious experimentation might have been for such pioneering initiatives and their organizers, the practice of conducting problem-solving workshops – small-group, facilitated discussions in an isolated setting involving participants from key levels of conflicting parties – took off very rapidly in the 1970s and 1980s. Leonard Doob launched workshop series on Cyprus and on Northern Ireland, while Burton undertook similar initiatives in Northern Ireland involving trade unionists, and also planned initiatives between Egypt and Israel and between India and Pakistan over the Kashmir question – both of which were frustrated by the outbreak of brief but violent wars which in themselves resolved very little. In the immediate aftermath of another brief war in the South Atlantic, he organized in cooperation with Edward Azar of the University of Maryland a series of workshops involving participants from Argentina and Britain, which is discussed further in one of the following chapters. Burton's colleagues, Herbert Kelman and Ronald Fisher, took up where Burton had shown the way and conducted long-term workshop series involving Israelis and Palestinians and the Greek and Turkish communities on Cyprus respectively. Others used the basic approach in the civil wars in Sri Lanka, in the conflict over apartheid within South Africa, in the struggle between the Sandanista Government and the "contras" in Nicaragua, and in some of the conflicts in the Baltic Republics and in the countries of the Caucasus following the break-up of the Soviet Union. All of these "experiments" have provided lessons that need to be studied and systematized about the technique of small-group problem solving and its likely impact on complex and deep-rooted conflict. Many have emphasized the need for some fundamental theory or theories that might need to be tested in such real world "experiments."

The need for a basic theory

Given the disparate backgrounds of many of these early scholar-practitioners who tentatively, and in some cases temporarily, moved from academia to the world of intractable conflict, it is hardly surprising that the theoretical bases for their activities tended to be eclectic and pragmatic. Many ideas that were applied were drawn from social psychology (misperception, cognitive dissonance, dehumanization, commitment theory), from group dynamics (role theory, groupthink), from industrial relations (concession-convergence bargaining, intra-group cohesion) or from international relations (escalation spirals, non-violent direct action). In the early experiments, it was enough to be able to say that the processes "worked" in the sense that participants changed in some positive way and came up with new ideas about possible options for the future. But why was this the case, and what was the real theoretical basis for arguing that intractable conflicts could ever be resolved by these – or any other – methods, as opposed to compromised, bargained away or temporarily settled – at least until the next round? One line of thought that slowly developed in the 1970s arose from the revival of interest in the idea, originally developed by Abraham Maslow, that all human individuals possessed a number of "basic" needs and that the frustration of these needs would lead to conflictful behavior and even to organized (or disorganized) violence.

This book explores this particular "fundamental theory" proposed for our field, articulated most empathically by John Burton: the idea that a set of ontological and non-negotiable basic human needs (BHNs), when unfulfilled, suppressed, or otherwise disregarded by authorities or institutions, will turn out to be the drivers of deep-rooted and intractable social conflicts. Significantly, along with the theory came guiding principles (indeed, "rules") for conflict resolution practice. The chapters that follow critically examine where BHN theory stands today, more than three decades after Burton strove to establish it as the "fundamental theory" (Burton 1979). To what extent does it remains a fertile ground for theory-building and for conflict resolution practice? Can we discern other ways in which the notion has influenced the field as the field itself has grown and ramified? Individually, each chapter focuses on either the "theory" or "practice" dimension of BHNs, but always with an eye for how the one affects the other.

In the 1970s and 1980s, incorporating this BHN concept into an overall "problem-solving" approach to conflict resolution seemed to provide a strong theoretical basis for the position that the search for alternative satisfiers offered at least one way out of the various types of impasse that attended many protracted and intractable conflicts. The question then became one of identifying how adversaries could be brought even to consider and then to discuss alternatives which could fulfill the basic needs that underlay the surface interests and positions that gave rise to their conflict. The answer seemed to be at hand in the form of Track Two, or unofficial, informal processes, whether these took the form of role reversals, problem-solving workshops, dialogues or simple conversations.

Basic Human Needs

The idea that there exist core and universal *needs* whose fulfillment is a necessary condition of human life and development – of Basic Human Needs (BHNs) – possesses a compelling face validity, an appeal to common sense, that has made it enduring if not always irresistible. As to enduring, one can find the notion of needs (usually translated as "desires") posited by Aristotle in the *Nicomachean Ethics*. (Indeed, Price's Chapter 6 begins by painting BNH theory as used in conflict resolution as essentially Aristotelian in structure and intent.) Aristotle contrasts "natural desires," part of intrinsic and universal human nature, with "acquired desires," which individuals accrue as they live in particular societies, cultures or polities. This may well be the first distinction made between "needs" and "wants." (It certainly wasn't the last.) Aristotle confidently contends that the objects of natural desires are always good ("virtuous") for us, because, well, they are "natural." What we want, by contrast, may or may not be good for us. A life lived in the fulfillment of "wrong desires" may be bad for us and also dangerously unethical. While the focus here is on the individual, the idea (and its ethical predicates) is expanded to society at large in Aristotle's *Politics*, where the polis itself arose as the necessary way to fulfill basic human needs, and where the notion of *virtue*, transcending the particular individual, is now attached to the idea of rightful and rational *authority*. Combining the *Ethics* with the *Politics*, Aristotle asserts that fulfillment of basic human needs is not only necessary for *human* (individual) life, but for *social* life as well. Here, as in many other areas, he anticipates by millennia a key dimension of Human Needs theory as it was to be applied to conflict resolution, and even before this in theories (and practices) related to economic development in the 1970s. In fact, as discussed below and in several chapters in this book, the axis around which the theory of BHN turns – integrating "healthy" individual functioning with consonant social and political processes – defines its major claims to theoretical and practical significance.

Social psychological approaches

So much for BHNs' enduring philosophical genealogy. If, on the other hand, some version of "science" is required to legitimate the idea, one might find it as a dedicated entry for "Basic Human Needs" in the eighth edition of Mosby's *Medical Dictionary*, where they are defined (2009: 195) as follows: "The elements required for survival and normal mental and physical health, such as food, water, shelter, protection from environmental threats, and love." Much as one might have wished for Mosby's corresponding entry medically defining "love," this is not forthcoming. Here, too, perhaps common sense is assumed. But if we think, minimally, of "love" as referring to certain qualities of social relationships, of emotionally important and gratifying connections between individuals, then the medical usage has much in common with many others, which stress the same socio-emotional theme, often in fact using the very same word (for example, famously, Maslow).

Perhaps we should say, this usage has much in common with many, *many* others, since one of the characteristics of BHN theory, and one of the reasons why, at least for many (mainly positivist) social and behavioral scientists, it is an idea easily resisted, is that the theory has tended to spawn almost innumerable lists of needs, each list claimed by its proponent to be *the* definitive one. For positivists, the provenance of these needs often appears idiosyncratic to the proponent, and their validation or testability highly uncertain. (Avruch and Väyrynen in Chapters 2 and 5 respectively take this up in discussion of John Burton's usage of BHN; most of the other chapters simply "get past" the positivist's critique.) This is not true, of course, of the purely biological or physical needs that feature in most of these lists – thirst and hunger, whose satisfiers are water and food (as measured in calories or nutrients), or shelter – where what some call "tissue deficits" can be measured and their consequences predicted. But Mosby's medical dictionary aside, what constitutes a measure of tissue (or other) deficits caused by the absence of love is less easily operationalized, and this reservation holds as well for such putative and often cited needs as belonging, self esteem or self-actualization.

Aristotle aside, it is Abraham Maslow's famous list of basic human needs, first published in a 1943 paper, that remains a touchstone for most BHN theorists. Usually portrayed as a pyramid, the five basic needs are posited to follow a developmental, stages of growth, sequence. They are: (1) Physiological needs; (2) Safety; (3) Love/belonging; (4) Esteem; (5) Self-actualization. Later, perhaps under the influence of Fromm or Victor Frankl, a sixth need, Self-Transcendence, was added to the sequence (Maslow 1943, 1954). Despite their wide recognition (several of the chapters in this book reference them), the social psychologists Pittman and Zeigler, in a recent review of BHN theory in contemporary social psychology, remark that, "It could be said, with only a bit of exaggeration, that Maslow's hierarchy of needs is a theory that everyone knows, and no one uses" (2007: 477). This is unfair, though not inaccurate so far as positivist experimentalists are concerned. In contrast, the theory has long resonated strongly in humanistic approaches to psychotherapy and, more pointedly, as a touchstone in teaching the social psychology of marketing, where the message is, "Have your product appear uniquely to satisfy the consumer's fundamental needs, and they will surely buy." In this transaction needs turn into wants and then (at least in "marketing for beginners") all needs/wants are reduced to *preferences*. This, of course, is the language of the Market, far from Mosby's *Medical*, and far, too, from the construal of needs for most theorists or practitioners in conflict resolution (and development: see below).

In their review of several social psychological theories that use the concept of BHN, Pittman and Zeigler distinguish among those that posit a single or core basic need from which others derive; those that posit many needs, operating either in a developmental sequence (per Maslow) or simultaneously arrayed and functionally differentiated but whose collective satisfaction is required; those that are focused mainly at the level of individual psychological functioning only; compared to those that situate the individual in a social environment and posit needs as both connecting the person to social groupings (as in social identity theory) and in serving to constitute the groups themselves. Clearly, the widely cited needs for belonging or relatedness (sometimes glossed as Attachment Theory or, in evolutionary terms, as the necessary social prerequisite for individual survival), are paramount here (Pittman and Zeigler 2007). When sociologists or anthropologists discuss basic human needs (rarely, as it happens) the focus is almost always beyond the level of the individual, on BHN connected to the functional "requirements" of the larger cultural or social systems (e.g. Thomas 1924; Malinowski 1944; Etzioni 1968; Sites 1973).

Compared to some BHN models, Maslow's is parsimonious. Henry Murray (1938) proposed 28 universal basic needs, both manifest and latent. Some of these needs, for example the "need for achievement," went on to generate a large literature in social psychological and – through the work of David McClelland (1961) – in modernization/development studies as well. (For more on the connection between needs and development, see below.) Significantly, examination of Murray's full list reveals the fact that many of them would be considered "negative," or at least as motivating less than obvious "prosocial" behavior. Some of these include needs for dominance, deference, aggression or abasement. A recent popular treatise on the "16 Human Needs" includes among the familiar positive ones (eating, physical activity and social contact) needs for power and vengeance (Reiss 2000). What is significant here is that much of the BHN literature either assumes that basic human needs are necessarily prosocial (their satisfaction necessarily a good or virtuous thing in Aristotle's sense) or ignores the possibility that the satisfaction of some needs by individuals (or groups) will entail some hurt or harm to others. Mitchell, in commenting on John Burton's use of BHN in his wider conflict theory (and practice), remarked long ago on the possibility that some needs might be "malign" (Mitchell 1990). If this is the case, then the entire "valence" of using BHN theory as proposed by Burton and others in conflict resolution would have to be reversed. Burton assumes that the mutual satisfaction of BHN by all the parties would result in positive-sum, "win–win" outcomes. But if some BHN are malign, a negative-sum, win–lose outcome is suggested. So far as practice is concerned, instead of allowing for the satisfaction of basic human needs, one would have to conceive ways to block (or otherwise redirect) the fulfillment of at least some of them.

Basic Human Needs: enter John Burton

So far as conflict resolution is concerned, any discussion of BHN will be dominated by the work of John W. Burton who, after the publication of *Deviance, Terrorism and War* (1979) fully identified himself with a version of the theory, which he came to claim determined his practice as well. Dennis Sandole reviews Burton's theory in some detail in Chapter 1, and virtually all of the chapters that follow grapple with Burtonian BHN theory and practice in some way; and so in this Introduction we note but a few salient aspects of his work: Borrowing his list of needs originally from the sociologist Paul Sites (1973), Burton was hardly at all interested in psychological, developmental or personality-related approaches to them. Even given his methodological individualism, his orientation was toward the individual in society, as a member of a group (usually a struggle or identity group) and toward the role of authorities or institutions insofar as they frustrated the fulfillment of individual basic human needs. Indeed, in that frustration, and in individuals' collective and relentless struggle to overcome it, lay the roots of intractable social conflict. For Burton, basic human needs were fixed, ontological and universal. In no way could they be construed as "preferences" (see also Doyal and Gough 1991). This, in essence, is Burton's theory of what he called deep-rooted conflict. In contrast, conflicts that were based mainly on less deeply rooted interests (e.g. commercial or industrial ones, or those amenable to preference analysis) he called "disputes." These were amenable to simple bargaining, negotiation or third-party mediation, as usually understood. In contrast, conflict rooted in frustrated basic human needs were non-negotiable, since individuals would not – or could not – compromise on them. Therefore another process entirely was called for, discussed in several chapters below as interactive problem solving, usually in the context of problem-solving workshops (PSWs). A number of the chapters that follow describe and analyze, sometimes critically, the nature of this process. Burton stressed that in the PSW the third party (typically a panel) was not a simple mediator, but among other things a specialist in the analysis of conflict and BHN. Examining the linkage between the theory of BHN and the practice of interactive problem solving is therefore a major concern of this volume.

Basic human needs in development theory and practice

Although most discussions of basic human needs (Burton's excepted) have taken place in the literature of social psychology, there is another field of endeavor that, for a time at least, featured centrally the idea of basic needs and their satisfaction. This was international development from the mid-1970s roughly to the mid-1980s. (Though, as we shall see later in this volume, echoes of this approach, unharnessed from "development" in a strictly economic sense of the term, connected now to human rights and human security, have reappeared in this different discourse, pointing perhaps to the future of BHN theory.) If Maslow is usually cited as representing the epitome of basic human needs in psychology, and Burton in conflict resolution, it is perhaps the Chilean economist Manfred Max-Neef whose conceptualization of "fundamental human needs" and "human-scale development" characterized much progressive thinking about economic development (and under-development), particularly in Latin America, in the 1980s and early 1990s (Elkins and Max-Neef 1992). For Max-Neef, in contrast to Maslow, needs are not hierarchical, but needs (excepting basic survival ones) can be "traded off" in the process of their satisfaction. While the fundamental needs are universal, "finite, few and classifiable," in contrast their satisfiers are many and vary from culture to culture, and through history. One of Max-Neef's central points is that the non-satisfaction of the fundamental needs leads to "poverty," though his definition of poverty goes beyond the "economistic" one connected mainly to income levels and the market. He writes of "*poverties*": of subsistence, of protection, of affection, of understanding, of participation, of identity. (Here one gets a sense of his list of fundamental needs.) Moreover (adverting to Mosby's Medical Dictionary), "each poverty generates pathologies" (Max-Neef 1992: 200). (See Väyrynen (1998) on the use of medical metaphors in peace research, and in Chapter 5 in this volume.) Max-Neef's scheme connects to theories of social conflict in an interesting way. Full development (he calls this Human-Scale Development) focuses on the individual, but its success "assumes a direct and participatory democracy" (1992: 198). One might argue that this is a close relative to the transformed political system (and political philosophy) that Burton imagines when he describes the ultimate effects of successful conflict resolution and *provention* (Burton 1990; and Sandole in this volume). Max-Neef assumes, that is, an end-state version of the very sort of social and political system whose absence (or deformation) Burton sees as the root of serious social conflict.

More broadly, the relationship of basic human needs to notions of poverty and *human* development is what characterized the dominant approach to development (if briefly) in the late 1970s. Writing as part of the "UN Intellectual History Project," Jolly *et al.* (2009) date the inception of Human Development based upon a people-centered, "basic needs strategy" to a 1976 conference of the UN's International Labor Organization (ILO) and the document that emerged from it: *Employment, Growth and Basic Needs: A One World Problem.* At the root of this strategy was the contrast between "economic prosperity and human development." The search, therefore, was for measures of human development besides GNP per capita, such as life expectancy, illiteracy, education, gender empowerment and political participation. They quote Amartya Sen's mordant comment: "We need a measure of the same level of vulgarity as GNP – just one number – but a measure that is not blind to social aspects of human lives as GNP is" (in Jolly *et al.* 2009: 3; see also Doyal and Gough 1991).

Begun and eagerly adopted in the mid-1970s, Jolly *et al.* (2009: 1) write that the basic needs strategy was short-lived.

> Its demise in the early 1980s was the result of a return to economic orthodoxy, which was driven by three factors: the rise of Thatcherism and Reaganism in developed countries, the onset of world recession, and banking policies designed to insure that developing countries repaid their debts.

The era of structural adjustment as conditions for IMF and World Bank loans, and neoliberal monetarist polices generally, buried the discourse of basic human needs in approaches to development. Even given the much vaunted Millennium Development Goals (MDGs) this is still largely the case.

Thus far we have touched on the notion of basic human needs as it arose in psychology and development, and briefly in Burton's usage in conflict resolution. The chapters that follow will elucidate this connection to conflict resolution theory and practice. For now, we can observe that in some ways Burton's usage represents a hybrid of the first two. The power of BHN as *motivators* of human behavior depends upon its (social) psychological qualities. The linkage of BHN to social conditions and to serious socio-political (as opposed to "tissue") "deficits" has much in common with human-centered BHN ideas of development, or lack of development. Burton, and BHN-oriented conflict resolution in general, basically focus on the conflictual "outputs" of seriously ("pathologically") undeveloped or maldeveloped social systems, and how those systems might change (perhaps in the direction of Max-Neef's participatory democracy) via the satisfaction of individual members' basic human needs.

Basic Human Needs: linking theory and practice

The successful marriage of problem-solving practice with the underlying theory of Basic Human Needs seems to have had its heyday mainly in the period from the early 1980s into the 1990s, when a wide variety of "Track Two" initiatives occurred. These used some variant of the basic approach outlined in the early writings of John Burton, Herbert Kelman and Ronald Fisher, together with a number of ideas from BHN to guide the actual course and hoped-for outcomes from such initiatives. A whole series of workshops involving Israelis and Palestinians took place prior to the better known Oslo process and to a considerable extent prepared the way for the latter (back-channel) meetings. Problem-solving meetings took place on Cyprus parallel to the ultimately abortive official negotiations over the Annan Plan, and were thus consonant with the label "para-negotiations" as coined by Ronald Fisher. A large and varied number of dialogues, workshops and conferences took place in Northern Ireland, involving members of civil society, trade unionists, political parties and even, on occasions, paramilitaries. Burton himself, together with Edward Azar, conducted the workshop series in the aftermath of the 1982 South Atlantic War briefly described in Christopher Mitchell's Chapter 8 in this work, as well as some more experimental processes involving parties from the civil wars in the Lebanon and in Sri Lanka. There were many other Track Two initiatives during this period.

However, by the last years of the twentieth century, it appears that the use of problem-solving approaches slowed down, as scholar-practitioners began to realize the resources that were required to keep even modest "Track Two" processes going, as the stubborn resistance to change involved in most complex conflict systems became more evident, and – more practically – as even the modest resources available for such academically peripheral activities dried up. Moreover, interest in Human Needs theory, never central to mainstream social science ideas about human behavior (as Solon Simmons points out in his chapter), waned as the search for ways to operationalize its central concepts and to test its core hypotheses failed to materialize. Proponents were left with arguments to the effect that it might be best to assume that human needs existed, that satisfiers of those needs could take a variety of forms, and to proceed on the basis of those assumptions (e.g. Kelman 1990).

Academic fashion aside, useful ideas often make a comeback and this seems to be happening with both the theory of Basic Human Needs and the practice of problem-solving workshops. In the latter case, a new generation of scholar practitioners has taken up the workshop method, examined and critiqued it, refocused it so that its aims have become more modest but also more realistic, and applied it to the intra-state, ethno-political struggles that have become a feature of the twenty-first century. In the case of the theory of Basic Human Needs, other scholars have reviewed its shortcomings and attempted to deal with these through new formulations of its central arguments and even by adopting entirely different claims about its nature and utility – for example, by introducing the idea that it might best be regarded through the lens of normative theory and as a basis for evaluating strategies, rather than as the empirical explanation for success or failure (themes taken up in Chapters 4 and 5 by Kriesberg and Väyrynen).

Both these innovations are represented in the chapters that follow, some written by members of this new generation of scholars and scholar-practitioners seeking ways to understand and deal with the new conflict systems that confront the twenty-first century, and others by members of the generation that developed and used these ideas while realizing how far short they fell of being the ideal conflict resolution tools they had promised in their early years. Each of the contributors has taken an individual approach to this focus on the relationship between the theory of Basic Human Needs and the practice of problem solving, some concerned mainly with "theory" and others focused on "practice," but in all cases referring to their mutual implications. Meanwhile, a number of clear themes have emerged that enabled us to group the contributions in a coherent fashion – interestingly enough, these were themes that mainly emerged from pointing out shortcomings in the original BHN/problem-solving approach. These themes have to do with the dilemma of power (asymmetry), the limitations of rational choice thinking at the heart of Burton's conception of BHN, culture as a missing dimension, and the often unacknowledged moral or ethical questions that adherence to a BHN framework entails.

Power

Several of the contributors have started with the justifiable background assumption that both the theory and the original practice have skirted around the whole problem of power and imbalance with the apparently blithe assumption that what is often superficially known as a major "power imbalance" would either disappear as rational solutions were generated through problem solving or could even be ignored completely. This hardly seems a safe assumption, given the number of asymmetric intra-state conflicts involving incumbents and insurgents which characterize the start of the twenty-first century – Sudan, Indonesia, the Philippines, Ossetia, Chechnya, Uganda, Mali, Syria, etc., etc. The issue is tackled head on in Kevin Avruch's Chapter 2, where the author begins by reviewing how the issue was skirted round by most earlier writers, who merely pointed to the rational assessment of long-term costs as the key driver towards peaceful resolution. This issue also forms a sub-theme running through Dennis Sandole's opening chapter, with its arguments about "pro-active prevention" based on fulfilling key human needs before frustration and violence set in and appear to demand the application of counter violence to preserve "stability" – that so desirable quality that obviates the need for any change at all.

Clearly implicated in any discussion of power is another neglected issue connected with asymmetry, taken up by Ingrid Sandole-Staroste in Chapter 3 who quite properly insists that, while Basic Human Needs theory and feminist theory grew up together, the two never seemed to connect at all until quite recently. Similarly, ignoring gender issues in protracted and complex conflicts tended to render many problem-solving approaches somewhat one-dimensional, to say the least. The recent inclusion of gender factors into practical peacemaking efforts – local economic support for women's enterprises, post-violence, women's groups' involvement in actual peace negotiations, insistence on including issues of domestic violence in peace arrangements – are all new ideas that enhance the chances of problem-solving approaches producing some kind of durable peace, post-violence.

Morality and the ethics of practice

A rather unexpected theme that emerged from some of the chapters in the book is the whole issue of the ethics of intervention (especially linked to the practice of problem solving) and the position of the third-party facilitators. Scholar-practitioners from the very early days of problem solving had simply assumed that intervening to produce "peace" through dialogues and workshops was a good thing, in and of itself, and in the MAD (mutual-assured-destruction) world of super-Power rivalry and classical inter-state conflict, this was perhaps enough. However, as more initiatives were undertaken into various kinds of intractable and protracted conflicts, the basis for doing so became less certain, and this uncertainty increased as problem solving was applied to a wider range of conflicts involving more obvious asymmetries – intra-family conflicts, ethnic minorities and dominant majorities, insurgents and incumbents. Tarya Väyrynen argues that the basis for intervening in the early days of problem solving – what she terms the medical analogy of cures for a disease – proves inadequate upon serious analysis and argues the need for a more subtle and sophisticated basis for daring to enter a complex conflict as a so-called "impartial" third party. Louis Kriesberg echoes this theme of the need for some solid ground from which to justify intervention into the problems of others. He suggests that, indeed, Basic Human Needs could supply such a basis, although he also argues for a variety of possible "solid grounds." In a sophisticated consideration of the whole Human Needs approach, Solon Simmons writes that the attempt to portray BHN as the "biological" engine driving action is mistaken. It might be more fruitful to conceive of basic needs as one normative yardstick for evaluating the impact of interventions, whether problem-solving or power-based. Simmons locates needs in political culture rather than the genome. In Chapter 6, Jamie Price joins in seeing the attribution of a genetic or ontological "misplaced concreteness" to BHN as a mistake, but nevertheless retains the "Galilean" (scientific/empirical) intention of seeking "explanation" through Bernard Lonergan's "Insight" approach.

Culture

One of the early and constant critiques of both Basic Human Needs theory and problem-solving practice, first articulated by Avruch and Black (1987) while they were colleagues of Burton at George Mason University, has been that of cultural insensitivity – a strong line of argument in Väyrynen's chapter and an underlying theme of many of the chapters in the book. The theme plays a major part in Avruch's opening sections and re-emerges in Mohammed Abu-Nimer's evaluation of Basic Human Needs theory's impact on practice in regions as far apart as Iraq, Sri Lanka, Israel-Palestine and Mindanao. All of these protracted conflicts have formed a part of Abu Nimer's extensive practice, so that his chapter presents an admirable introduction to the last section of the book, which focuses on the theme of problem-solving practice and how this has changed in the light of increasing experience with the approach's use in the real world of deep-rooted conflict. Chris Mitchell's chapter forms a useful starting point here, as it reviews what Mitchell refers to as "the classical model" of problem-solving workshops, devised in the 1960s and 1970s and encapsulated in John Burton's famous – or notorious – *Handbook* dating from 1987. The chapter takes a reader through Burton's "rules" and provides a commentary on the manner in which these were adapted or modified in a variety of problem-solving initiatives undertaken in the 1990s and early 2000s. Mitchell ends by arguing that one of the great blank spaces in the classical model is in "follow up" to workshops, which increasingly proved to be one of the central weaknesses of this whole process.

In greater detail, Ronald Fisher describes two innovations and extensions of the "classical model" which originally focused on the "primary parties" to a conflict. These involve crucial stakeholders in any process that seeks a durable peace. In the first example, Fisher describes an initial effort to create some degree of unity and coordination among the fractured opposition movements within the Sudan region of Darfur, united in their grievances and opposition to the government in Khartoum but in little else. In this case the underlying theory is that it will be necessary to make peace and create unity between competing factions on one side if any process at all is going to have a chance of creating a durable agreement between the primary adversaries. In the second example, Fisher describes a problem-solving effort to involve two important stakeholders formally outside the boundaries of a core conflict system who, nonetheless, have a major effect on interactions within those boundaries. This workshop series focused on the long drawn out conflict on the island of Cyprus but brought in representatives of the "parent" countries by including participants from Athens and Ankara – both currently desirous of a settlement – to help those directly involved in a search for solutions. Fisher emphasizes that both of these workshop series began to answer some questions left over from the classical model about how to deal with complex conflict systems in which the influence of internal factions or peripheral stakeholders turned out to be crucial in the search for a resolution.

A similar approach to broadening the focus of classical problem solving in cases of complex conflict systems is taken in Susan Allen Nan and Jacquie Greiff's Chapter 11, which describes a series of workshops involving participants from Georgia and South Ossetia in the wake of the short but vicious war that erupted within the formal boundaries of the State of Georgia in August 2008 and resulted in the kind of stalemate and a standoff that characterizes many early twenty-first-century intra-state conflicts. This chapter stresses the ongoing nature of interactive problem solving – the idea that successful workshops are rarely "one-off" events – and explores stages as the process unfolds. The authors see the notion of BHN as "implicit" in their approach, important particularly in the early stages where erstwhile enemies can recognize "shared human concerns" of, for example, families separated by the conflict. Nan and Greiff return all the way to some of Maslow's original ideas about human needs, and link their problem-solving approaches to the potential provision of goods that fulfill very practical needs, among them, information, energy and medical treatment. As they argue, there is no better way of helping to start an inevitably long process of resolution and reconciliation than by helping people find news of their loved ones missing as a result of violence.

Not all the interventions treated here follow the problem-solving workshop model, however defined. Kriesberg discusses a variety of interventions in Chapter 4, including such celebrated Cold War citizen exchanges or diplomacy as the Pugwash and Dartmouth conferences, sometimes gathered together under the term "Track Two." In Chapter 12, Frank Dukes describes the manner in which Basic Human Needs theories have affected his own practice, largely concerned with regional and environmental conflicts (often with strong social class overtones) within the United States. His primary intervention in this conflict occurred first in a university classroom, as part of a regularly scheduled class. Dukes discusses BHN as one of a number of "lenses" that he brings to each case of conflict he confronts and describes how each helps him understand some of the often hidden issues that underlie present positions and the contradictions that appear on the surface of conflicts, ostensibly about "rationally" negotiable issues. Dukes' example in this chapter arises from the history of the establishment of the Shenandoah National Park and the deep, residual resentments that fired up opposition even to exploring changes in the Park's boundaries. Price's application of "Insight" theory in the end takes him away from BHN entirely.

The limitations of rational choice thinking

What is especially apparent in the chapters that focus on practice, the bedrock assumption of Burton that parties, educated as to the power of Basic Human Needs, will come rationally to "cost" their conflict behavior and that this insight will presage some sort of resolution, is a part of the "classic model" that has not fared well. Abu-Nimer takes this on directly as one of the key limitations of BHN theory: here the missing dimension is not culture but affect, emotions. Dukes sensitively plumbs the emotional hurts, generations deep, that motivate those fervently opposed to what they regarded as further *illegitimate* and *unjust* government intervention in their lives. The "theory" chapters – Väyrynen, Simmons and Kriesberg's – make similar points.

Along with the diminution of the role of "rationality," these chapters revise a conception of Basic Human Needs as biologically grounded and "scientifically" valid (see Avruch's Chapter 2). This is in contrast to many social psychologist's understanding of the idea – in the past as well as today (Pittman and Zeigler 2007) – and in stark contrast to Burton's understanding, where BHN became "ontological" only when he felt forced to retreat from outrightly calling them "genetical." In contrast, the majority of the chapters that follow, perhaps in the spirit of these post-positivist times, seek simply "to get past" the question of the objective "scienticity" of BHNs, and treat them, rather, as metaphors, narrative devices, moral categories, even rhetorics. The exception is Dennis Sandole, Burton's student and sometime co-author, who stands resolutely in holding to the notion that basic human needs connect to neurochemical substrates (serotonin production) and brain function, and these to violence. With his contribution we can say with confidence that all the important "takes" on Basic Human Needs find representation in this volume.

Our brief account of the chapters that follow should be enough to convince a reader that our belief that the ideas of the pioneers of Basic Human Needs theory and its marriage to problem-solving processes are at least sufficiently alive and well to justify a return look at both – and to show how both the theory and the practice have evolved and continue to evolve in interesting and useful ways. We hope that the writings that follow can represent a reviving movement that will again make a contribution to academic thinking and to practical conflict resolution. At the very end of the book we will try to sketch out where we think both movements – theoretical and practical – might usefully head. In the meantime, our contributors can clearly speak for themselves.

References

Aristotle (2012) *The Nichomachean Ethics*, translated by R. Bartlett and S. Collins, Chicago: University of Chicago Press.

Avruch, K. and Black, P.W. (1987) "A generic theory of conflict resolution: a critique," *Negotiation Journal*, 3(1): 87–96, 99–100.

Blake, R.R., Shephard, H. and Mouton, J.S. (1963) *Managing Inter-Group Conflict in Industry*, Houston, TX: Gulf Publishing.

Burton, J.W. (1969) *Conflict and Communication*, London: Macmillan.

Burton, J.W. (1979) *Deviance, Terrorism and War*, New York: St. Martin's Press.

Burton, J.W. (1987) *Resolving Deep-Rooted Conflict: A Handbook*, Lanham, MD: University Press of America.

Burton, J.W. (1990) *Conflict: Resolution and Provention*, New York: St. Martin's.

Doob, Leonard W. (ed.) (1970) *Resolving Conflict in Africa: The Fermeda Workshop*, New Haven: Yale University Press.

Doyal, L. and Gough, I. (1991) *A Theory of Basic Human Needs*, New York: Guilford Press.

Elkins, P. and Max-Neef, M. (eds) (1992) *Real Life Economics: Understanding Wealth Creation*, New York: Routledge.

Etzioni, A. (1968) "Basic human needs, alienation and inauthenticity," *American Sociological Review*, 33(6): 870–885.

Fisher, R.J. (1997) *Interactive Conflict Resolution*, Syracuse: Syracuse University Press.

Follett, M.P. (1942) *Dynamic Administration: The Collected Papers of Mary Parker Follett*, edited by H. Metcalf and L. Urwick, New York: Harper.

Jolly, R., Emmerji, L. and Weiss, T.G. (2009), "The UN and human development," *UN Intellectual History Project*, Briefing Note Number 8. Online. Available www. unhistory.org/briefing/8HumDev.pdf (accessed August 16, 2012).

Kelman, H. (1990) "Applying a human needs perspective to the practice of conflict resolution: the Israeli-Palestinian case," in J.W. Burton (ed.) *Conflict: Human Needs Theory*, New York: St. Martin's Press.

Lewin, K. (1948) *Resolving Social Conflicts*, New York: Harper.

Malinowski, B. (1944) *A Scientific Theory of Culture*, Chapel Hill: University of North Carolina Press.

Maslow, A.H. (1943) "A theory of human motivation," *Psychological Review*, 50: 370–396.

Maslow, A.H. (1954) *Motivation and Personality*, New York: Harper.

Max-Neef, M. (1992) "Development and human needs," in P. Elkins and M. Max-Neef (eds) *Real Life Economics: Understanding Wealth Creation*, New York: Routledge.

McClelland, D.C. (1961) *The Achieving Society*, Princeton: Van Nostrand.

Mitchell, C.R. (1990) "Necessitous man and conflict resolution: more basic questions about basic human needs theory," in J.W. Burton (ed.) *Conflict: Human Needs Theory*, New York: St. Martin's Press.

Mitchell, C.R. (2005) "Ending confrontation between Indonesia and Malaysia," in R.J. Fisher (ed.) *Paving the Way: Contributions of Interactive Conflict Resolution to Peacemaking*, Lanham, MD: Lexington Books.

Mosby's Medical Dictionary (2009) 8th edn, St. Louis, MO: Elsevier.

Murray, H. (1938) *Explorations in Personality*, New York: Oxford University Press.

Pittman, T.S. and Zeigler, K.R. (2007) "Basic human needs," in A. Kruglanski and E.T. Higgins (eds) *Social Psychology: Handbook of Basic Principles*, 2nd edn, New York: Guilford.

Reiss, S. (2000) *Who Am I? The 16 Basic Desires that Motivate our Behavior and Define our Personality*, New York: Tarcher/Putnam.

Rogers, C. (1986) "The Rust Workshop: a personal overview," *Journal of Humanistic Psychology*, 26(3): 23–45.

Sites, P. (1973) *Control: The Basis of Social Order*, New York: Dunellen Publishers.

Thomas, W.I. (1924) *The Unadjusted Girl: With Cases and Standpoint for Behavior Analysis*, Boston: Little, Brown.

Väyrynen, T. (1998) "Medical metaphors in peace research: John Burton's conflict resolution theory and a constructionist alternative," International Journal of Peace Studies, 3(2): 3–18.

Walton, R.E and Robert McKersie, R. (1965) *A Behavioral Theory of Labor Negotiations*, New York: McGraw Hill.

Part I

Basic Human Needs in theory

Chapters 1–7 are all focused in one way or another on the theory of Basic Human Needs (BHN). Sandole's chapter provides the most comprehensive summary of the place of BHN in the work of its most emphatic proponent, John Burton, and extends the theory to conflicts involving direct violence. Avruch and Sandole-Staroste critique the Burtonian approach for its relative (Avruch) or absolute (Sandole-Staroste) neglect of power and gender, with implications for practice. Kriesberg and Väyrynen consider some of the moral or ethical implications of adopting a BHN perspective. Kriesberg places the most frequently associated BHN practice, the problem-solving workshop (PSW) among a range of different approaches to building peace. Väyrynen considers the heavily "medicalized" metaphors and the "scientific gaze" that many BHN approaches adopt towards understanding and "treating" conflict, and offers an alternative rooted in ethnography and phenomenology. Price and Simmons look beyond the usual understanding of BHN and conflict resolution entirely. Price critiques Burton's "Aristotelian" understanding of BHN and offers an approach to third-party involvement based upon the notion of "insight," adopted from the philosopher Bernard Lonergan. Completing the theory-focused section, Simmons looks at BHN through a narrative lens of "political talk," accepting the value of "thinking through" such needs as security, freedom, equality and tolerance, while moving beyond the requirement of anchoring such needs in biology or ontology.

1 Extending the reach of Basic Human Needs

A comprensive theory for the twenty-first century[1]

Dennis J.D. Sandole

Introduction

The purpose of this chapter is to contribute to the development of a comprehensive theory of conflict and conflict resolution by building upon the existing body of knowledge on basic human needs and their role in the initiation, exacerbation and resolution of violent conflict. This effort rests on an examination of the groundbreaking theoretical and practical work of conflict resolution pioneer, John W. Burton, who has done the most to advance knowledge on the relationship between frustrated basic needs and violent conflict. Following a brief overview of Burton's rich corpus of knowledge, I discuss what still seems to be missing from his work. Then, attempting to fill the void, I note the earlier contributions of others as well as my own in extending the theoretical and practical reach of current knowledge on the needs-conflict nexus, with implications for foreign and public policy in the ever more complex twenty-first century.

What do we know about the basic needs-conflict nexus?

Burton's contributions for our purposes comprise developments in four interrelated areas: (1) the World Society Paradigm (WSP); (2) Basic Human Needs (BHNs) Theory; (3) Analytical problem-solving facilitated conflict resolution processes; and (4) *provention.*

The World Society Paradigm

The World Society Paradigm (WSP) was Burton's response to the prevailing "billiard ball model" of the Realist-dominated field of International Relations (see Wolfers 1962). So-called "Realists" see a world comprised only of nation-states "bouncing off of each other" in their respective bids for power acquisition, maintenance and projection, with little or no attention paid to domestic politics, which are "black-boxed." By contrast, Burton's World Society Paradigm sees a world comprised of systems of multiple actors *in addition to* nation-states, e.g. business corporations, terrorist organizations, organized criminal networks, fiefdoms presided over by warlords, and the like (see Burton 1972: Ch. 4). An important feature of the WSP is that it incorporates the *billiard ball model* of Realists as well as the *cobweb model* of Idealists, showing the interactions, transactions and communications within, among and between non-state as well as state and transnational actors.

Basic Human Needs

Burton's thinking on the role of Basic Human Needs (BHNs) in the etiology of violent conflict began as a consideration of *values*, especially what he calls "social-psychological values" (1972: 127–128). These values, operative at the individual and small-group levels, may be pursued "even at the expense of life itself." Because they are fundamental to human behavior, they are "presumably universal [that is,] held by people within all cultures and ideological systems." Consequently, these values may be viewed as "social-biological values" – a subset of social-psychological values – because they reflect "biological drives and motivations," which are found even in "more primitive organisms" (Burton 1972: 127–128). As a "fundamental particle of human behavior," social-biological values are concerned with *homeostasis* (see Cannon 1963): "survival, personality development, and self-maintenance within any social environment" (Burton 1972: 128).

Regarding homeostasis, Burton (1972: 129, emphasis added) argues that:

> A hypothesis that there are social-biological values ... serves to explain the apparently *continuing struggle* for participation and freedom to develop personality within a social environment ... the *persistent demand* for independence of nations, and for identification of groups within states.

Burton's thinking presciently anticipates later developments, such as the ethnic wars in the former Yugoslavia and Soviet Union, plus the more recent Arab Spring. Indeed, Jean-Pierre Filiu (2011, emphasis added) sees the recent upheavals in North Africa and the Middle East as strident demands for "*dignity, pride, honour [and] a struggle for self-determination*, for liberation from a corrupt clique, for regaining control and power over a nation's and the individual's destiny." Further reinforcing this homeostasis thesis, Burton (1972: 129) argues that such "manifestations of nationalism have clear biological origins and protective functions."

Burton's theory of conflict, embedded within a values frame, postulated a clash between social-biological values and "institutional values, that is, values that relate directly to the survival of institutions or to the cultural goals of separately organized societies" (Burton 1972: 127). The nature of this conflict is that "in the course of social evolution, basic drives and motivations have been suppressed by institutional restraints, initially of a purely social or community character, and later by those resulting from economic specialization and organization" (Burton 1972: 129).

Burton's narrative on the potent role of social-biological values as drivers of human behavior, especially conflict, eventually gave way to a theory based on *needs*. In this later development, he was influenced more by sociologist Paul Sites (1973: Ch. 2) than by humanistic psychologist Abraham Maslow (1987), who is renowned for his work in developing a "hierarchy of needs" for (1) physiological (homeostatic) maintenance, (2) safety and security, (3) love and belongingness, (4) self-esteem and (5) self-actualization.[2]

Why did Burton decide to go with Sites instead of Maslow? In contrast to Maslow's hierarchy of five needs, "Sites (1973: Ch. 2) postulates eight, all of which require fulfillment and, therefore, none of which is necessarily more important than others": (1) consistency in response, (2) stimulation, (3) security, (4) recognition, (5) distributive justice, (6) rationality and the appearance of rationality, (7) meaning and (8) control (Burton 1979: 72).

To Sites' list of eight needs, Burton (1979: 73) added a ninth, *role defense:* the "protection of needs once they have been acquired." "Role defense" is concerned not only with the protection of a particular role (e.g. prime minister), but also the protection of measures necessary for the fulfillment of other needs commensurate with that role: "the individual attempts to secure a role and to preserve a role by which he acquires and maintains his recognition, security and stimulation" (Burton 1979: 73). This is an imperative that applies to all parties to conflicts, including those in privileged, elite, authority positions. For some, especially human rights advocates, this part of Burton's thinking is contentious, for he is arguing that successful conflict resolution depends in part on recognizing that the "bad guys" also have basic needs and not only those whom they oppress: "No explanation of a conflictual situation or the behavior of individuals, groups *and* authorities is complete without consideration of role defence as an important need" (emphasis added) (Burton 1979: 73; also see Burton 1979: Ch. 7).

Sites' comprehensive listing of needs and Burton's reframing of it eventually gave way to a much shorter listing – identity, participation, recognition and security – all of "which are an *ontological* part of the human development process" (emphasis added) (Burton 1984: 147). What remained consistent in Burton's theorizing as he shifted from social-biological values to basic needs was "that certain needs *will* be pursued, regardless of any force that might be used by authorities" (emphasis in the original) (Burton 1984: 141).

Analytical problem-solving facilitated conflict resolution processes

Burton's contributions to the development of conflict resolution processes originally took shape under the heading of "controlled communication"

(Burton 1969). The objective was to have a multidisciplinary third-party panel bring representatives of conflicting parties together to facilitate clear communication, statements of purpose and definitions of the problem about which they were conflicting. Conceived initially as a technique for dealing with *subjective* "social-psychological values" that had not yet achieved *objective* "social-biological," universal status, controlled communication was similar to the casework method employed by social workers, plus the methods of conciliation and mediation used in dealing with small group and industrial conflicts.[3]

As "needs" explicitly entered Burton's thinking, controlled communication was reinvented as "analytical problemsolving facilitated conflict resolution" (Burton 1990c: 328). The idea behind problemsolving is that conflict may not be about territory and similar grievances, but about underlying needs for security, recognition, participation and identity. For Burton, these basic needs are *social goals*, i.e. in contrast to physical resources, they are not scarce. Hence, conflicts originally perceived as zero-sum, "win-lose" contests, often with "lose-lose" outcomes, could be reframed as positive-sum with potential "win-win" outcomes. Since this is not an option in the traditional power paradigm, "then, clearly, it is in the interests of all parties to ensure that the opposing parties achieve these social needs" (Burton 1984: 147–148). The essential objective in analytical problemsolving facilitated conflict resolution, therefore, is to encourage the parties to bring to the surface their "underlying motivations" (e.g. their basic needs for identity, recognition, participation and security).

Accordingly, Burton argues that there is a need for a "paradigm shift" in thinking and behavior, from a power approach emphasizing coercion to a problemsolving or human needs perspective focusing on analysis, and a new vocabulary. Like controlled communication, problemsolving is an analytical approach that clears up misperceptions in a workshop format facilitated by trained, experienced third-party practitioners. Unlike controlled communication, however, problemsolving also deals with "objective" bases of conflict, which Burton referred to earlier as "social-biological values" and subsequently as basic human needs that are commonly held by humans and other organisms. Consequently, basic needs are universal and must be fulfilled, lest the frustrated actors concerned blast their way into our consciousness via terrorism and other forms of violence (see Burton 1979; 1984: Ch. 16; Sandole 2010: Ch. 4).

"Provention"

Burton created the neologism, "provention," to capture the "prevention of an undesirable event by removing its causes, and by creating conditions that do not give rise to its causes" (Burton 1990a: 3). In contrast to "*pre*-vention [therefore,] *pro*vention [signifies] taking steps to remove [underlying] sources of conflict, and more positively to promote conditions in which collaborative and valued relationships control behaviors" (emphasis in original) (Burton and Dukes 1990b: 161).[4]

Provention has implications for the robustness and resilience of civilizations that resolution may not have:

> Were consideration for the future given priority, civilizations would be threatened only by an inadequate understanding of human relations and systems operations. But civilizations have yet to discover the representative political system that gives priority to the future. Provention ... would be the core of such a political philosophy.
>
> (Burton and Dukes 1990b: 161)

Further:

> We have ... theories and empirical evidence that the source of a great deal of anti-social behavior stems from adverse living conditions. Yet there is little attempt to avoid the costs and consequences of deviant behaviors and incarcerations by diverting adequate resources to housing, education and health. Whether the conflict be drug violence or ethnicity conflict, there are means of provention that are probably less costly to society than attempts at control.
>
> (Burton and Dukes 1990b: 163)

Provention depends on proactive strategies. Whatever "human nature" is, however, it tends not to be proactive, but reactive. Nevertheless, extending Burton's thinking, provention should be an imperative toward which societies strive as policymakers and others contemplate a growing number of interdependent, interacting challenges comprising a complex "global problematique," e.g. climate change, pandemics, population growth, WMD proliferation, poverty, malnutrition, terrorism, environmental degradation (see Sandole 2010). Reinforcing this sentiment, Burton's biographer David Dunn (2004: 128) has framed provention as:

> a general theory of positive social change, where conflict is a central problem area, where the goal is the dynamic of a peaceful society (constituted at all levels of human behavior), where the relationships are sustained by legitimate mechanisms of reciprocated support and not by coercive measures or by elites, by virtue of their own authority.

In effect, for Dunn (2004: 132), "provention is at one and the same time a theory of general social systems and a reconstruction of political philosophy."

Accordingly, the World Society Paradigm is an ontological statement on the nature of the world within which conflicts occur; Basic Human Needs Theory accounts for why conflicts occur in that complex, multi-actor setting; Analytical Problemsolving Facilitated Conflict Resolution processes comprise a methodology for addressing those conflicts; and Provention is a strategic goal, with civilizational implications, that problemsolving can aim for, shifting from the small-group to the macro levels in the effort to head off complex, needs-related conflicts before they occur by resolutely addressing actual or potential deep-rooted causes and conditions.

What is still missing? The efforts of others to fill the void in Burton's thinking on the needs-conflict nexus

What has Burton not addressed in his comprehensive theory? This question was raised 25 years ago by some of Burton's colleagues at what is now the School for Conflict Analysis and Resolution (S-CAR) at George Mason University. Anthropologists Kevin Avruch and Peter Black, for example, argued that Burton did not say enough, if anything, about the role of *culture* in mediating the impact of frustrated "universal" needs on conflict (see Burton and Sandole 1986, 1987; Avruch and Black 1987, 1993; Avruch 1998). For Avruch and Black, *culture* is not merely one variable among others to be taken into account, but "a fundamental feature of human consciousness, the *sine qua non* of being human" (Black and Avruch 1989). Further, culture is not merely "constitutive of human reality," including the reality of conflict, but is also "a perception-shaping lens or ... grammar for the production and structuring of meaningful action" (Avruch and Black 1993: 132).

Accordingly, "when the parties to a conflict come from different cultures – when the conflict is 'intercultural' – one cannot presume that all crucial understandings are shared among them." There is a need, therefore, for a "cultural analysis" in intercultural conflict resolution to deal effectively with the parties' "respective *ethnotheories*, the notions of the root causes of the conflict, and *ethnopraxes*, the local acceptable techniques for resolving conflicts [which] may differ one from another in significant ways" (Avruch and Black 1993: 133, emphasis added).

One result of the Avruch/Black critique is explicit recognition that, while basic needs for identity, recognition, participation and security may be ontological and, therefore, universal, they are clearly embedded in, and therefore, mediated by cultural systems. The "local" meanings of actors' conflict behavior that are the objective of *understanding*, therefore, are embedded in those cultural systems.

At about the same time that Avruch and Black were critiquing Burton's work, Edward Azar (1986) was expanding on it to develop his theory of "protracted social conflict" (PSC). For Azar, the "enduring features" of PSC include "economic and technological underdevelopment, and unintegrated social and political systems" (Azar 1986: 28). These "real sources" of PSC "are *deep-rooted* in the lives and ontological being of those concerned" (Azar 1986: 29, emphasis added). Like Burton, Azar was led to the hypothesis that the source of protracted social conflict is the denial of those elements required in the development of all people and societies, and whose pursuit is a compelling need for all. These are *security, distinctive identity, social recognition of identity,* and *effective participation* in the processes that determine conditions of security and identity, and other such developmental requirements. The real source of conflict is the denial of those human needs that are common to all and whose pursuit is an ontological drive in all (emphasis in the original; see also Azar 1990 and Ramsbotham *et al.* 2011: Ch. 4).

Azar's contribution included making more explicit Burton's thinking on the *structure-agent nexus,* i.e. the role of the state in either facilitating or, more likely, frustrating the efforts of communal "identity groups" in pursuing and fulfilling their basic needs. It was frustration of needs that led to the "protracted conflicts" *within* states – what Mary Kaldor (2006) refers to as the "new wars" – that could eventually spill over to conflict *between* states ("old wars"), as such conflicts invite "the intervention of great powers, thus complicating even further the relationships of those powers" (Azar 1986: 37).[5]

Azar, also like Burton, was prescient in suggesting that the multidiscipline of conflict analysis and resolution has much to commend it as a body of theory and practice and as a basis for policymaking with regard to complex conflict situations that are impacting other global challenges, such as climate change, ecological degradation, poverty, proliferation of weapons of mass destruction, pandemics and terrorism (see Sandole 2010). In 1986, for example, 25 years prior to the Arab Spring, Azar wrote, "in the Middle East, the protest movements broke down into many factions as new leaders came to the fore with slightly different emphases" (Azar 1986: 37). Accordingly, "conflicts that commence as a clear confrontation between one authority and an opposition become complicated with many parties and issues that make the process of reconciliation all the more difficult" (Azar 1986: 37).

What is still missing? A personal effort to fill the void

The core omission in Basic Needs Theory: is it valid?

My own contribution to the discussion of what Burton has not addressed in his seminal work is not unique to him as it applies to many other scholars' work. Nevertheless, it is important; i.e. to what extent, if any, is Basic Human Needs theory empirically valid? In other words, to what extent, if any, are basic human needs *really* "ontological" and, therefore, "universal"? One possible answer lies in the complex relationship between social environment, status, self-esteem, serotonin and violence (see Wright 1995). Serotonin is a neurotransmitter "which plays a role in restraining aggressive impulses" (Goleman 1995: C10). Serotonin can be affected by one's self-worth (recognition, esteem, self-respect), which can itself be influenced by one's status (identity) and social environment (participation). Accordingly, a brutal social environment, reflective of physical and/or structural and cultural violence, with limited, if any, opportunities for personal growth and "social elevation," can correlate with low status, low self-esteem, low serotonin levels, "attendant states of mind" and an increase in the probability of violent behavior (including internalized violence in the form of depression and suicide) (see Sandole 1999: 181).

Another possible answer lies in research conducted by psychologist René Spitz on the "undeniable developmental effects of severe psychological deprivation and rejection, particularly in early childhood" (Garbarino 1999: 40). Spitz examined the differential impact of disrupted or non-existent attachment in babies born to women in Mexican institutions for unmarried mothers during the 1930s and 1940s. Some of these facilities required the mothers to withdraw from their babies six months after birth to allow for adoption. Other institutions forced the mothers to leave their babies days after they were born. Both groups of babies were looked after in terms of nutrition, personal hygiene and medical attention, *"but they were not loved"* (Garbarino 1999: 41, emphasis added):

> The first group of babies had a chance to form an attachment to their mothers, but were then psychologically abandoned. *Many of these babies died*, despite receiving good medical care and nutritious feeding … *they starved to death emotionally.*… The second group of babies never had psychological mothers, and they never connected with anyone. They, too, languished developmentally, although they did not die.
>
> (Garbarino 1999: 41, emphasis added)

The clear implication of Spitz's research is that basic needs for physical affection, love and affirmation of self-worth are present at birth and, therefore, are biological and homeostatic, i.e. relevant to survival and further development of humans in general. Reflective of the complex interaction between "nature" and "nurture," when needs are aroused by the environment and are then frustrated, catastrophic outcomes, including death, may ensue. In this particular case, just as adolescents and adults can die from depression, so can babies!

Is it conceivable, however, that the withdrawal of love and affection, resulting in the frustration of the needs for recognition, esteem and self-love, can lead to death in a newborn baby? James Gilligan (1996: 47), who has spent more than 25 years as a clinical psychiatrist treating hundreds of extremely violent men in the Massachusetts State Prison System, provides some clues: "the self cannot survive without love. The self starved of love dies.… Without feelings of love, the self feels numb, empty, and dead." Clearly, Dr. Gilligan is speaking of death *metaphorically*, but, yes, it is conceivable that when abandonment or rejection is intense enough, if the self dies in adolescents and adults, then the body may very well die in newborn babies.

Whatever the exact nature of the complex linkages between frustrated needs for recognition – for self-esteem, self-respect and self-love – and the expression of internalized violence in newborn babies, the message is clear: needs matter and we had better pay attention to them in public and foreign policymaking. For Gilligan, this is definitely the case, especially since the emotional experience of "the absence or deficiency of self-love is *shame*" (Gilligan 1996: 47, emphasis in original). In view of his practice-based research, "The emotion of *shame is the primary or ultimate cause of all violence,* whether toward others or toward the self" (Gilligan 1996: 110, emphasis added).

It would seem, therefore, that basic human needs are, indeed, universal and homeostatic – part of the biological make-up of all human beings and relevant to development and survival. This does not negate the Avruch/Black thesis on the role of culture in mediating the impact of needs or the experience of their frustration in the etiology of violence because, as indicated above, the environment ("nurture") plays a significant role in how basic needs ("nature") affect human behavior, including violent conflict. This reinforces Burton's basic argument that it is the frustration of basic needs for identity, recognition, participation and security by institutional authorities at various levels that results in violent conflict.

These propositions are implicit in another study, one with a large number of observations on many units of analysis over time. Epidemiologists Richard Wilkinson and Kate Pickett (2009) examined the relationships between income inequality and a number of indicators of physical and social dysfunction for the wealthiest countries of the world, plus all 50 US states, over a 30-year period. Subjecting their vast statistical datasets to regression analyses, they found clear relationships between income inequality – a form of *structural violence* (see Wilkinson and Pickett 2009: 134) – and community life and social relations (Ch. 4), mental health and drug use (Ch. 5), physical health and life expectancy (Ch. 6), obesity (Ch. 7), educational performance (Ch. 8), teenage births (Ch. 9), violence (Ch. 10), imprisonment and punishment (Ch. 11) and social mobility (Ch. 12).

Further confirming the hypothesized relationships between frustrated basic needs and violent behavior, Wilkinson and Pickett (2009: 134) report that:

> increased inequality ups the stakes in the competition for status: status matters even more. The impact of inequality on violence is even better established and accepted than the other effects of inequality that we discuss in this book.

What these "nature-nurture" studies have in common and with Burton's comprehensive theory is that low status, low feelings of self-worth, a feeling that one is not respected by others, can result in shame and then some form of internalized or externalized violence, even in new-born babies! Revisiting Gilligan's (1996) thesis on the role of shame in the etiology of violence, Wilkinson and Pickett (2009: 144, emphasis added) report that:

> In summary, we can see that *the association between inequality and violence is strong and consistent;* it's been demonstrated in many different time periods and settings. Recent evidence of the close correlation between ups and downs in inequality and violence show that if inequality is lessened, levels of violence also decline. *And the evolutionary importance of shame and humiliation provides a plausible explanation of why more unequal societies suffer more violence.*

Accordingly, not only does empirical reality correspond to Basic Human Needs theory, but frustrated needs for recognition, esteem, respect, self-love – which result in *shame* – are, in physically, structurally and culturally violent contexts, significant triggers of violence. This is especially the case among and between men: "Reckless, even violent behavior comes from young men at the bottom of society, deprived of all the markers of status, who must struggle to maintain face and what little status they have, often reacting explosively when it is threatened" (Wilkinson and Pickett 2009: 134). This accounts for the rising concern with the "youth-bulge," and not only in failed or failing states:

> The statistics are alarming. In crisis-hit Europe, the rates of under-25 joblessness are the highest since the OECD, the club of mostly rich nations, began recording them … youth unemployment adds to strains on government budgets, raises crime and threatens social stability.
>
> (Giles 2012)

According to David Stuckler of Cambridge University, unemployment in Europe correlates with a suicide epidemic (see Nadeau 2012: 36). As of June 2012, for example, more than 80 Italians have killed themselves since the beginning of the year; 1,727 Greeks have killed themselves since 2009; in Ireland, "deliberate self harm rates have doubled" since the beginning of the economic crisis; and in Spain, "the unemployment rate for people under 25 years old is now more than 50 percent [which] helps explain why that age group has the fastest-growing suicide rate in that country" (Nadeau 2012: 36).

In many cultures, few experiences are more guaranteed to make traditional males lose face and experience shame than to be unemployed. Whether that status translates into violent internalized or externalized aggression depends on other components of "The Journey" from unexpressed grievance to violent behavior – my second contribution to the discussion about what is missing from Burton's work – which we will now address.

The journey from unexpressed grievance to violent conflict behavior

The elements that I have identified as relevant components of "The Journey" represent theoretical and empirical studies that have been conducted by a number of scholars *independently* of each other, but which also overlap with one another's contribution, allowing the initially separate contributions to be reframed as *interdependent, interrelated* parts of a coherent whole. This reflects Burton's emphasis on "all available knowledge and experience," which is featured in his concept of "holism" (see Burton 1997) and his analytical problemsolving facilitated conflict resolution workshops. What these independent contributions all have in common is "dissonance" as conceptualized by Leon Festinger (1962) in his concept of "cognitive dissonance." For our purposes, *dissonance* represents a disconnect between a preferred state of affairs and an actual state of affairs. The greater and more intense the disconnect – the more frustrated actors' efforts are to synchronize the actual with the preferred (e.g. with regard to basic needs) – the more likely the disconnect will be expressed violently by the actors against the perceived sources of the problem.

The primary example of dissonance as the underlying common theme in "The Journey," is found in "structural" and "cultural violence," as conceptualized by peace studies pioneer Johan Galtung (1969, 1996). *Structural violence* is defined here as a situation in which members of an ethnic or other type of minority out-group are denied access to political, social, economic and other resources typically enjoyed and presided over by a mainstream in-group – resources that are relevant to the further development of the out-group members' capacities for meeting their basic needs. The minority out-group is denied access to these resources not because of what its members have done but because of *who they are*. Structural violence shifts to *cultural violence* when the structural violence is applauded and commemorated by the mainstream in-group in their framing of history and their educational systems, media and entertainment. What is intriguing about structural violence is that it may exist "objectively," i.e. independently of the perceptions of the aggrieved, disenfranchised, delegitimated out-group minority. Once structural violence shifts to cultural violence, however, perception of it on the part of the aggrieved out-group is assumed.

When members of aggrieved minority out-groups become aware of structural violence, it may take one of two forms: "relative deprivation" and/or "rank disequilibrium." *Relative deprivation* (Gurr 1970) occurs when *perceived* "value expectations" (what actors expect in terms of resources) are greater than *perceived* "value capabilities" (what actors feel they are capable of obtaining and holding on to). Again, the greater the disconnect – the greater the frustration – the greater the potential for a violent response to the perceived source. *Rank disequilibrium* (Galtung 1964) occurs when an actor is ranked as high on one particular dimension of socio-economic measurement (e.g. education), but low on others (e.g. class, occupation, race, social status).

Once structural violence is experienced as either relative deprivation and/or rank disequilibrium, *frustration-aggression* (Dollard *et al.* 1939) is likely to occur. Frustration has been defined by the Yale Group as an interference with an instigated goal-response at its appropriate time in a behavioral sequence. Once frustration has been experienced in attempting to fulfill basic needs for identity, recognition, participation and security by, for example, failing to hold on to a job that is essential for supporting one's family, aggression – e.g. "going postal" – may or may not follow, depending upon the interplay of the following four interrelated factors:

1   the *importance* of the blocked goal (e.g. the job that is essential to support one's family and sustain one's identity);
2   the *intensity* ("pain") of the blocking (e.g. losing the job, coupled with the shame and humiliation of being fired and rendered unemployed);
3   the *frequency*/duration of the blocking (e.g. not being able to find an adequate alternative job over time, coupled with persistent feelings of low self-worth); and
4   the *anticipation* of punishment for responding assertively to the perceived source[s] of the blocking (e.g. not being more "aggressive" in defending ones right to be [re-]employed because of a fear that such action would endanger their future employment prospects, get them in trouble with the law and degrade the sustainability of their family).

Regarding the policy implications of "The Journey," political authorities who adhere to a narrow Realist, power-based paradigm would tend to focus their efforts on enhancing the anticipation of punishment to deter aggrieved minority actors from taking direct action against those whom they perceive to be responsible for the structural, cultural and direct violence that has been employed against them. By contrast, authorities who adhere to a problemsolving/needs-based paradigm would likely concentrate on reducing, if not eliminating, the incidence and frequency of the frustration of minority actors' important objectives by establishing alternative systems for the fulfillment of their basic needs (e.g. by creating, in the short term, job retraining programs with pay).

In cases where the anticipation of punishment is reinforced, the successive, compounded frustration of needs is likely to generate dysfunctional societal outcomes. It is useful here to remind ourselves that, for Burton (1979: 59, emphasis added), needs describe those conditions or opportunities that are *essential to the individual* if he is to be a functioning and cooperative member of society, conditions that are *essential to his development* and which, through him, are *essential to the organization and survival of society*.

Most importantly,

> if the norms of the society inhibit and frustrate to the degree that he decides they are no longer useful, then, subject to values he attaches to social relationships, *he will employ methods outside the norms.... Threat of punishment, punishment itself, isolation from society will not control his behavior.*
>
> (Burton 1979: 78–79, emphasis added)

Burton's thinking clearly lends itself to the development of a theory of political extremism and violent behavior in general, for example, the riots in London and other British cities in August 2011. As *Washington Post* columnist Courtland Milloy (2011: B5) observed at the time, with implicit references to dissonance, relative deprivation, frustration, and basic needs for recognition, esteem and self-respect: "Feeling disrespected and often downright ignored, many [British youth] are threatening to destroy what they can't have."

By implication, Burton's work lends itself to the development of a theory of *terrorism* (see Sandole 2010: Ch. 4). For example, the 19 highjackers of September 11, 2001 were Muslim males, 15 of whom were from Saudi Arabia which currently has a youth unemployment rate that "is four times the older jobless rate" (Giles 2012). The unemployment status of the lead terrorist, Mohamed Atta, an Egyptian, prompted his father to ridicule him for not being a "real man" (see Lerner 2002). This personal experience of low self-worth, and shame and humiliation, was likely compounded by a profound sense that the terrorists' culture and religion have repeatedly been reviled by the Christian West that has been trying to marginalize, if not destroy, Islam since the 3rd Crusade of nearly 1,000 years ago. Indeed, these sentiments have been reinforced by the US-led wars in Iraq and Afghanistan plus Western (Judaic/Christian) military actions elsewhere (e.g. in Pakistan, Palestine and Yemen), which have served to further radicalize Muslims worldwide, in the process producing new cadres of fighters for the Global Jihad (see Pape 2005; Priest 2005a, 2005b).

Successive public and foreign policies that are designed to enhance the anticipation-of-punishment option for aggrieved minorities, e.g. the Global War on Terror (GWOT), can result in further escalating frustration of needs and then "tipping points" (see Gladwell 2000) between behavior that is still controllable and *self-stimulating/self-perpetuating violent conflict systems* of a quasi-deterministic nature that are difficult if not impossible to contain. Under such circumstances, actors will tend to *over-perceive* the threat emanating from "The Other," and *over-react* to the over-perceived threat (see Zinnes *et al.* 1961).

It is at this point that a third party intervention, perhaps along the lines of a multidisciplinary Burtonian panel, would be essential to encourage the parties to stop the bloodletting, thereby eliminating the symptoms of conflict (e.g. riots or terrorist attacks). The major danger, however, is that, once the parties turn off the violence – which is itself no mean feat – they may neglect to pursue provention, i.e. deal with the underlying sources of the conflict which has been expressed violently. This remains a major challenge for concerned members of the international community in their attempts to deal with the protracted, violent conflicts that continue to afflict world society. For instance, according to *Peace and Conflict 2010* (Hewitt *et al.* 2010: 1, emphasis added):

> Strikingly, of the 39 different conflicts that became active in the last 10 years, 31 were *conflict recurrences* – instances of resurgent, armed violence in societies where conflict had largely been dormant for at least a year. Only eight were entirely new conflicts between new antagonists involving new issues and interests.

A major reason for conflict recurrence is that "the internationally brokered settlement or containment of many armed conflicts since the early 1990s did not deal effectively with *root causes*" (Hewitt *et al.* 2010: 4, emphasis added). Such is one major consequence of the "default option" in international relations (see Beriker 2009), i.e. the tendency to employ the prevailing, traditional Realist paradigm which tends to focus only on symptoms at the total expense of deep-rooted, underlying causes and conditions. This leaves the underlying sources of conflict in place, like ticking time bombs, ready to be resurrected under the right conditions and causes.

Conclusion

In this chapter, I have attempted to contribute to the development of a comprehensive theory relevant to accounting for, and dealing with the complex conflicts of the twenty-first century. To achieve this goal, I reviewed the work of the conflict resolution pioneer who has done the most to advance knowledge on the relationship between frustrated basic human needs and violent conflict, John Burton. Accordingly, I examined Burton's World Society Paradigm (WSP), Basic Human Needs (BHN) Theory, analytical problem-solving facilitated conflict resolution processes and provention. I then identified some gaps, which, if filled, could extend the theoretical and practical reach of his work.

Pursuant to filling the gaps, I discussed two earlier responses to Burton's work, beginning with Kevin Avruch and Peter Black's critique of

Burton for his omission of any explicit reference to the role of culture in mediating the impact of basic needs on human behavior. I then examined Edward Azar's extension of Burton's work in developing a theory of *protracted social conflict* (PSC). According to Oliver Ramsbotham, Tom Woodhouse and Hugh Miall (2011: 103), who have distilled conflict and peace studies into a coherent knowledge system, PSC analysis is an attempt to "synthesize the realist and structuralist paradigms into a pluralist framework" that is more appropriate for explaining contemporary conflict patterns than alternative frames that are more limited in scope (Azar 1991: 95). Although not the final word on "the significance of mobilized identities, exclusionist ideologies, fragile and authoritarian governance, weak states and disputed sovereignty as chief sources of major armed [intrastate] conflict," Ramsbotham *et al.* (2011: 103, 104) claim that "Azar's model remains a rich framework" that deserves more attention than it has received.

In my own critique of Burton's work, I responded to his omission of any specific effort to explore the validity of his theory of the basic needs-violent conflict nexus. This analysis revealed the complex interaction between "nature" (basic needs, homeostasis, serotonin) and "nurture" (oppressed or otherwise frustrated needs, resulting in shame and humiliation) in the etiology of violent conflict behavior.

I then advanced "The Journey," revealing a sequence of interrelated stages in the shift from unexpressed grievance to manifest violence where experienced third-party interveners could, via facilitated problemsolving workshops, work together with the parties to manage the basic needs of all concerned, with the promise to craft public or foreign policy that achieves and maintains provention as "the main task" (Burton 1993: 63). This would be one clear example of an appropriate response to the "alarming void" that Burton (1993: 57) observed nearly 20 years ago: "power politics has failed domestically and internationally, but no alternative has been articulated and applied as policy. This is the bankrupt state of civilization at the end of the twentieth century." Hence, the continuing relevance of Burton's (1993: 60) claim that we need "a political philosophy that asserts that the satisfaction of human needs that are universal must be the ultimate goal of survivable societies". Until we develop and start to implement such a philosophy, with new forms of governance at multiple levels, the Human Experiment will continue to be reflective of "civilizations in crisis" (see Burton 1996).

Notes

1 The author respectfully acknowledges Dr. Ingrid Sandole-Staroste, Dr. Kevin Avruch and Dr. Christopher Mitchell, who read through and made comments on earlier drafts of this chapter.
2 Burton's preference for Sites over Maslow is surprising given that, prior to Burton's theorizing even of the role of social-biological values in the etiology of

violent conflict, James Chowning Davies (1962, 1973, 1986) had already developed a theory of political violence that made explicit use of Maslow's theory of needs, plus the Yale School's frustration-aggression theory (Dollard *et al.* 1939). Davies had hypothesized that it is the frustration of *substantive needs* (physical, social-affectional, self-esteem and self-actualization) or *implemental needs* (security, knowledge and power) that can lead to violent conflict: "violence … is produced when certain innate needs or demands are deeply frustrated" (Davies 1973: 251; see Sandole 1999: 119).

3 The "distinctive hypothesis" of controlled communication is that

> conflict behavior of communities and states comprises elements such as perception of external conditions, selection of goals, survey possible values, choice of different means of attaining goals, and assessments of values and means in relation to assessments of costs of conflict. The method hypothesizes that conflicts of interests are subjective and that experience and knowledge alter these components, thus producing altered relationships. By controlled communication misperceptions that parties to a dispute have of each other are exposed by introducing relevant theoretical and empirical knowledge.
>
> (Burton 1969: ix–x)

4 According to a construct I have developed, the "three levels of conflict reality" (see Sandole 2010), conflict can be viewed as existing at three levels. First, conflict can occur at the level of *symptoms*, for example, the number and intensity of terrorist bombings recorded for a given region during a particular year. This is the level at which traditional, Realist power approaches are directed. Second, conflict can occur at the level of the *challenged relationships* that give rise to symptoms. This is where third parties enter the "conflict space" of the parties concerned in order to assist them to deal with their conflicts, e.g. to either settle or resolve them. Finally, conflict can occur at the level of *deep-rooted, underlying causes and conditions* of the challenged relationships. Burton's *provention* deals with this fundamental level of conflict.

5 Azar identified 60, mostly identity-related, cases, particularly in the developing world, which have been increasing in frequency since the end of World War II. Examples include Lebanon, Sri Lanka, Ethiopia, Cyprus, Iran, Nigeria and Zimbabwe, but, in the "developed" world, Northern Ireland as well. Because political authorities rarely address deep-rooted, underlying causes and conditions of conflicts – the goal of provention – once particular PSCs develop, they tend to characterize world society for some time, because of the "simultaneous occurrence of conflict and underdevelopment," war and poverty, with each feeding on the other and making it "difficult for societies to overcome either condition alone" (Azar 1986: 39).

References

Avruch, K. (1998) *Culture and Conflict Resolution*, Washington, D.C.: US Institute of Peace Press.

Avruch, K. and Black, P.W. (1987) "A generic theory of conflict resolution: a critique," *Negotiation Journal*, 3(1), January: 87–96.

Avruch, K. and Black, P.W. (1993) "Conflict resolution in intercultural settings: problems and prospects," in D.J.D. Sandole and H. van der Merwe (eds) *Conflict Resolution Theory and Practice: Integration and Application*, Manchester: Manchester University Press and New York: St. Martin's Press.

Azar, E.E. (1986) "Protracted international conflicts: ten propositions," in E.E. Azar and J.W. Burton (eds) *International Conflict Resolution: Theory and Practice,* Sussex, UK: Wheatsheaf Books and Boulder, CO: Lynne Rienner Publishers.

Azar, E.E. (1990) *The Management of Protracted Social Conflict: Theory and Cases,* Aldershot, UK: Dartmouth.

Azar, E.E. (1991) "The analysis and management of protracted social conflict," in V.D. Volkan, D.A. Julius and J.V. Montville (eds) *The Psychodynamics of International Relationships,* Vol. 2, Lexington, MA: D.C. Heath.

Beriker, N. (2009) "Conflict resolution: the missing link between liberal international relations theory and realistic practice," in D.J.D. Sandole, S. Byrne, I. Sandole-Staroste and J. Senehi (eds) *Handbook of Conflict Analysis and Resolution,* London and New York: Routledge.

Black, P.W. and Avruch, K. (1989) "Some issues in thinking about culture and the resolution of conflict," *Humanity and Society,* 13: 187–194.

Burton, J.W. (1969) *Conflict and Communication: The Use of Controlled Communication in International Relations,* London: Macmillan and New York: Free Press.

Burton, J.W. (1972) *World Society,* Cambridge, UK and New York: Cambridge University Press.

Burton, J.W. (1979) *Deviance, Terrorism and War: The Process of Solving Unsolved Social and Political Problems,* New York: St. Martin's Press and Oxford, UK: Martin Robertson.

Burton, J.W. (1984) *Global Conflict: The Domestic Sources of International Crisis,* Brighton, UK: Wheatsheaf Books.

Burton, J.W. (1990a) *Conflict: Resolution and Provention,* London: Macmillan and New York: St. Martin's Press.

Burton, J.W. (ed.) (1990b) *Conflict: Human Needs Theory,* London: Macmillan and New York: St. Martin's Press.

Burton, J.W. (1990c) "Unfinished business in conflict resolution," in J.W. Burton and F. Dukes (eds) *Conflict: Readings in Management and Resolution,* London: Macmillan and New York: St. Martin's Press.

Burton, J.W. (1993) "Conflict resolution as a political philosophy," in D.J.D. Sandole and H. van der Merwe (eds) *Conflict Resolution Theory and Practice: Integration and Application,* Manchester, UK: Manchester University Press and New York: St. Martin's Press.

Burton, J.W. (1996) "Civilizations in crisis: from adversarial to problem solving processes," *International Journal of Peace Studies,* 1(1), January: 5–24.

Burton, J.W. (1997) *Violence Explained: The Sources of Conflict, Violence and Crime and Their Prevention,* Manchester, UK: Manchester University Press.

Burton, J.W. and Dukes, F. (eds) (1990a) *Conflict: Readings in Management and Resolution,* London: Macmillan and New York: St. Martin's Press.

Burton, J.W. and Dukes, F. (eds) (1990b) *Conflict: Practices in Management, Settlement and Resolution,* London: Macmillan and New York: St. Martin's Press.

Burton, J.W. and Sandole, D.J.D. (1986) "Generic theory: the basis of conflict resolution," *Negotiation Journal,* 2(4), October: 333–344.

Burton, J.W. and Sandole, D.J.D. (1987) "Expanding the debate on generic theory of conflict resolution: a response to a critique," *Negotiation Journal,* 3(1), January: 97–100.

Cannon, W.B. (1963) *The Wisdom of the Body,* revised and enlarged edn, New York: W.W. Norton.

Davies, J.C. (1962) "Toward a theory of revolution," *American Sociological Review*, 27: 5–19.

Davies, J.C. (1973) "Aggression, violence, revolution and war," in J.N. Knutson (ed.) *Handbook of Political Psychology*, San Francisco and London: Jossey-Bass.

Davies, J.C. (1986) "Roots of political behavior," in M.G. Hermann (ed.) *Political Psychology: Contemporary Problems and Issues*, San Francisco and London: Jossey-Bass.

Dollard, J., Doob, L.W., Miller, N.E., Mowrer, O.H. and Sears, R.R. (1939) *Frustration and Aggression*, New Haven: Yale University Press. Abridged and reprinted in E.I. Megargee and J.E. Hokanson (eds) (1970) *The Dynamics of Aggression: Individual, Group, and International Analyses*, New York and London: Harper and Row.

Dunn, D.J. (2004) *From Power Politics to Conflict Resolution: The Work of John W. Burton*, Houndmills, Basingstoke, Hampshire, UK and New York: Palgrave Macmillan.

Festinger, L. (1962) *A Theory of Cognitive Dissonance*, Stanford, CA: Stanford University Press.

Filiu, J.P. (2011) *The Arab Revolution: Ten Lessons from the Democratic Uprising*, London: C. Hurst. Cited in David Gardner (2011) "Enduring freedom," Life and Arts, *Financial Times*, September 10/11: 19.

Galtung, J. (1964) "A structural theory of aggression," *Journal of Peace Research*, 1: 95–119; reprinted in C.G. Smith (ed.) (1971) *Conflict Resolution: Contributions of the Behavioral Sciences*, Notre Dame, IN and London: University of Notre Dame Press.

Galtung, J. (1969) "Violence, peace and peace research," *Journal of Peace Research*, 6(3): 167–191.

Galtung, J. (1996) *Peace by Peaceful Means: Peace and Conflict, Development and Civilization*, International Peace Research Institute, Oslo (PRIO); London and Thousand Oaks, CA: SAGE Publications.

Garbarino, J. (1999) *Lost Boys: Why Our Sons Turn Violent and How We Can Save Them*, New York: Anchor Books.

Giles, C. (2012) "Soaring youth unemployment stokes fears of long-term harm," *Financial Times*, July 3: 4.

Gilligan, J. (1996) *Violence: Reflections on a National Epidemic*, New York: Vintage Press.

Gladwell, M. (2000) *The Tipping Point: How Little Things Can Make a Big Difference*, New York: Little, Brown.

Goleman, D. (1995) "Early violence leaves its mark on the brain," *New York Times*, October 3: C1, C10.

Gurr, T.R. (1970) *Why Men Rebel*, Princeton, NJ: Princeton University Press.

Hewitt, J.J., Wilkenfeld, J. and Gurr, T.R. (2010) *Peace and Conflict 2010*, Boulder, CO: Paradigm Publishers.

Hollis, M. (1994) *The Philosophy of Social Science: An Introduction*, Cambridge, UK and New York: Cambridge University Press.

Kaldor, M. (2006) *New and Old Wars: Organized Violence in a Global Era*, 2nd edn, Cambridge, UK and Malden, MA: Polity Press.

Lerner, J. (2002) "I was a terrorist," *Washington Post Magazine*, February 24: 24–28, 38–40.

Maslow, A.H. (1987) *Motivation and Personality*, 3rd edn, New York and London: Harper and Row.

Milloy, C. (2011) "From London to Philadelphia, youths erupting over theft of their futures," *Washington Post*, August 9: B1 and B5. Online. Available www.washingtonpost.com/local/from-london-to-philadelphia-youths-erupting-over-theft-of-their-futures/2011/08/09/gIQAZ3Ff5I_story.html (accessed August 15, 2011).

Nadeau, B.L. (2012) "Europe's 'white shadows'," *Newsweek*, June 25: 34–37.

Pape, R.A. (2005) *Dying to Win: The Strategic Logic of Suicide Terrorism*, New York: Random House.

Priest, D. (2005a) "Iraq new terror breeding ground: War created haven, CIA advisors report," *Washington Post*, January 14: A1.

Priest, D. (2005b) "War helps recruit terrorists, Hill told: Intelligence officials talk of growing insurgency," *Washington Post*, February 17: A1.

Ramsbotham, O., Woodhouse, T. and Miall, H. (2011) *Contemporary Conflict Resolution: The Prevention, Management and Transformation of Deadly Conflicts*, 3rd edn, Cambridge, UK and Malden, MA: Polity Press.

Sandole, D.J.D. (1999) *Capturing the Complexity of Conflict: Dealing with Violent Ethnic Conflict in the Post-Cold War Era*, London and New York: Pinter/Cassell.

Sandole, D.J.D. (2007) *Peace and Security in the Postmodern World: The OSCE and Conflict Resolution*, New York and London: Routledge.

Sandole, D.J.D. (2010) *Peacebuilding: Preventing Violent Conflict in a Complex World*, Cambridge, UK and Malden, MA: Polity Press.

Sites, P.M. (1973) *Control: The Basis of Social Order*, New York: Dunellen.

Wilkinson, R. and Pickett, K. (2009) *The Spirit Level: Why Greater Equality Makes Societies Stronger*, New York and London: Bloomsbury Press.

Wolfers, A. (1962) *Discord and Collaboration: Essays on International Politics*, Baltimore: Johns Hopkins University Press.

Wright, R. (1995) "The biology of violence," *New Yorker*, March 13: 68–77.

Zinnes, D.A., North, R.C. and Koch, Jr., H.E. (1961) "Capability, threat, and the outbreak of war," in J.N. Rosenau (ed.) *International Politics and Foreign Policy: A Reader in Research and Theory*, New York: Free Press and London: Collier-Macmillan.

2 Basic Human Needs and the dilemma of power in conflict resolution

Kevin Avruch

Introduction

Over the last several decades, as "conflict resolution" began to define itself as a distinct field of research and practice, that is, a *discipline*, certain gaps were discovered and addressed. Some were straightforward and arose from similar lacunae in the older disciplines that dominated conflict resolution at first, International Relations (IR) particularly. Attention had to be paid to culture and gender, for example. Other developments entailed broadening the field from an exclusive foundation in positivism to admit other epistemologies, such as phenomenology or Critical Theory. Yet another involved conceptualizing conflict as concerned with something more, and "deeper," than clashes of *interests*, and therefore conflict resolution as a practice requiring more than negotiation or mediation as modeled on the utilitarian heuristic of the buyer-seller (Avruch 2006, 2012). What lies beneath interests, something perhaps less amenable to rational bargaining? Some in the new field responded: think about *values*, or *identity*, or something called *basic human needs*.

There was one lacuna that the field long recognized but failed adequately to address (Scimecca 1991), "the dilemma of power." The dilemma presents itself at two levels. The first is conceptual and foundational and the second is manifest at the level of practice and ethics. Conceptually, power is a dilemma for the field because there already exists a dominant and dominating "theory" (what some of us, seeking to de-authorize, would instead call a *narrative*) of power and conflict with roots in Thucydides, Hobbes and Machiavelli, thence to Morgenthau and the entire edifice of realist and neorealist IR. In an important sense power is a dilemma for conflict resolution in direct proportion to the extent that it is *not* a dilemma for those "realist" thinkers for whom it is a self-evident social and political fact. Peace and conflict studies seeks to establish its foundations in a conceptualization of the world that is alternative to *Machtpolitik* thinking (and practice!). At the level of practice, the dilemma presents itself to the individual mediator or other sort of third party who intervenes in a conflict between parties with obvious and undeniable differences of power, and seeks a solution that is not predicated on Thucydides' prescription for the people of Melos "negotiating" with the powerful Athenians: "The strong do what they have the power to do and the weak accept that they have to accept."[1] Here is our dilemma: How to conceive of a "non-Melian" theory of power and conflict and having done so, how to design a conflict resolution practice that embodies it?

In this chapter, while touching briefly on how others in the field have responded both conceptually and practically to the dilemma of power (cf. Avruch 2012), I want to focus on a particular response and practice: John Burton's idea of *basic human needs* (BHN) as the drivers of deep-rooted conflict, and his original *problem-solving workshop* (PSW) as the practice that achieves their resolution.

As Dunn's (2004) portrayal of Burton's career in the academy, after his meteoric rise and fall in Australian politics and public service, makes clear, from very early on he opposed most of the key tenets of traditional IR thinking, exemplified in his heated debates with British colleagues in the early 1960s (Sandole 2006). In those days a central point of contention was Burton's challenge to the privileged position accorded to the state as the sole and autonomous "actor" in international politics, as well as the doctrinaire segregation, based on the presumed normless and amoral nature of the international system, of international from domestic politics. Burton was not alone in this critique of state-centric IR. But his challenge went deeper, to the whole structure of "power politics," and the hegemony of power in neorealist international relations. He also proposed a conflict resolution methodology (from early "controlled communication" to the later "analytical problem-solving workshop") to demonstrate why the power politics paradigm was the wrong way to understand, much less resolve, deep-rooted conflicts.

While the critique of power politics and neorealist international relations came very early to Burton, it was not until his "discovery" of basic human needs (BHN) – what Dunn (2004: 95) called the "ontological break" – that all the pieces necessary for the formulation of a conflict resolution practice fell for him into place. Postulating basic human needs, Burton argued, obviated the problem of power imbalance between parties, while the problem-solving workshop functioned to neutralize whatever imbalance remained. He claimed, in short, to offer a solution to the dilemma of power. This chapter seeks critically to examine this claim.

Basic Human Needs as a theory of conflict

Long a critic of state-centric IR and of power as its main explanatory variable (e.g. Burton 1962, 1965, 1972), Burton was challenged to offer an alternative practice to power-based diplomatic negotiation, and in late 1965 he crafted what he called "the controlled communication workshop," later to become the analytical problem-solving workshop (cf. Burton 1969,

1987). Although genealogically connected, what separated "controlled communication" from analytical problem solving was that the earlier form found Burton improvising as he went along, aiming for an improved version of negotiation divorced from power-plays. Controlled communication began as mainly a reformatory *process*, involving a rejection of *Macht* but otherwise unanchored in an articulated *theory of conflict*. In contrast, analytical problem solving was not at all improvisatory. Warranting a *Handbook* (1987), it featured exacting and prescriptive rules and was explicitly based on a theory of conflict as originating in the suppression by authorities of basic human needs. In basic human needs Burton believed he had found the compelling alternative explanatory variable to power as exercised by states or their elites.

Burton built on a long tradition positing some set of needs or requirements essential for personal and social growth and stability – some point to such an argument by Aristotle in the *Nicomachean Ethics* – but he was especially drawn to Maslow's (1954) influential work. Rather than conceiving of needs in terms of an individual's developmental stages, however, Burton understood them as simultaneous, and took his list from the work of the sociologist Paul Sites (1973). Sites named eight needs: consistency of response; stimulation; security; recognition; justice; meaning; rationality; and control. Burton added a ninth need, which he called role defense, "the protection of needs once they had been acquired" (1979: 73). Sites's argument was that these needs are both invariant and universal in their distribution and, crucially, that they cannot be "erased" through socialization. Not everyone can be molded to conformity. The exercise of raw power, brute force, can try to suppress needs and repress individuals, but resistance ensues, resulting in various "antisocial" behaviors. For Sites this was a causal explanation for criminality and social deviance. Burton applied Sites's theory far more broadly (Burton 1979). As these needs cannot be "socialized away" or permanently suppressed, concerted suppression by rulers or coercive authorities deploying power will only generate resistance, sometimes violent resistance. This is the source of *all* deep-rooted, protracted or intractable, social conflicts: the suppression of basic human needs by the application of dominating power. Logically, then, conflict resolution consists of finding ways toward the satisfaction of these needs.

At least four corollaries followed from these axioms. First, Burton claimed that because all applications of power (brute force or coercion) were directed against implacable and unalterable – *non-negotiable* – basic needs, power was always only contingently (temporarily) successful. Second, as he developed his ideas about deep-rooted conflicts and basic human needs he came to draw a bright line between the *management* of a conflict and its *resolution*. Conflict management implied bargaining and negotiation over interests. Being non-negotiable, basic human needs resisted negotiation, even the "principled" sort of interest-based and integrative solution-seeking championed by Fisher and Ury in their influential *Getting to Yes* (1981). The non-negotiability of basic human needs – they cannot be traded or bargained away even if "the individual" wanted to – was a key part of their essential character, and remained so for Burton in all his writings after *Deviance, Terrorism and War* (e.g. Burton 1997). In this way Burton differentiated "dispute" (over negotiable interests) from "conflict" (susceptible only to analysis and satisfaction of hitherto suppressed basic human needs). A corollary effect was to separate so-called dispute resolution from conflict resolution. This distinguished Burton's conception of conflict resolution from what was rapidly and simultaneously developing in the field as "alternative dispute resolution," ADR. Third, since "identity" was a key basic human need, the turn from management to resolution (from interests to needs) directed Burtonian resolutionists toward deep-rooted conflicts around identity – ethnicity, religion, race or nationalism – a move influenced by Burton's collaboration with Edward Azar.

Fourth, and finally, Burton argued that the need to conceive of true conflict resolution as the satisfaction of basic human needs implied an entirely new and different "political philosophy" from power politics and neorealism and, in practice, a radically different political system, one committed a priori to the individual's needs satisfaction, a commitment to what Burton termed "provention."

Although the theory was first elucidated at length in *Deviance, Terrorism and War* (1979), a particularly clear and forceful and summary, as well as a bold extension of the theory's "reach," was published in *Negotiation Journal* (Burton and Sandole 1986). The article was titled "Generic Theory: The Basis of Conflict Resolution." In it the authors confidently proclaimed nothing less than:

1 a revolutionary "paradigm shift" (à la Thomas Kuhn) in thinking about conflict, from a "levels" to a level- and discipline-spanning "generic" approach (in a flash undermining the rationale for an independent discipline called IR), thus;
2 a new "adiscipline" and *science* of Conflict Resolution, founded methodologically upon the replacement of "Popperian falsification" and empirical canons of induction and deduction (earlier Burton (1979: 198) had called BHN a "deduced hypothesis"), with C.S. Peirce's *abduction*, arriving at one's "hypothesis" through insight or a sort of common sense: "problem solving not by trial and error but by thoughtful and questioning analysis" (Burton and Sandole 1986: 335);
3 the rejection of conflict settlement or management as key goals of the new science's practice, to be replaced by the goals of resolution or prevention, abjuring traditional approaches to understanding conflict based upon such "normal science" ideas as: "the state system, power rivalries … cultural differences, the struggle for scarce resources" (Burton and Sandole 1986: 338).

Underlying all of this was the fundamental and axiomatic notion of basic human needs, described as not only a "generic theory but also a genetic one" (Burton and Sandole 1986: 338). In the genome, they are invariant and universal. They cannot be permanently suppressed. However, crucially related to practice, Burton asserted that BHNs were not scarce resources, trapping contestants in zero-sum contests. To increase, for example, the security of one is to increase the security of all. In this way Burton claimed to arrive at the ultimate positive-sum, Pareto-optimal solution. On the one hand, needs resisted mere political or social power because they were themselves all-powerful. On the other, they transcended scarcity and thus obviated destructive zero-sum conflict thinking – if only contestants could be made aware of this fact. This is what the problem-solving workshop was for.

Burton and Azar: linking individuals to structures

For others in IR who were critical of the state-centric assumptions of neo-realism Burton's idea of basic human needs resonated strongly. A collection titled *The Power of Human Needs in World Society* (Coate and Rosati 1988) featured essays (several by Burton himself) that explored the idea as an alternative to orthodox thinking about state power. But even his admirers could see problems stemming from the methodological individualism that undergirded the theory. For one thing, Burton was rather vague on what "structures" intervened between the level of the individual, his or her relentless basic needs, and society or the state. Burton leapt from the individual to the level of coercive, ruling elites. In their introductory chapter to *The Power of Human Needs in World Society* Coate and Rosati recognized this weakness. They wrote: "A human needs approach, however, must confront a major problem – the link between the micro (that is, individual) level and the macro (that is, societal – world and national) level" (Coate and Rosati 1988: 9). They suggested that focusing on "groups, social networks, and values" can address this weakness, but rather than specifying how, they went on in their concluding chapter (Coate and Rosati 1988: 269) to argue, rather unhelpfully, that

> Theorizing about the nature of social networks and relationships based on a human needs approach does not require explicit and definitively empirical linkages. The development of theory and a research agenda is not dependent solely on inductive, empirical analysis, but is also heavily dependent on deduction.

The first remark, abjuring explicitness and empiricism, seems contrary to some essential social scientific sensibility, and also contrary to the way Burton himself thought of his project – as "science." Meanwhile, by their subsequent remark, on induction versus deduction, Coate and Rosati merely placed themselves in the awkward and methodologically incoherent position that formed one of the bases of Avruch and Black's (1987) critique of Burton (see below), and one that Burton later claimed to transcend by doing away with Aristotle entirely in favor of Charles Sanders Peirce: by rejecting both induction and deduction in favor of abduction.

Something more productive in the matter of micro to macro linkages was achieved by Burton's brief collaboration with Edward Azar (Azar and Burton 1986). Like Burton, Azar was a critic of traditional IR thinking. Unlike Burton who came to academic IR after a career in diplomacy and became a vocal critic of orthodoxy almost as soon as he encountered it, Azar was educated and socialized in the discipline. Nevertheless, he moved away from dominant IR analysis with its assumptions of state "actors" rationally pursuing interests in power-based settings. Instead, he began to look "inside" states for signs of conflict and instability that had the potential of overflowing state borders into the international arena or, alternatively, of international forces piercing borders, and destabilizing states in turn. Doubtless it was his own experience as a Lebanese citizen from a multi-communal society governed by a state reliant on fragile "confessional" alliances and the thin fiction of shared national interests rationally arrived at and pursued, and as a scholar studying conflict in the Middle East more generally, that sowed whatever reservations he came to have about orthodox neorealist theory. He was also interested from early on in the relationship between development and social conflict, particularly uneven development and (perhaps thinking of the Shi'a Lebanese in those days) the state-sanctioned misdistribution of valued resources (Ramsbotham 2005).

Azar's theory of "protracted social conflicts" (PSC) focused on what he called the "disarticulation between state and society" (Azar 1990: 10). Structural disarticulation, dysfunctional governance and potentially destabilizing international linkages provided the initial conditions for protracted conflict. But whence the final *motivation* for action by individuals and groups? Where is the "engine" that puts this fraught state-society structure in motion and drives the conflict? Collaborating with Burton, Azar fixed on the power of basic human needs: "The source of protracted social conflicts is the denial of those elements required in the development of all people, and whose pursuit is a compelling need of all." He went on to name the elements: "These are security, distinctive identity, social recognition of identity, and effective participation..." and concludes: "The real source of conflict is the denial of those human needs that are common to all and whose pursuit is an ontological drive in all" (Azar 1985; see also Azar 1990).

The suppression of basic human needs provided Azar with the motivational "engine" driving protracted social conflicts. Balancing this, what Burton found in Azar were the explicit and empirical linkages, the groups, social networks and values that bridged micro and macro levels. Azar's theory was also structural in the sense that he stressed the linkage between conflict and systematic inequality, poverty and under-development. Burton's theory of deep-rooted conflict benefited from his collaboration with Azar. But conceptual problems with the very idea of basic human needs remained unaddressed.

The critics respond

The bold agenda-setting article Burton published with Dennis Sandole (Burton and Sandole 1986) directly occasioned the so-called Avruch–Black critique, which came out in *Negotiation Journal* the following year (Avruch and Black 1987).[2] As cultural anthropologists it is not surprising that we found the geneticism of Burton's conception of basic human needs, as well as their universality and invariance, matters for debate. But we criticized the Burton–Sandole piece as well on methodological grounds, for its scientism and for their claim (invoking Kuhn) to BHN as "paradigm busting." Ours was, admittedly, a rather pugnacious piece.

We rejected claims to Kuhnian revolution. We pointed out that needs-theory has a long history, in philosophy, theology, as well as the social sciences, and an equally long history of critique. In anthropology, for example, there was Bronislaw Malinowski's "scientific theory of culture" (Malinowski 1944). Malinowski asserted seven needs and even, going beyond Burton, listed the precise cultural institutions by which they were satisfied.[3] Malinowski's theory was dismissed by many in anthropology as banal functionalism. In Burton's usage of BHN theory we saw a functionalism "in reverse": how sociocultural institutions worked mainly to suppress needs and how this resulted in the opposite of functionalism's epitome, social equilibrium, producing instead deep-rooted social conflict.

Other questions put forth by needs critics were raised: why those needs? Why not others? Harold Isaacs (1975) wrote of two basic human needs, belonging and self-esteem. Joseph Scimecca (1990), coming from humanistic sociology, citing Fromm and Rollo May and influenced by Ernest Becker, asserted self-reflexivity and freedom. Somewhere Galtung had his list, Etzioni his, and almost everyone cited Maslow at least once. Burton had added a ninth need to Sites's canonical eight, role defense or the need to protect other needs once acquired. We pointed out that this need rendered all the others logically irrelevant. One can have eight needs or 800: all one must do is claim role defense as a basic human need and every other need is guaranteed. "Role defense" disappeared from Burton's later writing, and Sites's original eight alone remained.

It was Burton's claim to have found *the* generic theory in establishing "the *science* of conflict resolution" that had us critically engage BHN theory on his chosen ground of positivist science (e.g. Hempel 1965). How were the needs derived? Are they deduced, and if so, from what covering law or theory? How might they be operationalized so as to be empirically tested?

Burton and Sandole (1986) had done away with "Popperian falsification" in a sentence. Fair enough, but if one is claiming "science" what takes its place? Although in earlier writing Burton claimed that BHN were deductively discovered, he too saw the problem with this and thereafter invoked Peirce's idea of "abduction" as a way to get around deduction/induction methodology entirely. The problem with this is that for Peirce abduction refers to how a scientist might insightfully or creatively formulate an *hypothesis* on the basis of informed conjecture or "educated guess." While in formal logic abduction may indeed constitute a fallacy of "affirming the consequent," what makes it, Peirce argues, a valid method in scientific investigation is that having formulated a plausible explanation (the hypothesis) on the basis of insight or knowledge of the phenomenon under study, one can then proceed to evaluate or test the hypothesis. Abduction is, to put it differently, something that may well occur in the *context of discovery* in science, but there still remains to be satisfied the canonical (positivist) standards involved in the *context of verification.* Hypotheses abductively adduced still need to be validated before they "count" as a scientific explanation. This is what Burton never did, nor could he ever do while claiming "scientific" status for BHN. For Peirce, one might adduce basic human needs as an hypothesis in support of a theory, but Burton was intent on "abducing" the existence of basic human needs in support of the theory of Basic Human Needs: precisely the fallacy logicians call *post hoc ergo propter hoc.* According to Dunn (2004), Burton solved this in that he moved away from the language of sociobiology or genetics and wrote instead of the "ontological" status of basic human needs. In so far as he still laid claim to a science of conflict resolution, it is hard to see the gain here. Indeed, to replace "biology" with "ontology" is to substitute metaphysics for physics, and Kant for Galileo or Francis Bacon. Building conflict resolution on Kantian principles may not be, in the end, such a bad strategy, a point I shall return to in the chapter's conclusion. But it probably wasn't what Burton had in mind, the sort of scientific authority he sought.[4]

Hempelian logical positivism was not the only basis for our critique. Closer to their own sensibilities as cultural theorists, we cited A.R. Louch (1966) who stood in for a range of post-Wittgenstein, natural language philosophers. Not only did Burton's geneticism occlude culture, but in doing so he was unable to realize that he hid as well the potentially culturally constructed nature of such "basic" needs as security, identity and so on. This, indeed, is the tack Tarja Väyrynen (2001) took in critiquing BHN with a social constructionist framework derived from the phenomenological sociology of Alfred Schutz. One could also say, in the spirit of Louch and others, that the particular language game of science that Burton relied upon was not the only such game possible – or even the most desirable.

Our cultural critique was not the only one. Essays by Burton's close colleagues, Richard Rubenstein and Christopher Mitchell, published in the

1990 collection on Human Needs theory (one of the four in the Conflict Series Burton produced in his year as a visiting fellow at the United States Institute of Peace) were in some ways more pointed than ours. Rubenstein averred that BHN theory flies very close to the sun of Natural Law theory. "One uses it to restate or confirm conclusions already arrived at." Rubenstein went on to call for a theory of BHN that "avoids the pitfalls and limitations of a Natural Law perspective: that is, it restores the qualities of historicity, concreteness, and theoretical unity to a doctrine that often seems vague, abstract, and conclusory" (Rubenstein 1990: 344). Rubenstein looked mainly to Marx and class as the source, at least of "historicity." Mitchell went further. After posing the usual questions (how many? why these needs? how do we know?) and one or two not usually considered (to avoid conflict must all needs be satisfied at once? a few? which few? must they be wholly or can they be partially satisfied?), he wrote (Mitchell 1990: 159–160) that even if one can actually produce a "complete list" of needs one must ask

> whether such a list will lead (1) to a revelation of the underlying causes of the conflict under review and (2) to a solution.... If there is no such list, then efforts to develop a theory of conflict resolution based on removing the factors frustrating BHNs seems doomed to failure – or, at least, to a hit and miss strategy that can hardly be said to be based on sound theory.

Mitchell also questioned the relative inattention Burton gives to satisfiers (where "cultural" variability may be more significant than previously assumed) and, most telling, he raised the possibility that some basic human needs may be *malign.* What if "security" is actually best satisfied through dominance? Or "identity" necessarily implies ethnocentrism?

As one the authors of the 1987 "cultural" critique there is nothing I would retract. Yet, more than 25 years later, I can also say that in some essential way the article also reflected our ignorance of the totality of Burton's work and his place in the contemporary controversies in IR theory. Black and I mentioned, but passed over, his claims about bursting the paradigm of power politics in neorealist IR. In this case the blinders of our own disciplinary socialization picked up "culture" but passed over "power" almost entirely. Burton's "ontological break" was from traditional IR theory and its basis in power, to a conception of conflict resolution and problem solving based on the significance of irrepressible BHN. It was in his opposition to the "normal science" of realist power politics that Burton claimed revolutionary status. And indeed, in the UK at least, he was very much treated by some colleagues as a dangerous revolutionary (Dunn 2004; Sandole 2006). Basic human needs, ontologically rooted in the individual and *all-powerful* in their demand for satisfaction, was Burton's Jacobin retort to the putative primacy of the all-powerful state.

The dilemma of power and conflict resolution

Alongside the primacy of the state as realist IR's fundamental idea, *power* is understood as axiomatic. In a world where power among states is self-evidently maldistributed the explanation of inter-state conflict is also self-evident. Strong states seek to dominate one another, weaker ones succumb or seek power-balancing alliances. Therefore IR is naturally much better at explaining the causes of war than outbreaks of peace (but see Vasquez 1993). Conflict management (hardly ever "resolution," except perhaps following a total victory of one side) is a matter of deterrence, stable balances of power or, around the edges, striving to reduce the dangers inherent in perceived security dilemmas by enhancing some measure of information-sharing through communication (e.g. "hotlines") among rivals. In any case, as axiomatic, power is essentially uncontested, never the object of critical inquiry.

Such is not the case for conflict resolution, even for sub-state domains. We agree that in "the real world" power is unevenly distributed. We disagree that the world must be governed under Melian rules, or that *management* is our only option. How then are we to deal with power? Kenneth Boulding's response, for example, was to expand the idea of power by deconstructing it into three "faces," maintaining that the Melian, coercive and destructive face was not the only one possible (Boulding 1989).

One problem is that much conflict resolution theory and practice have been built on assumptions of power symmetry. The prototypical example comes from our most elegant and mathematically "powerful" template, game theory, where the very parameter that specifies perfect (equal) knowledge of the game for each player is so obviously unreflective of conditions in the real world. Beyond formal game theory, we can find similar assumption of essential symmetry carried forward to much negotiation theory and practice. In contrast, a serious engagement with problems of power can be found in the literature on third-party involvement in conflict resolution, particularly in mediation. The common response is some variation on the notion of mediator "empowerment" of the weaker party (Birkhoff 2002).

Empowerment is a complicated idea, not without its critics (e.g. Groom and Webb 1987), and means different things to different practitioners. In ADR-based mediation empowerment is usually achieved through assuming strict neutrality or impartiality toward the parties and imposing standards of "process equality" (turn-taking and so on) within the mediation itself. The assumption here is that "processual equality" maps seamlessly onto "processual justice." For other practitioners, whose conception of justice and its requirements are more comprehensive and rigorous, empowerment implies something quite a bit more, something that extends far beyond the mediation setting. Beyond specifying formal rules of process, Mitchell (1993, 2003) has written about different sorts of third-party roles with respect to the skills or resources they can bring, some of them capacity-building, aiming to improve the negotiating position of the weaker party.[5] Meanwhile, when Adam Curle (1971) wrote about *conscientization* he had in mind a much broader enterprise on the part of the third party in relation to the weaker contestant. In common with Paulo Freire's (1970) *Pedagogy of the Oppressed* – or, indeed, the disequilibrating outside agitator activities of Saul Alinsky's (1971) *Rules for Radicals* – Curle meant for empowerment to entail making the weaker party fully aware of their position and their options. Not surprisingly, if successful, the first result of this sometimes was increased conflict. Curle understood this could be serious, even violent conflict. This pointed us (or should have, anyway) to some of the ethical concerns that this sort of empowerment entailed.

The larger point is that the field of conflict resolution cannot evade the realities of power asymmetry since we reject from the outset the Machiavellian calculus of *Machtpolitik* as our only choice. I have mentioned a few responses here; there are others (Avruch 2012: Ch. 9). Against all of these, however, there remain consistent critics of our enterprise, even from within the field, who argue we have not in fact adequately addressed the problem, and until we do conflict resolution as a normative discipline and practice is doomed to *moral* failure (Rouhana 2004, 2010).

Burton's resolution of the dilemma of power?

What was John Burton's response? Recall that from the beginning he was a vocal critic not only of state-centricity in traditional IR, but of its very foundations in conceptions of the primacy of coercive power. By the late 1970s Burton read Sites and, "discovering" basic human needs, had the final piece in managing his break with IR and forging an entirely new (conflict resolution) discipline and methodology. This is what justified his claims to paradigm change. Clearly, we ought then to expect that Burton's "solution" to the dilemma of power be equally far-reaching both in the realm of conflict theory and also crucially for the practice of conflict resolution. I argue it was not.

On the side of theory it can be said that the vigor of Burton's argument that deep-rooted conflict stems from the suppression of basic human needs is only as strong as the arguments (including methodological ones) that can be made for the specific needs he adduces, and here we cite the several critics (of needs theory generally and Burton's in particular) to question this. The best that can be said is that Burton's encounter with Azar's PSC took BHN theory from being a simple variant of the frustration-aggression hypothesis (which bears its own critical literature), focused on individuals, to a more comprehensive theory positing social groups and collective "actors," thus spanning micro to macro levels of analysis. The radical idea that Burton proposed was that ultimately power resided in basic human needs that demanded satisfaction at all costs, not in the overarching cultural-social systems within which individuals were "socialized" to conform, nor in the state or governmental structures that sought coercively to compel conformance. What is the effect here? It is to *displace the locus of power* from agents of the social system (including the state) to residence "inside" the individual. It would be a serious mistake to say this has conferred "agency" on the individual, however. To the contrary, BHNs here function much like the "selfish" genes of sociobiology. The individual is merely the vessel through which the irrepressible and imperious needs are expressed. Individuals have no choice. This is about as far from the liberatory sense of individual "agency" as critical theorists understand it, as one can get.

Burton's is admittedly a very different conception of power from that of the realists. Power here derives from ontological needs inexorably seeking satisfaction. In contrast, power in the realist's sense is hardly "ontological." It is constructed, not given. A state may be blessed in having deep water harbors, vast deposits of valuable resources, plentiful water, a temperate climate and much arable land, but even such "givens" of realist power must be exploitable (*turned into state power*) through public policy and government action, industry or the efficient organization of capital and labor. Other sources of realist state power, such as military and technological capacity, are self-evidently "made" and not given. Boulding (1989) would argue that the realist's conception of power is monodimensional or lacks nuance. Nevertheless, "power" for the realists *is* a variable along some kind (or multiple kinds, from "hard to "soft") of continuum. Variation is its essence. For Burton, "power" appears monolithic, or at best in a sort of binary variation: it is "on" when BHN are suppressed and conflict ensues, or it is "off" if and when needs are satisfied.

Assuming some conceptual connection between theory and practice, what does all this look like from the practice side? I think it is entirely plausible to argue that Burton's greatest contribution to conflict resolution was not in the area of theory but in practice, from the early idea of "controlled communication" to the facilitated conflict resolution in the form of the analytical problem-solving workshop (Burton 1969, 1987). The origins of the first workshop in December 1965 have been described by several of Burton's colleagues (Fisher 1997; Dunn 2004; Mitchell 2004; Sandole 2006). It was held in response to a challenge by Burton's IR opponents that he do something to "prove" the worth of his ideas. The first workshop was the result, and its success led to others and more importantly to attempts on Burton's part, as well as colleagues who had participated in some of them, including Kelman and Mitchell, to systematize their thoughts and try to *theorize* what, in fact, was going on (see Kelman 1990; Mitchell 2004). Burton did not "come to" the workshop idea with anything close to an articulated theory. He came instead from his earlier life with a strong sense of what was wrong with the traditional practices of state diplomacy and power-based foreign affairs. For Burton, practice preceded theory.

Burton's most explicit and programmatic description of the workshop format is to be found in *Resolving Deep-Rooted Conflict: A Handbook* (1987). It is written around 56 rules of procedure, with accompanying explanation. The workshop is not to be confused with ADR-type mediation or any sort of facilitated negotiation. Indeed, Burton argues against final texts arising from it. Rather, the goal is *analytical:* to enable "parties in conflict to ascertain the hidden data of motivations and intentions and to explore means by which common human-societal needs can be achieved" (1987: 16). It is a sort of "archeological" enterprise, aiming to excavate beyond the surface of issues and positions to deeper (and motivating) strata (Avruch and Black 1990). In this sense it is similar to the Fisher and Ury model of interest-based negotiation, but for the crucial difference that Burton sees interests as variable and negotiable, while BHN, ontological and buried much deeper, are neither.

Given this, what is most disappointing is that power asymmetry as a problem for practice is not discussed in the *Handbook*. This is surprising given how much attention to it is given in much mediation literature on practice, usually linked to strategies of processual fairness, neutrality and empowerment. Burton certainly writes about neutrality and rules of workshop process but these are never linked to power asymmetry because asymmetry is *ab initio* not at all problematic. Of course, Burton sees power at work in the conflict: the application of power to suppress BHN is after all at the root cause of it. But it is *not* a factor requiring attention in the workshop itself. Burton (1987: 46) writes:

> [I]t may appear that there is a clear struggle between two factions for political power for its own sake. The power struggle could be a sufficient explanation for the conflict, suggesting the need for some third party intervention to control violence [or empower the weaker party – KA].

But this would be an incorrect explanation. Not power, but BHN is the sufficient explanation. And the more powerful party must be brought through analysis to see the real "costs and consequences" of their actions. This what the workshop aims to accomplish.

The idea of bringing parties to rationally *cost* their continued course of action is the central problem-solving mechanism that Burton proposes. *Analysis* is entirely cognitive and educatory, leading parties to realistic *costing of the consequences of their actions.* Learning of the cost, parties (stronger parties as well) will *rationally* come to decide that it is better to resolve the conflict than to continue it. Avruch and Black (1990) briefly described this conception of the parties as sorts of rational decision-making *Homo economicus*, but it is Tarja Väyrynen (2001) who has more completely explored the consequences of this sort of instrumental rationality as the basis for Burton's practice. The application of acute analysis by the facilitating panel, of sufficient learning of costs by the parties, will "output" in the form of cost-reduction/utilities maximizing rational behavior. Empowerment is beside the point because power as conventionally understood is simply not relevant.[6]

How singular is Burton's approach can be seen in the record of a series of public conversation held at ICAR in 1988, between Burton and ICAR colleague James Laue. Laue was a superb practitioner with experience in the American Civil Rights movement (the subject of his Harvard doctorate in sociology) and in Bobby Kennedy's Community Relations Service in the Department of Justice. He put issues around the ethics of third-party interventions in the forefront of his practice, and held that "conflict resolution must be put in the service of three core values: empowerment, justice, and freedom" (Black and Avruch 1999: 31). Under no circumstances should a third party intervene in such a way that benefits the stronger party or blocks the attainment of justice for the weaker (Laue and Cormick 1978). We are fortunate that Richard Rubenstein recorded the substance of these several conversations and published an account of them. Laue and Burton disagreed strongly on the notion of "social justice." Laue understood it in an absolute form. Burton (uncharacteristically relativist!) argued that the only definition of social justice was one the parties themselves had: the third party had no role to play here. When the issue of power imbalance arose the disagreement became even sharper. Rubenstein (1999: 40) recounts the exchange:

> With the mention of "empowerment" Burton would lean forward with a strained smile. "But Jim," he would inquire, "if you really intend to 'empower' the weaker party, why should the stronger party stay at the table for a moment? And what do you mean by 'justice'? When the parties discover a solution to their problem that satisfies their basic needs, they recognize that access to the satisfier is power, and that the satisfaction of basic human needs is justice." Other forms of apparent power are illusory, John maintained, like the alleged superiority of American might in the Vietnam War.

In the face of insuppressible BHN, power is "illusory." Asymmetries of power are absorbed and disappear, in a sense, into the dynamics and process of a well-run problem-solving workshop. But then why *do* stronger parties ever agree to come to one? Presumably because they have begun to see or feel some of the "costs" involved in continuing the conflict? This bears some resemblance to I.W. Zartman's (2000) notion of negotiation proceeding when a "mutually hurting stalemate" between the parties has been reached. Perhaps, though notice that even "mutual hurt" implies a sort of equality or equivalence of power. This equality is precisely what situations of profound power asymmetry lack. Put differently: the "hurt" imposed on the weaker party by the stronger can be much greater, and go on for a much longer time, before the stronger party begins to feel any-thing mutually perceptible. A lot of sorrow may be harvested, napalm dropped and blood spilled, in proof of the illusory nature of power, Jim Laue might say.

Conclusion: Basic Human Needs are dead. Long live Basic Human Needs!

In the end, Burton's conception of basic human needs can be found wanting on two counts. First, Peirce notwithstanding, it is difficult to see them satisfactorily accounted for within the framework of hypothesis-testing positivism or "behavioral science." One can't see Galileo or Bacon here. But one might easily pick out Kant. Second, in the crucial matter of connecting theory to practice, Burton failed in the end to link the idea of power and BHN coherently to his hyper-rational conception of facilitated conflict resolution. In short, I think he never resolved the dilemma of "real-world" power asymmetry in practice. But I do see the power of basic human needs all around me. Students respond almost viscerally to the notion. It has tremendous face validity for them, even if it resists opera-tionalization. In 2011 they saw a young Tunisian street merchant endure decades of abuse from authorities and crack after he is publicly slapped by a police officer. (A *female* police office. Is the social construction of gender in the Arab world of significance, here? Do we need a dollop of cultural context?) Following his dramatic suicide the Arab world explodes. They call for dignity and freedom. Are these needs "basic"? Can they be accu-rately measured? They are certainly palpable.

One also sees the concept of basic human needs in the theoretical work of some younger scholars who strive to revise the idea in their own ("post-positivist") vocabularies: phenomenology (Väyrynen 2001); narrative gen-erativity (Simmons 2008); psychoanalysis and critical theory (invoking both Marcuse and Ricoeur; see English 2010; Park 2010). One sees it in many different manifestations in the descendants of the analytical problem-solving workshop that Burton's (prescriptive, overly rigid and rationalistic) form has given birth to: in the practice of Herb Kelman, Chris Mitchell, Ron Fisher, Mohammed Abu-Nimer, Diana Francis and Susan Allen Nan.

And one sees the idea stretched onto a much broader canvas. Twenty-five years ago perhaps no-one (save the visionary John Burton, himself) would have foreseen the idea of "human security" arise and gain wide acceptance as an imperative, at times competing in a political-moral dis-course with the old imperative of "national security." One sees it under-lying Amartya Sen's linkage of development and freedom. And one sees it, of course (here adverting to Kant) in the entire globalizing discourse of human rights wherein it is argued that these are the rights "one has simply because one is a human being" (Donnelly 1989: 1). Basic human needs are not inducible, deducible or abducible. They are however the central element, the motivating thematic, of very important narratives we tell ourselves and others tell us, about how to understand serious or deadly social conflict in this century. And in this way they are powerful indeed.

Notes

1 Thucydides, *History of the Peloponnesian War*, Book V (85–113).
2 Let the record show that Burton and Sandole contacted Bill Breslin, *Negotiation Journal*'s editor, suggesting he publish an Avruch-Black response (Sandole 2006).
3 Malinowski's seven needs and associated cultural satisfiers: metabolism-commissariat; reproduction-kinship; bodily comforts-shelter; safety-protection; movement-activities; growth-training; health-hygiene (Malinowski 1944: 91).
4 On verification, Chris Mitchell tells me (having once expressed to him similar doubts about method) that Burton would have responded by arguing that the theory would be "verified" (or at least tested) insofar as the ideas were recognized as relevant by the workshop participants. I would argue this simply puts us in a different epistemological muddle if "science" is our grail. But it certainly makes Burton appear a Peircean pragmaticist of the first order.
5 Mitchell also found it productive to focus less on the nature of "power" and more on the varied manifestations of "asymmetry" (Mitchell 1991, 1995, 2009; also Avruch 1998, 2012).
6 One ought also to treat rational decision-making itself as an empirical question. Political and social scientists studying decision-making and conflict have taught us too much about predictable cognitive distortions to give free and full confidence in decision-making rationality. "Higher" distortions include reactive devaluation, groupthink, self-fulfilling prophecy, mirror imaging, entrapment and autistic hostility, among others (Jervis 1976; Kahneman 2011).

Bibliography

Alinsky, S. (1971) *Rules for Radicals*, New York: Random House.
Avruch, K. (1998) *Culture and Conflict Resolution*, Washington D.C.: United States Institute of Peace Press.
Avruch, K. (2006) "Toward an Expanded Canon of Negotiation Theory," *Marquette Law Review*, 89(3): 567–582.
Avruch, K. (2012) *Context and Pretext in Conflict Resolution: Culture, Identity, Power and Practice*, Boulder, CO: Paradigm Publishers.
Avruch, K. and Black, P.W. (1987) "A Generic Theory of Conflict Resolution: A Critique," *Negotiation Journal*, 3(1): 87–96, 99–100.
Avruch, K. and Black, P.W. (1990) "Ideas of Human Nature in Contemporary Conflict Resolution Theory," *Negotiation Journal*, 6(3): 221–228.
Avruch, K., and Black, P.W. (1991) "The Culture Question and Conflict Resolution," *Peace and Change*, 16(1): 22–45.
Azar, E. (1985) "Protracted Social Conflicts: Ten Propositions," *International Interactions*, 12: 59–70.
Azar, E. (1990) *The Management of Protracted Social Conflict: Theory and Cases*, Brookfield, VT: Gower.
Azar, E. and Burton, J.W. (eds) (1986) *International Conflict Resolution: Theory and Practice*, Sussex, UK: Wheatsheaf Books.

Birkhoff, J. (2002) *Mediators's Perspective on Power: A Window into a Profession?* Unpublished Ph.D. Dissertation, ICAR, George Mason University.

Black, P.W. and Avruch, K. (1999) "Cultural Relativism, Conflict Resolution, and Social Justice," *Peace and Conflict Studies*, 6(1): 21–36.

Boulding, K. (1989) *Three Faces of Power*, Beverly Hills, CA: Sage.

Burton, J.W. (1962) *Peace Theory*, New York: Knopf.

Burton, J.W. (1965) *International Relations: A General Theory*, Cambridge: Cambridge University Press.

Burton, J.W. (1969) *Conflict and Communication: The Use of Controlled Communication in International Relations*, London: Macmillan.

Burton, J.W. (1972) *World Society*, Cambridge: Cambridge University Press.

Burton, J.W. (1979) *Deviance, Terrorism, and War*, New York: St. Martin's.

Burton, J.W. (1987) *Resolving Deep-Rooted Conflict: A Handbook*, Lanham, MD: University Press of America.

Burton, J.W. (1990) *Conflict: Resolution and Provention*, London: Macmillan and New York: St. Martin's.

Burton, J.W. (ed.) (1990) *Conflict: Human Needs Theory*, London: Macmillan and New York: St. Martin's.

Burton, J.W. (1997) *Violence Explained*, Manchester, UK: Manchester University Press and New York: St. Martin's.

Burton, J.W. and Dukes, F. (eds) (1990) *Conflict: Readings in Management and Resolution*, New York: St. Martin's.

Burton, J.W. and Dukes, F. (eds) (1990) *Conflict: Practices in Settlement, Management, and Resolution*, New York: St. Martin's.

Burton, J.W. and Sandole, D.J.D. (1986) "Generic Theory: The Basis of Conflict Resolution," *Negotiation Journal*, 2: 333–344.

Burton, J.W. and Sandole, D.J.D. (1987) "Expanding the Debate on Generic Theory of Conflict Resolution: A Response to a Critique," *Negotiation Journal*, 3(1): 97–100.

Coate, R.A. and Rosati, J.A. (eds) (1988) *The Power of Human Needs in World Society*, Boulder, CO: Lynne Rienner.

Curle, A. (1971) *Making Peace*, London: Tavistock.

Curle, A. (1986) *In the Middle: Non-Official Mediation in Violent Situations*, Oxford: Berg.

Donnelly, J. (1989) *Universal Human Rights in Theory and Practice*, Ithaca: Cornell University Press.

Dunn, D.J. (2004) *From Power Politics to Conflict Resolution: Assessing the Work of John W. Burton*, Revised edn, London: Palgrave/Macmillan.

English, M. (2010) "For Liberation or Exploitation: Reviving the Human Needs Debate," *Unrest Magazine*. Online. Available www.unrestmag.com/unrest-magazine-issue-one-september-2010 (accessed August 28, 2012).

Fisher, R.J. (1997) *Interactive Conflict Resolution*, Syracuse: Syracuse University Press.

Fisher, R., Ury, W. and Patton, B. (1991) [1981] *Getting To Yes*, 2nd edn, New York: Penguin Books.

Freire, P. (1970) *Pedagogy of the Oppressed*, New York: Continuum.

Groom, A.J.R. and Webb, K. (1987) "Injustice, Empowerment and Facilitation in Conflict," *International Interactions*, 13(3): 263–280.

Hempel, C.G. (1965) *Aspects of Scientific Explanation*, New York: Free Press.

Isaacs, H. (1975) *Idols of the Tribe: Group Identity and Political Change*, Cambridge, MA: Harvard University Press.

Jervis, R. (1976) *Perception and Misperception in International Politics*, Princeton: Princeton University Press.

Kahneman, D. (2011) *Thinking Fast, Thinking Slow*, New York: Farrar, Straus & Giroux.

Kelman, H. (1990) "Applying a Human Needs Perspective to the Practice of Conflict Resolution: The Israeli-Palestinian Case," in J.W. Burton (ed.) *Conflict: Human Needs Theory*, New York: St. Martin's.

Laue, J. and Cormick, G. (1978) "The Ethics of Intervention in Community Disputes," in G. Bermant, H. Kelman and D. Warwick (eds) *The Ethics of Social Intervention*, Washington, D.C.: Halstead Press.

Louch, A.R. (1966) *Explanation and Human Action*, Berkeley: University of California Press.

Malinowski, B. (1944) *A Scientific Theory of Culture*, Chapel Hill: University of North Carolina Press.

Maslow, A. (1954) *Motivation and Personality*, New York: Harper.

Mitchell, C.R. (1990) "Necessitous Man and Conflict Resolution: More Basic Questions about Basic Human Needs Theory," in J. Burton (ed.) *Conflict: Human Needs Theory*, New York: St. Martin's.

Mitchell, C.R. (1991) "Classifying Conflicts: Asymmetry and Resolution," *Annals of the American Association of Political and Social Sciences*, 518: 23–38.

Mitchell, C.R. (1993) "The Process and Stages of Mediation: Two Sudanese Cases," in D. Smock (ed.) *Making War and Waging Peace: Foreign Intervention in Africa*, Washington, D.C.: United States Institute of Peace Press.

Mitchell, C.R. (1995) "Asymmetry and Strategies of Regional Conflict Reduction," in I.W. Zartman and V. Kremenyuk (eds) *Cooperative Security: Reducing Third World Wars*, New York: Syracuse University Press.

Mitchell, C.R. (2003) "Mediation and the Ending of Conflicts," in J. Darby and R. MacGuinty (eds) *Contemporary Peacemaking: Conflict, Violence, and Peace Processes*, London: Palgrave/Macmillan.

Mitchell, C.R. (2004) "Ending Confrontation between Indonesia and Malaysia," in R.J. Fisher (ed.) *Paving the Way: Contributions of Interactive Conflict Resolution to Peacemaking*, Lanham, MD: Lexington Books.

Mitchell, C.R. (2009) "Persuading Lions: Problems of Transferring Insights from Track-2 Exercises Undertaken in Conditions of Asymmetry," *Dynamics of Asymmetric Conflict*, 2(1): 32–50.

Morgenthau, H. (1967) *Politics among Nations*, New York: Knopf.

Park, L. (2010) "Opening the Black Box: Reconsidering Needs Theory through Psychoanalysis and Critical Theory," *International Journal of Peace Studies*, 15(1): 1–17.

Ramsbotham, O. (2005) "The Analysis of Protracted Social Conflict: A Tribute to Edward Azar," *Review of International Studies*, 31: 109–136.

Rouhana, N. (2004) "Group Identity and Power Asymmetry in Reconciliation Processes: The Israeli-Palestinian Case," *Peace and Conflict: Journal of Peace Psychology*, 10(1): 33–52.

Rouhana, N. (2010) "Key Issues in Reconciliation: Challenging Traditional Assumptions on Conflict Resolution and Power Dynamics," in D. Bar-Tal (ed.) *Intergroup Conflicts and their Resolution: Social Psychological Perspectives*, New York: Psychology Press.

Rubenstein, R.E. (1990) "Basic Needs Theory: Beyond Natural Law," in J. Burton (ed.) *Conflict: Human Needs Theory*, New York: St. Martin's.

Rubenstein, R.E. (1999) "Conflict Resolution and Distributive Justice: Reflections on the Burton-Laue Debate," *Peace and Conflict Studies*, 6(1): 37–45.

Sandole, D.J.D. (2006) "Traditional 'Realism' versus the 'New' Realism: John W. Burton, Conflict Provention, and the Elusive 'Paradigm Shift'," *Global Society*, 20(4): 543–562.

Scimecca, J.A. (1990) "Self-Reflexivity and Freedom: Toward a Prescriptive Theory of Conflict Resolution," in J. Burton (ed.) *Conflict: Human Needs Theory*, New York: St. Martin's.

Scimecca, J.A. (1991) "Conflict Resolution in the United States: The Emergence of a Profession?" in K. Avruch, P. Black and J. Scimecca (eds) *Conflict Resolution: Cross-Cultural Perspectives*, New York: Greenwood.

Simmons, S. (2008) "Generativity-Based Conflict: Maturing Microfoundations for Conflict Theory," in D.J.D Sandole, S. Byrne, I. Sandole-Staroste and J. Senehi (eds) *A Handbook of Conflict Analysis and Resolution*, New York: Routledge.

Sites, P. (1973) *Control: The Basis of Social Order*, New York: Dunellen Publishers.

Thucydides (1998) *History of the Peloponnesian War*, Trans. B. Jowett, Amherst, NY: Prometheus Books.

Vasquez, J.A. (1993) *The War Puzzle*, New York: Cambridge University Press.

Väyrynen, T. (2001) *Culture and International Conflict Resolution*, Manchester, UK: Manchester University Press.

Zartman, I.W. (2000) "Ripeness: The Hurting Stalemate and Beyond," in P. Stern and D. Druckman (eds) *Conflict Resolution after the Cold War*, Washington, D.C.: National Academy Press.

3 Through gender lenses

Human Needs theory in conflict resolution[1]

Ingrid Sandole-Staroste

Introduction

This chapter grows out of a conversation that began about 20 years ago with leading conflict resolution theorist and practitioner, John W. Burton. As a feminist, I was skeptical of his Human Needs Theory and was not convinced about his claims of universality. Here I revisit the issue, building on my earlier contribution to this debate (see Sandole-Staroste, 1992, 1994).

Organization of the chapter

In the first part of the chapter, I explore Burton's Human Needs Theory (1990a, 1990b, 1997) and his claim that needs are ontological and, therefore, the very essence of an individual; further, that unless social, political, economic and cultural institutions are designed in such a way that they address and fulfill basic human needs, conflicts cannot be resolved and wars cannot be prevented. In the second part of the chapter, I explore feminist theories and the critique that feminists levy on traditional power relations, which they identify as the very obstacle to making gender a central category of analysis. In the third part of the chapter, I explore human needs and feminist theories together to determine whether, and to what extent (if at all), they converge and/or diverge, and whether feminist thinking can strengthen the explanatory power of Human Needs Theory. In the fourth and final part, I explore the implications for practice of the feminist–Human Needs theory nexus.

The historical context

Nearly half a century ago, International Relations and other social science scholars began to call into question the dominant paradigm of power politics and the ability of the traditional social sciences to deal with complex social conflicts (see Boulding 1962; Burton 1972; Burton, *et al.* 1974). They advocated a radical shift in perspective, rejected disciplinary constraints and created a new *inter*disciplinary field: conflict resolution. A new language and new concepts emerged that are now employed across disciplines to analyze, explain and solve conflicts. A new theory evolved and from it common practices were developed (Kelman 2009; Kriesberg 2009; Ramsbotham, *et al.* 2011; Pruitt and Rubin 2004; Sandole 2006, 2010; Sandole and Sandole-Staroste 1987).[2]

John Burton (1990a, 1990b, 1997), a leading theorist and, some say, "one of the most important and controversial founders" in the emerging field of conflict resolution (Jabri 1997: x), advanced a theory based on a set of non-negotiable, universal human needs. A witness to the turbulent events of the twentieth century, Burton was motivated to find and explain the causes of war and prescriptions to avoid it. He realized that when "times change radically ... thought [must] ... change [radically] as well" (Dunn 2004: 47). Consequently, he set out to find new ways not only to think about, but to solve and *provent* violent conflicts.[3] He considered assumptions underlying power politics, such as "peace ... [is] a period of preparation for war" (Veblen [1917] 1998: 299) as passé for the dawning twenty-first century. In place of traditional power politics, Burton proposed Basic Human Needs (BHN) Theory,[4] claiming that human needs are generic, applying to humans across historical time and cultural space. He also proposed that conflict resolution processes can be deduced from BHN theory and that wars can be *provented*.

Second wave feminist theories evolved at about the same time as conflict resolution theory. In contrast to the discipline of International Relations – which was by then well established in universities across the USA and Europe – second wave feminism was brought into university classrooms as a result of women's social activism during the 1960s, 1970s and 1980s. Feminists introduced the concept of *gender* and "like any other social science concept ... [including human needs, gender has been] shaped by the political and intellectual contexts of the time" (Bradley 2007: 5, 33). Second wave feminists also wanted a radical shift in perspective. They rejected disciplinary constraints, and created a new *inter*disciplinary field: feminist studies.

Feminists had grown profoundly skeptical of the dominant paradigms in all academic disciplines and developed numerous feminist theories – liberal, Marxist, radical, psychoanalytic, socialist, existential, cultural, gay and lesbian, and eco-feminist. Later, various *post*discourses – postmodernism, poststructuralism, postcolonialism and third wave feminism – informed feminist thinking as well.[5] Although feminist theories differ from each other in sometimes significant ways and are critical of each other, they all reject the status quo, arguing that existing paradigms and social systems generally have been inadequate, or failed outright, to address women's experiences and needs and solve the resulting conflicts. Some see "women's oppression [as] the most fundamental form of oppression," because it "is the most widespread, existing in virtually every known society" (Jaggar and Rothenberg Struhl, cited in Tong 1989: 710; Bartky

1990). Feminists also see the oppression of women as "a conceptual model for understanding all other forms of oppression" (Tong 1989: 710).

Human Needs theory

Burton assumes a link between human needs and conflict and argues that, within a conflict resolution framework, an effective analysis can be made and solutions formulated because the field of conflict resolution is "adisciplinary ... [cutting] across all disciplines: a synthesis, a holistic approach to a problem area" (Burton and Sandole 1986: 333). Indeed, he claims that the field of conflict resolution "knows no boundaries of thought ... transcends ... separate compartments of knowledge ... cannot be broken up into aspects of behavior ... and cuts ... across cultures" (Burton 1990b: 20). Consequently, adopting a holistic view of human conflictual behavior is considered politically realistic, and in no sense superficial.

Burton (1990b: 21) maintains that the only value orientation inherent in conflict resolution "is the goal of resolving conflict." Therefore, the study of conflict resolution is analytical and has no ideological orientation. Human Needs Theory in this context is believed to have the power to explain and to "transcend observable differences in human behavior" (Burton and Sandole 1986: 334).

Burton and Sandole (1986: 334) question the assumption inherent in the traditional power paradigm that "the problem source is people and their nature" and not the conditions under which they live. The authors identify institutions and structures as the source of the problem, because their function is to preserve themselves by controlling members of society. Burton offers an alternative paradigm that focuses on the *relations* between individuals and structures. It proposes that there are limits to the extent to which a person can be socialized or manipulated, and that unless human needs are fulfilled, social stability, even with the use of force, cannot be achieved. In effect, human needs cannot be suppressed or socialized away (Burton 1990b: 23, 32). The roots of social conflict are, therefore, to be found, not in "human deformities [but] rather [in] structural and institutional deformities." In this sense, human needs are "more compelling in directing behaviors than many possible external influences" (Burton 1990b: 33). This, for Burton, is not a deterministic view because human beings respond to "opportunities of development, and ... are malleable in this sense" (Burton 1990b: 32). Human beings cannot, however, be socialized to accept "denial of needs such as [identity, security, development,] recognition, autonomy, dignity, and bonding, for they are preconditions of individual development" (Burton 1990b: 32). Because "[i]ndividuals cannot be socialized into destroying their identity, [they are compelled to] react against social environments that do" (Burton 1990b: 33).

Burton's proposition that individuals can be molded only to a limited extent has had an influence on the perception of the nature of conflict, its resolution, and *provention.* Because individuals are compelled to pursue their needs, "regardless of circumstance and consequences" (Burton 1990b: 33), they will seek to satisfy these needs inside or outside the legal norms of society. In other words, needs "reflect universal motivation" and "will be pursued by all means available" (Burton 1990b: 36). This means "deterrence cannot deter in conditions in which human needs are frustrated" (Burton 1990b: 34). The focus on needs, therefore, enhances the political power of individual human behavior at all levels because social stability can be established and maintained only if human needs are met.

Feminist theories

Feminist scholars, too, searched for more inclusive systems, decision-making processes, greater decentralization, new philosophies, and created a body of scholarly work that has drawn attention to alternative ways of organizing societies and of solving conflicts within and between families, and local, national and global communities.

Feminist theories developed when women questioned the assumed "naturalness" of their position in society, declaring that their issues deserved public attention. In the process, they uncovered the workings of masculinity and femininity in patriarchal society, including the structural and ideological systems that privilege masculinity. They laid bare the patriarchal foundations of culture and social institutions and gained a deeper understanding of how to bring about social change to meet the needs of all people. And while not all women are feminists, feminist knowledge grew out of women's experience and can be stated as follows:

> the female perspective is both legitimate and illuminating of *human* experience and that to marginalize this part of the human experience is to construct a false picture.
>
> Feminism directly challenges the power relationships resulting from dominant viewpoints, theories, categories, and understandings of the world, and thus it directs a revolutionary, emancipatory practice. This practice demands that existing economic, political and social structures be changed.
>
> (Weir and Faulkner 2004: xii, emphasis added)

In other words, the practice of feminism aims to abolish the structures of patriarchy, that is, male-dominated, male-identified and male-centered structures. Both women and men participate in patriarchy, and although patriarchy privileges men and masculinity, it could not function without the complex notions of femininity and a sufficiently large number of women accepting patriarchal relations as "normal" (Johnson 2006). Patriarchy divides the world into a private (non-political) sphere typically associated with women, and a public (political) sphere occupied by men. Its hierarchal organization guarantees that the public world not only rules the private world, but that it is also regarded as more valuable with serious consequences that manifest themselves most notably in the distribution of resources and, thus, in the distribution of power.[6]

On the national as well as global levels, an increasing share of resources flow to public institutions such as military establishments – still predominantly male-dominated, male-identified and male-centered. Thus,

> the ... Stockholm International Peace Research Institute (SIPRI), [reported that] during 2005 the world's total military expenditures reached a stunning all time high of 1.1 *trillion* ... that amounted to spending, in just one year, $173 on militaries for every single woman, child, and man on the planet.
>
> (Enloe 2007: 157)[7]

At the same time, vital resources that impact the private world are cut. Consequently, "[w]omen bear a disproportionate burden of the world's poverty.... According to some estimates, women represent 70 percent of the world's poor" (United Nations 2011a):

> Statistics indicate that women are more likely than men to be poor and at risk of hunger because of the systematic discrimination they face in education, health care, employment and control of assets. Poverty implications are widespread for women, leaving many without even basic rights such as access to clean drinking water, sanitation, medical care and decent employment ... [and] little protection from violence and ... no role in decision making.

The absence of women's voices in the public sphere has meant, for example, that a US$77 *billion* budget for eight post-conflict needs assessments allocated less than *eight* percent to addressing the needs of women (United Nations 2011b). Feminist efforts to make visible masculinized ways of thinking and policy preferences have arguably become more urgent (Frye 2010: 149–153) because it cannot be taken for granted that the institutionalization of feminine values and ways of thinking and acting are recognized as valid alternatives to patriarchal relations. A decade into the twenty-first century, too many people are still holding on to the traditional power paradigm – its patriarchal values, norms and beliefs – unable to recognize the urgency to fundamentally change our approach to solving conflicts that are rooted in the marginalization of the majority world, global militarization, climate change and dwindling resources (see Abbott *et al.* 2007; Narayan *et al.* 2000).

Convergence and divergence of feminist and Human Needs theories

According to Rubenstein (1990: 1), we view conflicts within and between societies through the "lenses" of theory, "whether conscious or unconscious." The lenses of theory determine how events are perceived and analyzed. And, if the "lens" is defective or the frame is poorly constructed, perception and analysis, as well as policy, will be distorted. Consequently, the question arises: does Human Needs Theory provide a non-defective lens and a well constructed "frame of interpretation"? Does it illuminate features that enrich the analysis of conflict and prescriptions for its resolution? Alternatively, are the lens and frame poorly constructed, distorting both the analysis and resolution of conflicts?

Both Human Needs and feminist theories advocate a fundamental restructuring of our thinking and approaches to analyzing and solving the conflicts that we face in the twenty-first century. As mentioned earlier, Burton (1997, 1990b) makes sweeping claims that arguably reflect a masculine orientation that confidently assumes universal truths, while seemingly being unaware of gender and other differences (e.g. cultural). Mary Clark (1990: 34) noted that "Human Needs Theory ... has taken for its model of human nature the individual of Western thought," or more precisely, "the [masculine] individual of Western thought," the "necessitous man" (Mitchell 1990). Given that gender plays a fundamental role in how conflicts are initiated and carried out on all, but particularly the national and global, levels, where it is mostly a masculine enterprise, the question arises: is "a holistic view of *human* conflictual behaviour" (emphasis added) indeed "politically realistic [and] not superficial" (Burton 1990b: 20), when gender as an analytic category is ignored? Further, is it fair to ask whether Burton's Human Needs approach to conflict resolution "transcends separate compartments of knowledge"? Disregarding the entire body of feminist knowledge, Burton seems unaware that Western "culture is deeply and fundamentally structured socially, politically, ideologically, and conceptually by gender as well as by race, class, and sexuality" (Bleier 1986: 2). It then follows that "the dominant categories of cultural experience e.g., (white, male, middle/upper class, and heterosexual) are reflected in its structure, theories, concepts, values, ideologies, and practices" (Bleier 1986: 2). Unless conflict resolution scholars "theorize gender – define gender as an analytic category within which humans think and organize their social activity" (Harding 1986: 17), they will be blind to the magnitude to which gender meanings permeate value, belief and normative systems, institutions and even such apparently gender-free phenomena as Human Needs Theory.

Despite Burton's omissions, feminist and Human Needs perspectives share "frames of interpretation" in that they both critique the traditional power paradigm for its failure to resolve conflicts at all levels due to its adherence to the status quo and its determination to preserve, with force if necessary, outdated structures and institutions to maintain control. However, feminists go further in their analysis and point to the inherent identity of the traditional power paradigm (inclusive of the state and all the interlocking elements of that system) with patriarchy, where "power emerged as male power" (MacKinnon 1989: xi). Thus, Burton's focus on "the whole person, the nation or identity group of the person, the political system, the physical environment" (Burton 1990b: 20) is incomplete, because his "whole person" is conceptualized as gender neutral. Likewise, "the nation or identity group of the person, the political system, [and] the physical environment" are devoid of gender and gendered experiences, making difference of any kind invisible.

Addressing political systems and physical environments, international relations scholar, Ann Tickner (1992: 1) notes that "politics is a man's world, inhabited by diplomats, soldiers, and international civil servants most of whom are men." If women occupy positions of power like the former US Secretary of State Hillary Rodham Clinton (2003) (and Condoleezza Rice (2011) and Madeleine Albright (2003) before her), she is perceived by many as holding that position despite being a woman. Many still hold the belief that the areas of politics, military and foreign policy-making

> are least appropriate for women. Strength, power, autonomy, independence, and rationality, all typically associated with men and masculinity, are characteristics we most value in those to whom we entrust the conduct of our foreign policy and the defense of our national interest.
>
> (Tickner 1992: 3)

Moreover, the fact that a woman heads an institution such as the US Department of State does not change the institution itself. Indeed, patriarchal values and beliefs are deeply rooted in the hierarchical order of such institutions where, at the "Senior Foreign Service officers [level],... men still outnumber women three to one" (Hovanec 2008: 12). This gender distribution is not exceptional and can be found in most institutions. The higher up the professional pyramid one moves, the fewer positions of authority are occupied by women (Baker 2011; Havemann 2007; Henderson 2008; Yeager 2007; *The Economist* 2010).

Without a gender analysis – given the well researched influence of gender socialization on individuals and institutions – one cannot state reliably that women and men relate to and identify with the nation, political system and the physical environment in exactly the same way. Likewise, by omitting a gender analysis, Human Needs Theory's claim to have "universal application" and a "holistic view of human behavior" is being met with skepticism precisely because "each ungendered term serves to hide the political workings of masculinity and femininity," thereby missing the major structures of power (Enloe 2007: 3).

Although feminist and Human Needs theorists concur with the notion that conflicts arise because of structural and institutional deformities, feminists disagree with Burton's claim that conflicts do not arise because of individual human deformities. Through a feminist lens, individuals *and* social systems are locked in a mutual relationship and, therefore, shape each other. Individuals are shaped or "deformed" by social systems as they participate through socialization and by choosing, all too often, "the path of least resistance," that is, gender "appropriate" behavior, thereby reinforcing the status quo of traditional power relations (Johnson 2006: 78–80; also see Giddens' concept of *structuration*, 1984).

If women choose the "path of greater resistance," and strive to succeed in a male-dominated, male-identified and male-centered world, they have to weigh the risks by "walking a fine line" – a predicament that men do not face. Women who aim for leadership positions have to balance their culturally defined role of femininity with the male-identified professional position they seek to occupy. This poses a dilemma that is not easily resolved. If they exhibit masculine-identified behaviors (aggressive, competitive), they run the risk of either being ignored or criticized, or of being perceived as strident, incompetent, or "deviant." If they remain soft-spoken and diplomatic, they won't be taken seriously (Hovanec 2008). This has potentially serious implications with regard not only to interpersonal conflict, but to global conflict and its effective resolution. Because women are judged by masculine – not *human* – standards, they have to play by men's rules; they also have to work harder and think smarter. Under such conditions, it is difficult for them to realize their full *human* potential. Thus, not only do they have to deal with structural deformities, but individual deformities, because to succeed in male-dominated, male-identified and male-centered institutional settings, women and men, consciously or subconsciously, are expected to – and do – behave in accordance with patriarchal values, beliefs and norms. In this regard, Clark (1990: 36) comments that:

> our current fission of the concepts of "the individual" and "society" into separate, often warring, compartments blinds us to the fact that these are *one* thing. To the extent that a society is dysfunctional, then so are its individual members, for every person is inescapably a social being, formed by and forming others within his or her circle of contacts.

The field of conflict analysis and resolution itself provides examples of how individuals and social systems are interlocked and shape each other. Leaders in the field barely acknowledge the utility of gender analysis and feminist scholarship, even though gender relations are an essential aspect of any conflict situation.[8] This is not surprising or new. Almost two decades ago, Taylor and Beinstein Miller (1994: 1–2) noted that, although, "many ... practitioners of interpersonal conflict management are women, most of those involved in the academic study of conflict and its resolution are not [and] ... little in conflict resolution theory explicitly addresses issues of gender." In a field that purports to be "a synthesis that goes beyond separate disciplines ... [and] accepts no boundaries of knowledge" (Burton 1990b: xi), the marginalization of feminist knowledge and female experience suggests that both institutional and human imperfection must be addressed if conflicts are to be effectively resolved and *prevented* at any level.

Despite the "defects" of Human Needs Theory, feminists share Burton's vision of a social environment in which *humans* can engage in an ongoing process of dialogue and interaction and freely express and fulfill their needs, values and interests without fearing physical and psychological oppression. In such an environment, each solution to a problem is not seen as an end-product, but rather as part of an ongoing process: each solution is perceived as establishing new relationships that entail their own set of issues to be solved. Feminist and Human Needs theorists imagine that such an environment will inspire "a new synthesis of knowledge, new techniques and a change in conceptualization of a problem" (Burton 1990b: 202), locating that corpus of knowledge not in a static but in an ever changing political, economic, social and cultural context.

Feminists note that societies reflecting such social environments and practices are not new; they have existed in the past (Elise Boulding 1976; Eisler 1988), underscoring the importance of knowing not only male, but also female history. Without such knowledge, earlier environments and practices remain invisible, and a false understanding of human identity is constructed. Only an understanding of *human* history will allow individuals to gain an appropriate sense of meaning, purpose and direction that increases their autonomy of choice, which is an essential part of solving and *preventing* conflicts (Elise Boulding 1976).[9]

Burton's (1990b, 1997) idea of creating a social environment based on *human* needs is not in opposition to feminist thinking. Feminist skepticism arises because human needs are assumed to be gender neutral. The notion that individuals cannot be socialized to deny their needs is problematic precisely because Burton's underlying assumptions remain hidden, and human needs suspiciously mirror male needs, assuming that social environments impact girls' and women's and boys' and men's lives in the same way. Yet, as ample evidence indicates, in many parts of the world, women are effectively deprived of the preconditions for their individual development and are socialized to deny needs such as autonomy, dignity and recognition. Power is culturally conferred on male members of households and communities who are given the authority to impose a subordinate status on girls and women. Consequently, many girls and women do not have access to education, paid employment, reproductive health care, property and divorce rights. All too often they are subjected to abuse, sexual exploitation, trafficking and are killed in peace as well as war (Engle 2006; Hunt 2004; Leatherman 2011). In this regard, Noeleen Heyzer (2003: 5–6) notes that:

> violence against women, once an unfortunate side-effect, is now a deliberate part of many … armed conflicts impacting women's and men's, girls' and boys' lives profoundly and in different ways. I have been to Bosnia where women described abduction, rape camps and forced impregnation, and to Rwanda where women had been gang raped and purposely infected with HIV/AIDS…. Stories like these have been repeated again and again, in different languages, in different surroundings: [Columbia], East Timor, the Democratic Republic of the Congo, and Guatemala. Only the sorrow and the pain were the same.

What Human Needs Theory "lens" fails to illuminate are the gendered aspects of human experience, i.e. that

> women and men have bodies and hence have multiple experience of emdodiedness, especially in violent conflicts…. [A]ll current protracted-social and international conflicts show how issues of embodiment and the body become vitally important: The body is constantly confronted with death, physical or psychological pain.
>
> (Reimann 2002: 9)

Burton's (1990b: 33) claim that individuals are compelled to react against social environments that destroy their identities presupposes rational (male) individuals with the same (male) bodies, having control, at least to a certain extent, over their bodies and the social environment.

Burton would respond that, according to Human Needs Theory, gender, race, class and culture are features of *values* and, thus, analytically separate from *needs*; that values play an important part in the development of identity (i.e. defending needs of security and identity), and "impinge upon needs and can be confused with them" (Burton 1990b: 37). What remains unexplained is how we discern that needs are not derived from values, i.e. gender, culture, race and class (Avruch and Black 1987). To relegate gender, culture, race and class to a less influential level denies the constitutive role that these social categories play in the development of the individual (Avruch and Black 1990: 227).

In light of the uncertainty of what ontological *human* needs are and whether they exist, the creation of a social environment based on them must be looked at cautiously. Human needs may be no more than traits common to many people who belong to privileged social categories.

Creating an environment based on human needs with no attention to how gender, cultural, race, class, sexual and non-disabled identities are acquired, may not be a neutral undertaking into which women can be assimilated without loss. Such an undertaking may be a particularly masculine project, disguised as a human project. It may obscure the power structure, allowing it to go unchallenged. After all, in Western culture the central reference point is still associated with privileged social categories – male, white, heterosexual, non-disabled and upper/middle class.

Yet, Burton's concepts of "valued relationships" and "reciprocity" as preconditions for creating a social environment in which conflicts are not merely settled, but solved and *prevented*, find support in feminist thinking. Gilligan's (1982: 167) research on moral development, for example, found that "people have real emotional needs to be attached to something." She contends that the notion of rights, which is predicated on equality and centered on the understanding of fairness, is in itself not satisfying because it "fractures society and places on every person the burden of standing on his [her] own feet" (Gilligan 1982: 167). The notion of responsibility, on the other hand, which "relies on the concept of equity, that is, the recognition of differences in need," fulfills the emotional need for attachment. It rests on an understanding that gives rise to compassion and care, or what Burton calls "reciprocity" and "valued relationships." Clark (1990: 46) observes that "meaningful social bonds are an absolute need of the human organism, and rupture of these bonds is – as novelists and playwrights have been telling us for centuries – a tragedy."

Feminist and Human Needs theorists recognize the importance of autonomy in creating a new social environment. From a Human Needs perspective, an autonomous person "has self-esteem and a sense of competence that is socially recognized" (Burton 1990b: 93). Feminists assert that self-esteem and a sense of competence derive from exercising real power in all areas of life where power does not mean the domination and exploitation of others, "but rather the freedom and space to express [one's] own desires, creativity and potential" (Segal 1984, cited in Coole 1988: 254). Eisler (1988) referred to it as *actualization* power, where neither women nor men are subordinate to the other. This notion of power converges with Burton's (1990b) assertion that non-material needs – e.g. identity, security – are often fundamental to parties in conflict, and that the increase in the satisfaction of such needs for one party leads to the increase in satisfaction for the other. Conflicts, paradoxically, are often not over scarce material resources, but over identity and security, which do not necessarily involve short supplies of resources.

Implications for practice

John Burton used to say that there is nothing more practical than a good theory, and to him Human Needs Theory was, above all, practical. He and some of his followers had the confidence – and some might say arrogance – to declare that the human needs he identified are universal and *all* individuals are compelled to satisfy them, "regardless of circumstance and consequences" (Burton 1990b: 33). Such a declaration will immediately alert a gender-aware practitioner to consider the conflict promoting potential of human needs. From a gender perspective, it is important to ask whether "need for recognition, stimulation and security can ... lead to a need for dominance, control over and arrogance (and hence to the need for an out- and in-group)" (Mitchell, 1990 cited in Reimann 2002: 22). The gender-aware practitioner would analyze existing patriarchal – male-dominated, -identified and -centered – power structures, and be vigilant to the fact that women often serve to fulfill the basic need for an enemy, particularly during war time when that status is used by perpetrators to justify atrocities against women, including rape.

> Vamik Volkan's ideas that human beings have a basic need for ... enemies as well as allies (Mitchell 1990: 156) [suggest that if] human beings are driven by the need for dominance (as a form of security, recognition, and meaning), then one cannot think of needs as fundamentally neutral or conflict inhibiting. Rather from a gender-sensitive perspective "universally, ontological human needs" have to be discussed as conflict promoting (ibid). Far from being value-neutral, a need becomes a "political instrument, meticulously prepared, calculated and used."
>
> (Reimann 2002: 22)[10]

Conclusion

The tenets of feminist and Human Needs "lenses" converge as well as diverge. They diverge because Human Needs Theory renders invisible gender as a social category. Thus, through feminist lenses, Human Needs Theory constitutes an important, but incomplete body of knowledge; its power is diminished because it fails to recognize that "gender difference is the most ancient, most universal, and most powerful origin of many morally valued conceptualizations of everything else in the world around us" (Harding 1986: 17). Hence, gender is an essential component of the traditional power paradigm that Burton sought to dismantle. By not defining gender "as an analytic category within which humans think and organize their social activity," Human Needs theorists fail to "appreciate the extent to which gender meanings have suffused our belief systems, institutions, and such apparently gender-free phenomena as [human needs]" (Harding 1986: 17). Cynthia Enloe (2004: 94) observes that not every scholar has to be a gender specialist, "but what they have to do is say that leaving out the serious asking of the gender question ... will mean that their theorizing ... will not just be incomplete. It will be unreliable."

It will fail to identify "gender as a form of power and power in its gendered forms" (MacKinnon 1989: xi).

At the same time, however, feminist and Human Needs approaches to conflict resolution converge at crucial points, thereby redefining the traditional model of reality reflecting what Eisler (1988: xix) describes as *partnership* societies that make possible Burton's practice of conflict *provention*. Partnership societies tend to be more peaceful because they are less hierarchical and authoritarian, satisfying what Clark (1990: 48) regards as a fundamental human need: a "sense of temporal continuity between an unexperienced yet culturally present past and a never to be experienced yet personally significant future." Partnership societies allow feminist and needs-oriented conflict theorists to achieve more of their *common* goals than might otherwise be the case – the establishment of "different systems, different decision-making processes, greater decentralization, and different philosophies" (Burton 1990b: 115).

By ignoring feminist knowledge, Human Needs Theory is limited to an analysis that does not understand the gendered implications of the conflicts that conflict researchers and practitioners try to resolve and/or *provent*. Satisfying human needs without addressing gender undermines the real prospects of Burton's aspiration: finding new ways to explain the causes of violent conflict and prescriptions for peaceful relations. To accomplish these complex, interrelated objectives, the taboo of structural and individual hegemonic masculinity must be addressed and overcome.

Notes

1 I want to thank Marcella Ridlen Ray and Dennis Sandole for reading the first draft of this chapter and for their thoughtful comments.
2 In this regard, also see "Parents of the Field Video Interview Series" by Christopher R. Mitchell and Johannes Botes (http://scar.gmu.edu/parents, accessed February 10, 2013).
3 See Burton (1990b: 3):

> *Conflict provention* means deducing from an adequate explanation of the phenomenon of conflict, including its human dimensions, not merely the conditions that create an environment of conflict, and the structural changes required to remove it, but more importantly, the promotion of conditions that create cooperative relationships. The term *provention* was invented because *prevention* has a negative connotation.

4 I will refer to Basic Human Needs and Human Needs interchangeably throughout the chapter.
5 See, for example, Bradley 2007; Bryson 1999; Bulbeck 1999; de Beauvoir 1974; Collins 1990; Dworkin 1989; Flax 1990; Freedman 2001; Greer 1971; hooks 1984, 1989; Humm 1990, 1992; Jaggar and Rothenberg Struhl 1978; Keller 1985; MacKinnon 1989; Spender 1985; Tong 1989; Walby 1990, 1997.
6 For example, the United States "ranks first in the world in ... military power and just 40th in child mortality (under age five)" (Sklar 2010: 313). At the time of the writing of this chapter, the Pentagon received a $17 billion increase from the US House of Representatives, which approved a $649 billion defence

budget (Cassata 2011), while, according to the US Department of Agriculture, 12 million American families (11.2 percent of all US households) struggled to put food on the table and often failed to do so (Herbert 2010: 323).

7 Heyzer (2003: 6) notes that "while women are sometimes complicit in war, they are almost completely absent in the decisions to go to war – or in the appropriation of funds that make weapons and war possible."

8 Stiegler (2001) provides an apt metaphor:

> If the field [of conflict analysis and resolution] and the many scholarly disciplines on which it draws represent the strands of a *braid*, then feminist scholarship represents the bow at the end of the braid. In other words, feminist scholarship is not an integral part of the field. Like a bow, it is "added on." Because of its marginalized status, it is not well understood how feminism participates in power relations generally and in [conflict analysis and resolution] in particular.
>
> (Sandole-Staroste 2011: 235)

9 Thus, for example, in the past there appear to have been long periods of peace and prosperity, during which great strides were made in social, technological, and cultural developments (Bleier 2000). Eisler (1988: 66) describes this fact as "the best kept secret[:] practically all the material and social technologies fundamental to Western civilization were developed before the imposition of a patriarchal society." During these periods, societies were neither patriarchies nor matriarchies (ibid., xvi). Indeed, they appear to have been *partnership* societies in which women and men were able to express their needs, values and interests freely without fearing for their physical and psychological safety. They appear to have been societies in which perhaps the most fundamental human need – social bonding – was satisfied (Clark 1990: 39), because "humans evolved with the desire to *belong*, not to *compete*" (Eisler 1988: 39).

10 In a similar vein, it could be argued that Catholic priests as members of the dominant in-group, satisfied their needs while enjoying the protection of the Church – a male-dominated, -identified and -centered institution – from being held accountable for the sexual abuses against children who were entrusted to them.

References

Abbott, C., Rogers, P. and Sloboda, J. (2007) *Beyond Terror*, London: Rider.

Albright, M. (2003) *Madam Secretary: A Memoir*, New York: Hyperion.

Avruch, K. and Black, P.W. (1987) "A generic theory of conflict resolution: a critique," *Negotiation Journal*, 3(1): 87–96.

Avruch, K. and Black, P.W. (1990) "Ideas of human nature in contemporary conflict resolution theory," *Negotiation Journal*, 6(3): 221–228.

Baker, S. (2011) "This CEO's goal: more women in the boardroom," *The Washington Post*, June 5, G3.

Bartky, S.L. (1990) *Femininity and Domination: Studies in the Phenomenology of Oppression*, New York and London: Routledge.

Bleier, R. (1986) *Feminist Approaches to Science*, New York: Pergamon Press.

Bleier, R. (2000) "Theories of human origins and cultural evolution: man the hunter," in R. Satow (ed.) *Gender and Social Life*, Boston and London: Allyn and Bacon.

Boulding, E. (1976) *The Underside of History: A View of Women Through Time*, Boulder, CO: Westview Press.

Boulding, K. (1962) *Conflict and Defense: A General Theory*, New York: Harper and Row.

Bradley, H. (2007) *Gender*, Cambridge, UK: Polity.

Bryson, V. (1999) *Feminist Debates*, London: Macmillan.

Bulbeck, C. (1999) *Re-Orienting Western Feminism: Women's Diversity in a Postcolonial World*, Cambridge: Cambridge University Press.

Burton, J.W. (ed.) (1990a) *Conflict: Human Needs Theory*, New York: St. Martin's Press.

Burton, J.W. (1990b) *Conflict: Resolution and Provention*, New York: St. Martin's Press.

Burton, J.W. (1972) *World Society*, London: Cambridge University Press.

Burton, J.W. (1997) *Violence Explained*, Manchester: Manchester University Press.

Burton, J.W. and Sandole, D.J.D. (1986) "Generic theory: the basis of conflict resolution," *Negotiation Journal*, 2(4): 333–344.

Burton, J.W., Groom, A.J.R., Mitchell, C.R. and De Reuck, A.V.S. (1974) *The Study of World Society: A London Perspective*, Occasional Papers Series, Pittsburgh, PA: International Studies Association.

Cassata, D. (2011) "House approves $649 billion defense budget bill. Frank criticizes $17 billion increase in time of austerity," July 9. Online. Available http://articles.boston.com/2011–07–09/news/29756144lchaplains-pentagon-budget-defense-spending (accessed July 15, 2012).

Clark, M. (1990) "Meaningful social bonding as a universal human need," in J.W. Burton (ed.) *Conflict: Human Needs Theory*, New York: St. Martin's Press.

Clinton, H.R. (2003) *Living History*, New York: Simon and Schuster.

Collins, P.H. (1990) *Black Feminist Thought*, London: Harper Collins Academic.

Coole, D.H. (1988) *Women in Political Theory*, Brighton, Sussex, UK: Wheatsheaf Books.

de Beauvoir, S. (1974) *The Second Sex*, New York: Vintage Books.

Dunn, D.J. (2004) *From Power Politics to Conflict Resolution: The Work of John W. Burton*, Houndmills, Basingstoke, Hampshire and New York: Palgrave Macmillan.

Dworkin, A. (1989) *Pornography: Men Possessing Women*, New York: Dutton.

Eisler, R. (1988) *The Chalice and the Blade*, San Francisco: Harper & Row.

Engle, M.S. (2006) *Human Rights and Gender Violence: Translating International Law into Local Justice*, Chicago and London: University of Chicago Press.

Enloe, C. (2004) *The Curious Feminist: Searching for Women in a New Age of Empire*, Berkeley, CA: University of California Press.

Enloe, C. (2007) *Globalization and Militarism*, Lanham, Maryland: Rowman and Littlefield.

Flax, J. (1990) *Thinking Fragments: Psychoanalysis, Feminism, and Postmodernism in the Contemporary West*, Berkeley, CA: University of California Press.

Foucault, M. (1979) *Discipline and Punish: The Birth of the Prison*, New York: Random House.

Freedman, J. (2001) *Feminism*, Buckingham: Open University Press.

Frye, M. (2010) "Oppression," in P.S. Rothenberg (ed.) *Race, Class, and Gender in the United States*, 8th edn, New York: Worth Publishers.

Giddens, A. (1984) *The Constitution of Society: Outline of the Theory of Structuration*, Berkeley and Los Angeles: University of California Press.

Gilligan, C. (1982) *In a Different Voice*, Cambridge, MA: Harvard University Press.

Greer, G. (1971) *The Female Eunuch*, New York: McGraw-Hill.

Harding, S. (1986) *The Science Question in Feminism*, Ithaca, NY: Cornell University Press.

Havemann, J.M. (2007) "Great expectations," *Wilson Quarterly*, Summer: 46–53.

Henderson, K. (2008) "Ready to kill," *Washington Post*, February 24. Online. Available   www.washingtonpost.com/wp-yn/content/article/2008/02/20/AR2008022001954_pf.html (accessed March 1, 2012).

Herbert, B. (2010) "Shhh, don't say 'poverty'," in P.S. Rothenberg (ed.) *Race, Class, and Gender in the United States*, 8th edn, New York: Worth Publishers.

Heyzer, N. (2003) "Gender, peace and disarmament," in K. Vignard (ed.) *Women, Men, Peace and Security*, Geneva, Switzerland: United Nations Institute for Disarmament Research (UNDIR).

hooks, b. (1984) *Feminist Theory from Margin to Center*, Boston, MA: South End Press.

hooks, b. (1989) *Talking Back: Thinking Feminist, Thinking Black*, Boston, MA: South End Press.

Hovanec, S.C. (2008) "Speaking out: where have all the women gone?" *Foreign Service Journal*, 85(6), June: 12–14.

Humm, M. (1990) *The Dictionary of Feminist Theory*, Columbus: Ohio State University Press.

Humm, M. (1992) *Modern Feminisms: Political, Literary, Cultural*, New York: Columbia University Press.

Hunt, S. (2004) *This Was Not Our War: Bosnian Women Reclaiming the Peace*, Durham, NC: Duke University Press.

Jabri, V. (1997) Foreword to John W. Burton, *Violence Explained*, Manchester: Manchester University Press.

Jaggar, A.M. and Rothenberg Struhl, P. (eds) (1978) *Feminist Frameworks*, New York: McGraw Hill.

Johnson, A.G. (2006) *Privilege, Power, and Difference*, New York: McGraw Hill.

Keller, E.F. (1985) *Reflections on Gender and Science*, New Haven, CT: Yale University Press.

Kelman, H. (2009) "A social-psychological approach to conflict analysis and resolution," in D. Sandole, S. Byrne, I. Sandole-Staroste and J. Senehi (eds) *Handbook of Conflict Analysis and Resolution*, London and New York: Routledge.

Kriesberg, L. (2009) "Waging conflicts constructively," in D. Sandole, S. Byrne, I. Sandole-Staroste and J. Senehi (eds) *Handbook of Conflict Analysis and Resolution*, London and New York: Routledge.

Leatherman, Janie L. (2011) *Sexual Violence and Armed Conflict*, Cambridge, UK: Polity Press.

MacKinnon, C.A. (1989) *Toward a Feminist Theory of the State*, Cambridge, MA: Harvard University Press.

Milloy, C. (2011) "The middle class is being bamboozled. But why?" *Washington Post*, July 27: B1, B4.

Mitchell, C.R. (1990) "Necessitous man and conflict resolution: more basic questions about basic human needs," in J. Burton (ed.) *Conflict: Human Needs Theory*, New York: St. Martin's Press.

Mitchell, C.R. and Botes, J. (2011) "Parents of the field video interview series." Online. Available http://scar.gmu.edu/parents (assessed February 10 2013).

Narayan, D., Patel, R., Schafft, K., Rademacher, A. and Koch-Schulte, S. (2000) *Voices of the Poor: Can Anyone Hear Us?* Oxford, UK: Oxford University Press.

Pruitt, D.G. and Rubin, J.Z. (2004) *Social Conflict: Escalation, Stalemate, and Settlement*, Boston: McGraw-Hill.

Ramsbotham, O., Woodhouse, T. and Miall, H. (2011) *Contemporary Conflict Resolution*, Cambridge, UK and Malden, MA: Polity Press.

Reimann, C. (2002) *All you need is love … and what about gender? Engendering Burton's Human Needs Theory*, Working Paper 10, Centre for Conflict Resolution, Department of Peace Studies, University of Bradford, UK, January.

Rice, C. (2011) *No Higher Honor: A Memoir of My Years in Washington*, New York: Crown Publishers.

Rubenstein, R. (1990) *Interpreting Violent Conflict: A Conference for Conflict Analysts and Journalists*, Summary of Proceedings, Center for Conflict Analysis and Resolution, George Mason University, Fairfax, Virginia, April 1990.

Sandole, D.J.D. (2006) "Traditional 'realism' versus the 'new realism': John W. Burton, conflict provention, and the elusive 'paradigm shift'," *Global Society*, 20(4), October: 543–562.

Sandole, D.J.D. (2010) *Peacebuilding*, Cambridge, UK and Malden, MA: Polity Press.

Sandole, D.J.D. and Sandole-Staroste, I. (1987) *Conflict Management and Problem Solving: Interpersonal to International Applications*, New York: New York University Press.

Sandole-Staroste, I. (1992) "Feminist thought: a powerful voice in conflict resolution," *ICAR Newsletter*, 5(1): 7–10.

Sandole-Staroste, I. (1994) "Overlapping radicalisms: convergence and divergence between feminist and human needs theories in conflict resolution," in A. Taylor and J. Beinstein Miller (eds), *Conflict and Gender*, Cresskill, NJ: Hampton Press.

Sandole-Staroste, I. (2011) "Gender mainstreaming: a valuable tool in building sustainable peace," in D. Sandole, S. Byrne, I. Sandole-Staroste and J. Senehi (eds) *Handbook of Conflict Analysis and Resolution*, London and New York: Routledge.

Sklar, H. (2010) "Imagine a country – 2009," in P.S. Rothenberg, *Race, Class, and Gender in the United States*, 8th edn, New York: Worth Publishers.

Spender, D. (1985) *Man-Made Language*, London: Routledge & Kegan Paul.

Stiegler, B. (2001) *How Gender Enters the Mainstream: Concepts, Arguments and Practical Examples of the EU Strategy on Gender Mainstreaming*, Labour and Social Policy Department, Bonn, Germany: Economic and Social Policy Research and Consulting Centre of the Friedrich Ebert Foundation (FES).

Taylor, A. and Beinstein Miller, J. (eds) (1994) *Conflict and Gender*, Cresskill, NJ: Hampton Press.

The Economist (2010) "Briefing women in the workforce: female power," January 2: 49–51.

Tickner, J.A. (1992) *Gendering World Politics*, New York: Columbia University Press.

Tong, R. (1989) *Feminist Thought: A Comprehensive Introduction*, Boulder, CO: Westview Press.

Weir, S. and Faulkner, C. (eds) (2004) *Voice of a New Generation: A Feminist Anthology*, Boston: Pearson Education.

United Nations (2011a) "Women, Poverty and Economics." Online. Available www.unifem.org/gender_issues/women_poverty_economics (accessed June 14, 2011).

United Nations (2011b) "Facts and figures on peace and security." Online. Available www.womenwarpeace.org (accessed June 17, 2011).

Veblen, T. [1917] (1998) *The Nature of Peace*, New Brunswick, N.J.: Transaction Publishers.

Walby, S. (1990) *Theorizing Patriarchy*, Oxford: Blackwell.

Walby, S. (1997) *Gender Transformations*, London: Routledge.

Yeager, H. (2007) "Soldiering ahead," *Wilson Quarterly*, Summer: 54–62.

4 Moral judgments, Human Needs and conflict resolution

Alternative approaches to ethical standards[1]

Louis Kriesberg

Many proponents of the Human Needs approach to severe conflicts argue that such conflicts arise from unsatisfied basic human needs and that the conflicts can be resolved when adversaries in a conflict, aided by facilitators, recognize that those unsatisfied needs and/or the perception of them were generated by their conflict. Building on that recognition, the adversary parties may change the conditions and/or their understanding of each other's human needs. Those changes can then transform the conflict positively. Experience in problem-solving workshops provides evidence that these ideas often resonate with workshop participants. This combination of theory and practice in facilitated workshops and dialogue sessions is attractive to many workers in the conflict resolution field.

An additional attraction of a Human Needs approach for some practitioners and theoreticians in the conflict resolution field is that it seems to provide firm ground to stand on in order to assess when a conflict's resolution or outcome is likely to be regarded as just and sustainable. By positing the existence of specific, universal human needs, thwarting the perceived satisfaction of those needs can be judged to be morally wrong. The combination of having a basis for judging the morality of conflict outcomes together with knowing the factual basis for severe conflicts and knowing ways to resolve such conflicts enhances the value of each set of ideas.

In this chapter I examine the validity of this particular combination of three sets of ideas as they relate to relatively non-institutionalized large-scale conflicts. Admittedly, some proponents of the existence and importance of basic human needs emphasize the link between conflict and satisfying those needs, as a matter of science and not of morality. This is the case for John Burton, for example, who views the universal needs as rooted in social psychology (Sites 1973; Burton 1990). Maslow's theory of a hierarchy of human needs from physiology through social needs is also essentially analytic (Maslow 1970).

Nevertheless, the positing of human needs seems to invite the belief that it is morally right to try to satisfy them and wrong to obstruct human efforts to satisfy them. In any case, the wish among workers in the field of conflict resolution to have a basis to judge the rightness of different ways to fight, goals sought and outcomes reached is strong. At the outset of this chapter, I discuss the reasons that having a firm basis by which people can judge the morality of different ways to wage and to resolve social conflicts is so important. I then examine the Human Needs approach articulated by Burton as providing an explanation for the waging and resolving of conflicts, doing so from the perspective of the conflict resolution approach. The place of the problem-solving workshop in the context of the broad spectrum of conflict resolution practices is then examined. Throughout, I discuss alternative claims regarding moral judgments of the ways conflicts are conducted and resolved, and contrast these with moral claims that might be made for Human Needs theory as a basis for moral judgments.

The importance of having solid ground to judge conflicts

There are several reasons to have clear and well-grounded standards to judge the propriety of alternative ways to conduct and various outcomes of conflicts. Most mundanely, persons engaging in conflict resolution work as interveners are increasingly being asked to assess the effectiveness of their work at the behest of funders of their work. Furthermore, anyone engaged in social action and efforts at social change should seek feedback about the effectiveness of their efforts so that appropriate adjustments in those efforts may be made.

Those assessments too often are quite limited, frequently focusing on reports of satisfaction with training or other conflict resolution measures by the persons who experienced them. Indicators are usually taken of possible outcomes sought by the conflict resolvers working to advance peace; they focus on the changes that the people providing intermediary services are trying to bring about. But other possible changes, desired and undesired, may not be subjects of inquiry. Yet such unplanned effects may be highly significant, for example, for longer-term impacts or other parties engaged in the conflict not directly targeted by the conflict resolvers.

Having principles by which to assess how a conflict is waged and ended can help partisans and interveners recognize and minimize unfortunate costs and consequences. Reflecting on such possible assessments can encourage consideration of better ways to wage conflicts, to intervene in them, and to settle them. Standards to assess how well conflicts are conducted and settled can help foster constructive conflicts and peace. Those benefits are greater insofar as the standards are widely shared by all parties in a conflict and by the would-be interveners. Another criterion for the standards is that they are comprehensive in encompassing the gamut of peoples impacted by a conflict. The benefits are enhanced insofar as the standards are congruent with good theory and evidence about the course of social conflicts in varying circumstances. Determining what those standards should be, however, is extremely difficult, as discussed in this chapter.

Assessing Basic Human Needs in conflict resolution theory

Several chapters in this book and other writing discuss the Human Needs approach and how it provides a helpful guide to conflict resolution practice. And other chapters and publications offer critiques of this approach, notably by challenging the universality of particular human needs and their manifestations (Avruch 1998; Väyrynen 2001). But I will focus on problems in the Basic Human Needs approach deriving from conflict resolution theory and research and also from the practice of conflict resolution, all broadly understood. This focus can contribute to the integration of social conflict theory with conflict resolution practice, as the link between Basic Human Needs approach and problem-solving workshop practice are examined.

In this chapter, I discuss major tenets of social conflict theory as they are articulated or enacted by self-identified conflict resolvers and other persons engaged as conflict partisans or intermediaries. These conflict resolution tenets will be compared with the ideas of the Basic Human Needs approach.

The principles I discuss are particularly prominent in the conflict transformation or constructive version of the conflict resolution approach (Lederach 1997; Dayton and Kriesberg 2009; Kriesberg and Dayton 2012). There is no consensus on a comprehensive theory about the emergence, escalation, de-escalation and resolution of all kinds of conflicts. Therefore, I discuss principles and propositions of the evolving perspective underlying explanations of how conflicts are conducted and transformed. A basic premise in this perspective is that social conflicts are not inherently bad or destructive and to be avoided. Indeed, as widely understood, conflicts can be recognized not only as inevitable in social life, but they are often beneficial in discovering and advancing truth, justice, and other aspects of human well-being. Accordingly, there is a close relationship between moral concerns and how conflicts are conducted and resolved. Therefore we should try to maximize constructive ways of waging and resolving conflicts and minimize destructive ways.

A Human Needs approach, however, may imply that conflicts will not arise when basic human needs are sufficiently "satisfied"; sometimes there is a tendency to treat satisfaction dichotomously, as attained or not.

Another related tenet regarding large-sale social conflicts is that the emergence of a conflict and its course, moving through escalation, de-escalation and termination, is constructed in interaction among numerous actors. Those actors are made up of many different constituent groups, each of which has its own set of needs and concerns. To regard a large entity such as a nation or ethnic community as having a particular set of basic human needs entails reifying that entity. It assumes the entity is much more homogenous and unitary than it actually is. Human needs are too often discussed in terms appropriate for an individual human being but not for a large collectivity.

The broad conflict transformation approach emphasizes the multiplicity of actors in every conflict, as they vary over time. Consequently, costs and benefits, pains and pleasures are experienced to different degrees among different elements within each side and they change over the course of a conflict. Moreover, the parameters of each socially constructed conflict can change significantly because all the groups engaged in that conflict are connected to numerous other conflicts (Kriesberg 1980; Bar-Siman-Tov 2006). When the salience of one conflict falls relative to another conflict's increasing salience, it is likely to de-escalate and may even become dormant.

Despite all this complexity, each conflict is too often considered to be a two-sided fight, particularly by the partisans. They readily structure it as a fight between "them" and "us." The fundamental trajectory of conflicts is largely shaped by the primary adversaries in the conflict, with intermediaries usually having only limited effects. Conflicts tend to move through stages as they emerge, escalate, de-escalate and move toward resolution. They are constantly in flux, shifting in multiple dimensions, at varying speeds.

In explaining the emergence of a conflict, deprivation and unsatisfied needs are not sufficient. A sense of grievance is only one of the conditions that minimally are combined for a conflict to emerge; a grievance entails a set of people feeling that they do not have what they should have or that others are offending their values. But, in addition, the emergence of a conflict requires that the people with the grievance believe that they have a shared identity, separate from people with different identities. The identity may be based on ethnicity, geographic location, occupational position, citizenship, ideology or any other presumed commonality. Which basic needs are more or less unrealized depends on the salient identities.

Furthermore, for a conflict to be manifested and waged, the members of a potential contentious party must believe that their unsatisfactory condition is attributable to the actions of some other identified group whose actions can be altered. A conflict will not arise if suffering unfulfilled human needs is attributed to God's unfathomable will or to one's own inadequacies. Members of the aggrieved group must envisage a goal whereby their grievance would be reduced if the people responsible for their grievance would change or go away.

Finally, the members of the aggrieved group must believe they are capable of acting so as to bring about the desired change in the group that is responsible for the grievance. They may believe that they can coerce the other side to change or use various non-coercive means to bring about the desired change, by persuasion or by promised benefits. This condition is important, and it helps explain why so often a conflict does not erupt and if it does, it is the relatively powerful who start the fight.

Social conflict theory also has much to say about the course of a conflict: how it escalates, de-escalates, becomes transformed or terminated, and how the outcome is sustained. Considerable attention is given to means of struggle and managing them with minimal destructiveness. A fundamental idea is that conflicts are conducted in more or less institutionalized fashion. Within organizations, cities, countries and even internationally, there are rules about how to handle disputes and even major conflicts. The regulations vary in detail and in the effectiveness with which they are implemented.

In recent decades, considerable attention in conflict resolution theory and practice is being given to the transformation of destructive conflicts into sustained constructively conducted conflicts, particularly after periods of large-scale violence or oppression. Conduct that results in the emergence and escalation of conflicts is not the same as the conduct resulting in the persistence or the de-escalating transition of conflicts. Actions relating to negotiating conflict settlements, building legitimate conflict-management institutions and maintaining equitable relations are also different. The distinctions among these conflict stages varies among partisans and analysts; thus, a given situation, a war, may be seen as the outcome of past conduct or as a means to achieve a particular future outcome. Significantly for this chapter, the salience and interpretation of various human needs tend to vary in these different conflict stages.

Another complication is that opponents in every conflict are connected with each other by many ties and also by some degree of mutual interdependence. They also are embedded in larger social systems, which are characterized by shared values and interests as well as cross-cutting differences. Such factors generally help constrain conflicts from destructive escalation and diffusion. If the cross-cutting ties are numerous and very strong while the shared values are few and weak, however, the result would likely be widespread destructive conflicts.

These complexities stressed in social conflict theorizing pose another problem for applying a narrow Human Needs approach. The fulfillment of human needs is not a dichotomous matter; it is not likely to ever be fully met or unmet. In any circumstances a person may have various needs varyingly satisfied. Moreover, in any large-scale conflict, the members of each side will differ in the degree diverse needs are unsatisfied.

In short, it is not the existence of any particular human need that explains when a conflict becomes manifest or how it is conducted. Basic human needs do not, by themselves, explain the great variability in the patterns of the many different kinds of human conflict. Framing a conflict largely in terms of the satisfaction of basic human needs, nevertheless, may be useful in moderating and resolving a social conflict in certain circumstances. I turn to that consideration next.

Problem-solving workshops in the context of conflict resolution practice

Problem-solving workshops have been a major contributor to the development of the field of contemporary conflict resolution. The practice of bringing together a few persons from adversary countries, ethnic communities, business organizations, or government agencies for intensive interactions that are guided by facilitators has been an important vehicle for research into ongoing conflicts and also a way to help transform and resolve severe conflicts (Kelman 1992; Fisher 1997). Initially, in the 1960s, these workshops were usually organized and facilitated by academics.

Notably for the concerns of this chapter, they were specifically undertaken in the context of international and intra-state conflicts to foster movement toward a peaceful resolution. An early significant case related to the conflict in 1963–1966 among Indonesia, the newly formed Federation of Malaysia and Singapore; the conflict is often identified by its Indonesian name, Konfrontasi (Mitchell 2005). The conflict escalated despite many official mediated and unmediated efforts to settle it. A group of academics based at University College, London, led by John Burton, had been developing an alternative to traditional international relations scholarship. Given Burton's knowledge and connections acquired when he was a senior Australian diplomat, in December 1965 the group was able to initiate quiet discussions among high-level non-officials associated with the contending governments. The meetings among them, along with a panel of social scientists, went on into June 1966.

The discussions indicated the value of having social science ideas about conflicts introduced into the discussions by external facilitators. In this case, the ideas related to the functions of conflicts and the reasons for misunderstandings, not evidently about human needs. In this atmosphere, communication between persons from contending parties developed so that they better understood each other and could explore possible solutions to their conflict. The understandings and possible resolutions contributed to final official negotiations resulting in a settlement.

Many other problem-solving workshops followed, within the context of several intractable conflicts, most notably between Greek and Turkish Cypriots, Palestinians and Israelis, and Republicans and Unionists in Northern Ireland (Rouhana and Kelman 1994; Rouhana 1995). In varying degrees, these facilitated workshops drew from evolving practice and thinking, sometimes including ideas pertaining to the Basic Human Needs approach. These workshops generally could not be credited with major breakthroughs, but they often helped to prepare for negotiations, complemented the negotiation process, or contributed to sustaining peace agreements. When they have contributed significantly to the transformation of a major conflict, the workshop participants were generally at high official levels.

A related kind of conflict resolution practices began in the 1950s and has continued to expand, often under the rubric of "Track Two" diplomacy, a non-official channel of communication between leading figures from adversarial countries. The Pugwash and the Dartmouth conferences have made important contributions to conflict resolution theory and practice. In 1957, nuclear physicists and others involved in the development and possible use of nuclear weapons, working in the United States, Great Britain and the Soviet Union, began meeting to exchange ideas about technical matters related to reducing the risks of nuclear warfare. The first meetings, held in Pugwash, Nova Scotia, Canada, evolved into the Pugwash Conferences on Science and World Affairs. Discussions at these meetings contributed to the later signing of many arms-control agreements (Rotblat 1972; Pentz and Slovo 1981). In 1995, the Pugwash conferences and Joseph Rotblat, the executive director, won the Nobel Peace Prize for their work.

The Dartmouth conference began at the urging of President Dwight D. Eisenhower. At his request, Norman Cousins, then editor of the *Saturday Review*, brought together a group of prominent US and Soviet citizens to help keep communication open when official relations were especially strained. The first meeting was at Dartmouth College in 1960, and many meetings followed, providing a venue for the exchange of information and ideas such that participants could serve as quasi mediators (Chufrin and Saunders 1993).

After the Cold War, reflection on the process and the phases of development of the Dartmouth conference provided the basis for two members, Gennady I. Chufrin and Harold H. Saunders, to co-chair another set of conferences, called the Tajikistan Dialogue (Saunders 1995). A vicious civil war erupted in Tajikistan after the Soviet Union dissolved and Tajikistan became independent. Meetings among a wide range of high-ranking Tajikistanis were begun in 1993; their sustained dialogue facilitated by Saunders and Chufrin contributed to building interpersonal relations and developing ideas that significantly aided a settlement of the civil war.

It should be noted that persons who identify themselves as conflict resolvers or have been trained in conflict resolution are not the only people who apply diverse techniques and strategies that are excellent examples of mainstream conflict resolution thinking. In actuality, many people do so, unwittingly as well as wittingly. Indeed many of the ideas about negotiation, mediation and conflict transformation have been drawn from the doings of persons who were unschooled in the field. This includes government officials and former officials, religious figures and experts in technical affairs (Yarrow 1978).

Of course conflict resolution undertakings entail many other kinds of activities, aside from problem-solving workshops, dialogue groups, or Track Two diplomacy. One broad area of essential work is carried out largely by academically based persons. They conduct research, assess various conflict resolution practices, and analyze the trajectory of diverse kinds of social conflicts. They strive to synthesize the results of such efforts and infer implications for conflict resolution practice. They also often teach and train people who are engaged in social conflicts or anticipate being so engaged regarding the ideas and practices of conflict resolution.

Another major set of activities focuses on developing alternative policies to those being pursued, which sustain and even exacerbate destructive conflicts. Thus, during the Cold War, peace and conflict analysts in Western Europe developed non-offensive defense strategies that were particularly influential for Soviet leaders and contributed to transforming the Cold War (Evangelista 1999; Wiseman 2002). This entailed, for example, ways to restructure defense forces so that they were clearly defensive, and not forces readily capable of rapid forward advances that could be regarded as designed for offense.

Many other persons and organizations working in the conflict resolution field analyze particular conflicts and propose policies for mitigating those conflicts. They publish books, magazine articles, or op-ed newspaper columns, suggesting general strategies or specific tactics to avoid destructive conflict escalation, to end a violent conflict, or to establish an enduring peace (Fisher *et al.* 1996; Galtung *et al.* 2002). They may also consult with conflict partisans providing advice and counsel to help transform a destructive conflict.

There are several other major areas of conflict resolution practice. They include direct mediation, as practiced by President Jimmy Carter while president and afterwards, by United Nations officials, and by members of non-governmental organizations. They include helping to build institutional arrangements that contribute to managing conflicts constructively, which may involve strengthening the relevant social infrastructure. That entails changing norms and modifying resource allocations, as well as establishing structures to conduct conflicts legitimately.

A great enlargement in conflict resolution work has emerged in recent decades, relating to recovering from disastrous mass violence and overcoming large-scale oppression. These grave problems, in the context of increasing globalization, have resulted in more frequent interventions to assist in needed societal transformations. Governments have not developed great capacities for such undertakings and international governmental organizations (IGOs) and non-governmental organizations (NGOs) have stepped in to perform the needed tasks, contributing to economic, political and social development. This work may entail facilitating group interactions fostering reconciliation, aiding and monitoring elections, and building systems to manage inter-communal conflicts.

The Human Needs approach seems particularly pertinent in many externally facilitated problem-solving workshops, perhaps especially when the participants are non-officials. An important kind of relevance is that the language of human needs may be accessible and attractive to the participants and therefore useful for the facilitators. This is noted in Chapter 11 by Susan Allen Nan. However, in many other domains of conflict resolution practice, the ideas of the Human Needs approach do not play highly significant roles. Often, quite conventional ways of thinking about power and interests are applied and techniques of diplomacy, negotiation and mediation are used. In matters of conflict transformation, of constructive conflict escalation and of reconciliation the ideas of conflict analysis and resolution examined earlier are applied.

Alternative solutions for judging conflict conduct

In the light of this broad view of conflicts and their resolution and the limitations of the Basic Human Needs approach to explain the course of all kinds of social conflicts and therefore to provide standards of judgment of them, I turn to discuss possible alternative solutions.

One view of moral standards related to conducting social conflicts is that they derive from religious faith. Undoubtedly, many people in the world rely on their religious beliefs to provide moral guidance in conducting and intervening in conflicts. There are even some religious imperatives that are shared by many religions, for example, about doing unto others as one would want done to oneself.

However, in specific conflicts such religious directives generally provide parochial views rather than universal ones that would encompass enemies. Indeed, people on the basis of their religious faith characterize certain other people as evil and damnable. Although pacifist tenets can be found in many religious traditions, most leaders and followers in almost all religions tend to support the conflict choices made by civil authorities in the countries where the religious organizations function.

There are also some specific guidelines for particular kinds of conflicts that have philosophical and religious origins. For example, the just war doctrine is often presented as a way to limit warfare on moral grounds (Waltzer 1997). According to this reasoning, going to war justly requires a just cause, the probability of success, a legitimate public authority, proportionality, being a last resort and undertaken with a right intention. Furthermore, combatants should not conduct war actions against non-combatants; not use weapons such as mass rape or weapons with uncontrolled effects; war actions should be proportional and militarily necessary; and prisoners of war should be fairly treated. In actuality, political leaders can easily ignore such prescriptions or even claim their adherence to them as they make war as they please.

At another extreme, some people believe that moral standards are relative, deriving from culture and personal experience. No universal consensus about absolute standards exists or can exist. Furthermore, morality is based on value preferences, and according to an important social science tradition, value preferences cannot be derived from beliefs about reality. Morality is articulated in the form of "should" statements, not factual statements (Weber 1946). Moral standards are given authority when people share understandings, for example, about God, which makes morality a matter of faith. According to widely accepted social science traditions, however, there is an objective reality that can be approached by empirical methods of research. Full and accurate understanding of the objective reality may never be attained, but by seeking it, more can be learned about it. That is the goal of the social as well as the natural sciences.

These conceptions of beliefs and values have been subjected to criticism and newer views should be considered here because they help lessen the dilemmas about what it means to act morally in conducting and resolving a conflict (Kriesberg 1999). The existence of a reality separable from the observation of it is sometimes questioned. The argument is that what we know must derive from observations and those are filtered through our senses, even if they are augmented by instruments (Rubinstein *et al.* 1984; Putnam 1987). It follows that reality can be known only under specific conditions of observation, and therefore reality varies under different conditions and from differently situated perspectives. However, this does not mean that we can construct reality any way we like. Matters vary in the strength of their predispositions to be perceived one way rather than another. After all, some things are generally viewed similarly, regardless of the bases of observations.

Recent research also has affected our understanding of morality. One development has been the growing recognition that certain kinds of conduct are generally deplored. Two kinds of research are particularly interesting in this regard. One is the study of human evolution and human tendencies regarding cooperation, trust and fairness. Another major area of relevant research pertains to the development of norms regarding conflicts.

A remarkable body of recent research revives Charles Darwin's original recognition that natural selection sometimes acts on groups as well as individuals (Sober and Wilson 1998). He pointed out that a tribe that included many members who were always ready to aid one another and to sacrifice themselves for the common good would defeat most other tribes with few such members. Therefore, the standard of morality would tend to increase everywhere. In the 1960s, on the contrary, many analysts of evolution argued that natural selection could act only on individuals and not on groups, and established the concept of selfishness as paramount in evolutionary biology. At the same time, the concept of psychological egoism became prominent, minimizing the tendency of people to consciously choose to act altruistically. Beginning in the 1970s, however, group selection and intentional altruism became recognized and demonstrated in anthropological field work, psychological experimentation, philosophical reasoning and analyses in evolutionary biology.

For example, there have been numerous studies of food sharing among hunters and gatherers in human societies that reveal the widespread practice of the more successful members of a group sharing food with those who are less successful. How extensive this is and the conditions that contribute to it vary with ecological and social conditions (Kaplan and Hill 1985). There is evidence that humans favor fairness and cooperation, innately dislike extreme hierarchical differences, and punish persons acting unfairly (Gintis *et al.* 2001; Fahr and Gächter 2002). Of course, as with human needs, such innate tendencies do not determine conduct. Their manifestation is shaped by cultural definitions of fairness and equality and by many social circumstances. They vary for relations within a "tribe" or between "tribes," and membership in a tribe or other identity group is socially constructed. But the existence of such traits among humans should be kept in mind in discussions of human nature.

Norms that guide conduct related to conflict are increasing studied, revealing that certain kinds of actions are almost universally deplored. Even those persons who perpetrate condemned acts often hide or deny that they or members of their group actually committed such acts. But sometimes they even come to acknowledge that their group was wrong or that they themselves did wrong. The extension of shared norms may be seen in the growing acceptance of the existence of universal human rights and the widening condemnation of torture, rape and genocidal acts (Mueller 1983; Pinker 2011). The study of normative regimes in international affairs also indicates the existence of moral standards that influence the conduct of governments sharing those standards (Krasner 1983).

Shared normative standards provide a basis for moral imperatives. This is exemplified by the argument for conventionalism as the basis for ethics in international relations and other domains. Ethics is based on principles that people use to justify and win acceptance from others for their actions. To be effective, the concerned parties must share the principles. Rather than promulgating any particular ethical tradition as the foundation for moral theory, moral obligation can be and is based on agreement to regard "certain rules as authoritative, and certain practices as legitimate.... Whatever the parties concerned agree to regard as just or legitimate is just or legitimate," according to this view (Welch 1994). The present discussion is based on this conventionalist approach. Accordingly, I neither assert that there is a universally agreed-on moral code, nor assume that a particular moral code is supreme. However, the argument does not assert that every conventional moral code is equally supportable (Edgerton 1992).

Furthermore, in recent decades, increased use has been made of social science research to assess and help formulate social policies. The results often remind us that good intentions do not guarantee good results. Therefore, it is useful to carefully examine the actual consequences of alternative policies. Analyzing the consequences of different ways of fighting and of intervening does help ground morality in empirical and practical considerations.

The expanding work in conflict resolution has stimulated practitioners and analysts to reflect on the nature of their knowledge and of their morality. These concerns compel attention to the varying interpretations of the past and the present that adversaries construct, even about the same events. Moreover, as noted earlier, many practitioners and advocates of non-violence and conflict resolution believe that through mutual probing all parties can gain a more complete truth (Gandhi 1940). The probing can occur in many channels, including interactive workshops, confrontations in a non-violent campaign, or community meetings.

I believe that conflict resolution efforts require attention to moral issues (Nader 1991). For example, mediators and other kinds of interveners face choices about whether to intervene, when to intervene and how to intervene. Moreover, the partisans waging a struggle endeavor to morally justify their actions to their constituents and allies and also to their adversaries. If they take a conflict resolution approach, the moral issues are particularly salient. Some conflict resolvers concerned about the morality of various kinds of interventions declare particular basic values or moral principles that should guide conflict resolution work. James Laue, for example, argued that conflict resolution ethics rest on "the basic premise … that persons are inherently valuable, and to be treated as ends-in-themselves" (Laue 1982: 34; also Laue and Cormick 1978). He derived three core values from this premise: proportional empowerment, justice and freedom; and on the bases of these values, he offers several ethical principles for interveners.

The analysis of conflicts makes evident that no means of struggle and no settlement has purely good or bad consequences. Every course of action embodies a mixture of moral characteristics. Thus, people may fight for a future with greater social justice, but in doing so they often reduce freedom for many, engage in killing, and suffer severe losses; or a settlement may end the killing, but only briefly and in a way that engenders new injustices. Indeed, to insist on the primacy of one's own value-ordering and moral principles contradicts some aspects of the conflict resolution perspective. I am convinced that reflecting on the growing empirical evidence about social conflicts can help guide partisans and intermediaries to more effectively mitigate the destructiveness of conflicts.

In the light of thousands of years of human civilizations, it is possible to discern trends toward larger realms of inclusion for humans. More and more forms of exclusion and subjugation have become widely viewed as unacceptable. This is evident regarding the practice of slavery, harsh treatment of young children and subordination of women. Such conditions continue in varying degree in some places around the world. Nevertheless, they have been increasingly deemed wrong and have diminished through the millennia.

Since the end of World War II, there has been a great movement to promote adherence to human rights. The movement has included an expansion in the domains and countries in which there is official and public recognition of them; there also has been increasing institutional structures and ad hoc practices to punish violators. The Universal Declaration of Human Rights, which was adopted by the United Nations General Assembly in 1948, was a founding document for the movement. It stressed principles of liberty and equality and individual rights; this was criticized by some governments and additional covenants were adopted in subsequent years. In 1966, the International Covenant on Civil and Political Rights and the International Covenant on Economic, Social and Cultural Rights were adopted by the United Nations. Subsequently, conventions were adopted opposed to discrimination against any races, women and persons with disabilities, against torture and for the rights of migrant workers.

In addition to the broad standards of human rights, another way in which moral standards are set forth and implemented is by specifying them in particular arenas of conflict behavior. Elements of this were set forth in the Geneva Conventions, beginning in 1864. This has been greatly elaborated, often by drawing from both the analysis of actual conflict behavior and from widely shared norms and prescriptions, which may be embodied in international and national laws. The expansion of non-governmental advocacy groups for the protection of human rights has contributed greatly to this. Work by people in the field of human rights and in the field of conflict resolution can and do complement each other (Babbitt and Lutz 2009).

Policy recommendations based on empirical experience and normative concerns are exemplified in the formulation of a new doctrine: the Responsibility to Protect (R2P). It is responsive to the failure of international actors to intervene when that seems to be needed and the inadequacies of interventions when they actually are undertaken (Hall 2010; Mills and O'Driscoll 2010). During the wars breaking up Yugoslavia, the debates around the world about whether or not and how to intervene while mass atrocities were underway propelled efforts to agree about what should be done to deal with such circumstances. Addressing the General Assembly in 1999 and 2000, Secretary-General Kofi Annan called for international consensus about not allowing gross violations of human rights and yet not assaulting state sovereignty. In September 2000 the Government of Canada joined by major foundations established the International Commission on Intervention and State Sovereignty (ICISS), co-chaired by Gareth Evans and Mohamed Sahnoun.

A year later, the Commission released its report, enunciating two basic principles:

1. State sovereignty implies responsibility and the primary responsibility for the protection of its people lies with the state itself.
2. Where a population is suffering serious harm, as a result of internal war, insurgency, repression or state failure, and the state in question is unwilling or unable to halt or avert it, the principle

of non-intervention yields to the international responsibility to protect.

(www.responsibilitytoprotect.org/index.php/publications)

The R2P has three components: 1. the responsibility to *prevent* the harms identified above by addressing root causes and direct causes of those harms; 2. the responsibility to *respond* appropriately to the situations of compelling need, and only in extreme cases respond with military intervention; 3. the responsibility to *rebuild*. Furthermore, the responsibility to prevent should have the highest priority. Military intervention should be the last resort and be the minimal amount needed to reach the objective. Security Council authorization should be sought in all cases and if the Security Council does not authorize action, the General Assembly may be asked to consider the proposal.

Acceptance of the idea that the international community has a responsibility to protect, as prescribed in the report, has speedily grown (von Schorlemer 2007). This was recognized at the September 2005 United Nations' World Summit by the world's heads of state and governments. In 2007 Secretary-General Ban Ki-moon took steps to institutionalize the Responsibility to Protect. An international coalition of NGOs is engaged in strengthening the normative and institutional character of R2P (http://responsibilitytoprotect.org). It is also noteworthy that on March 28, 2011, President Obama used some of the language of R2P in explaining and justifying the US intervention in Libya.

Efforts to assess particular kinds of peace actions can propose policy guidelines derived from widely shared norms and empirical analyses of such actions. This is demonstrated in Diehl and Druckman's (2010) book, *Evaluating Peace Operations*. The authors derive three core peace operations goals from the statements and mandates of the major stakeholders in such operations, national and international agencies and organizations. The core goals are violence abatement, conflict containment and conflict settlement.

Diehl and Druckman identify several measures of progress for each core goal, discussing limitations of each measure. They do the same for goals that are more specific to a particular mission. Analyzing the attainment of goals at that operational level focuses attention on actual effects of peace efforts and not on general intentions or remaining at the level of quite general goals. By formulating the template for evaluating a wide array of peace operations relatively broad principles of judgment are recognized. This also tends to expand the moral standard by which the operational actions are to be judged.

Conclusions

It should be clear that the quest for firm ground to stand on in ethically judging all kinds of ways to wage and to settle diverse conflicts is not likely to be wholly successful. Particular persons and groups may prescribe standards, but without very widespread agreement about them, they cannot be effective. Such agreement is unlikely on a global scale in the foreseeable future. Moreover, such prescriptions unavoidably must be stated at a very abstract level and result in contradictions as multiple prescriptions are applied to specific cases under specific conditions.

The availability of a well-grounded comprehensive theory about all kinds of conflicts and their trajectories is also needed to formulate effective ethical standards for making and sustaining peace. Again, there is no consensus about any such comprehensive conflict theory. I doubt its feasibility in adequate detail. There is an inherent problem in developing a comprehensive theory when partisans and intermediaries are nearly always focused on a single case within a particular time period. The clinical medical model is one way to deal with that matter. But a public health model may be a better one. In the clinical model, a physician draws from many disciplines and applies them to a unique patient. In the public health model, general preventive measures are taken for the benefit of populations.

A public health approach also includes engaging non-professionals so that they behave in ways that prevents damaging their health. This relates to not spreading diseases and avoiding disabling accidents, as well as eating and exercising properly. An important aspect of conflict resolution work is the diffusion of knowledge and skills about preventing, containing and recovering from destructive conflicts. A risk in such diffusion is that isolated techniques in conflict resolution are adopted or only the words of conflict resolution are taken. Ignoring the basic ideas of the field can easily result in mistakes and ineffective actions. Some of the core ideas of the approach should diffuse with specific words or techniques. Furthermore, moral considerations are advantageously associated with the diffusion of the ideas and practices of conflict resolution. More research and reflection is needed about various packages of theory and practices as they are brought to bear in different circumstances.

The Human Needs approach to conflict resolution might be usefully viewed as one solution for a particular set of intervention methods to be applied to a particular set of conflicts, under certain conditions. That is not bad. However, this is only one of a number of possible moral yardsticks, as I have previously argued. The analysis made in this chapter indicates that islands of mini-theory and sets of limited practices are a way to develop ethical standards to guide conduct. Such islands would be for the use of partisans in a conflict and for intermediaries who do not view themselves as conflict resolvers, as well as for those who so define themselves (Kriesberg 2011).

The world is incredibly messy. Even if neat universal moral or theoretical guides are unattainable, it is not advisable to ignore the issue of morality in waging and settling conflicts. Conflict resolution practitioners can be clear about the moral standards they choose to use. They should recognize other standards are possible, and are likely to be held by other stakeholders. All who strive to advance peace and widely equitable relations should strive for greater normative consensus and also bring to bear the best evidence possible about the trajectories of various social conflicts and what affects them.

Note

1 An earlier version of this chapter was presented at the conference "Reconsidering John Burton: Conflict Resolution and Basic Human Needs," April 29–May 1, 2011, The School for Conflict Analysis and Resolution. I thank the participants of the conference for their comments and also Bruce W. Dayton, Paula Freedman, Robert A. Rubinstein, and Carolyn M. Stephenson for their comments.

References

Avruch, K. (1998) *Culture and Conflict Resolution*. Washington, D.C., United States Institute of Peace.

Babbitt, E.F. and E.L. Lutz (eds) (2009) *Human Rights and Conflict Resolution in Context*. Syracuse, NY, Syracuse University Press.

Bar-Siman-Tov, J. (2006) "Interlocking Conflicts in the Middle East." *Conflict and Conflict Resolution in Middle-Eastern Societies: Between Tradition and Modernity*. H.-J. Albrecht, J.-M. Simon, H. Rezaei, H.-C. Rohne and E. Kiza. Berlin, Duncker & Humboldt.

Burton, J. (1990) *Conflict: Resolution and Provention*. New York, St. Martin's.

Chufrin, G.I. and H.H. Saunders (1993) "A Public Peace Process." *Negotiation Journal*, 9 (April 1993): 155–177.

Dayton, B.W. and L. Kriesberg (eds) (2009) *Conflict Transformation and Peacebuilding: Moving From Violence to Sustainable Peace*. Oxford, UK, Routledge.

Diehl, P.F. and D. Druckman (2010) *Evaluating Peace Operations*. Boulder, London, Lynne Rienner.

Edgerton, R. (1992) *Sick Societies*. New York, The Free Press.

Evangelista, M. (1999) *Unarmed Forces: The Transnational Movement to End the Cold War*. Ithaca and London, Cornell University Press.

Fahr, E. and S. Gächter (2002) "Altruistic Punishment in Humans." *Nature*, 415 (January 10): 137–140.

Fisher, R. (1997) *Interactive Conflict Resolution*. Syracuse, Syracuse University Press.

Fisher, R., E. Kopelman and A.K. Schneider (1996) *Beyond Machiavelli*. New York, Penguin.

Galtung, J., Carl G. Jacobsen and Kai Frithjof Brand-Jacobsen (2002) *Searching for Peace: The Road to TRANSCEND*, 2nd edn. London, Pluto.

Gandhi, M.K. (1940) *An Autobiography of My Experiments with Truth*. Almedabad, India, Nvajivan.

Gintis, H., E.A. Smith and S. Bowles (2001) "Costly Signaling and Cooperation." *Journal of Theoretical Biology*, 213(1): 103–119.

Hall, B.W. (2010) "International Law and the Responsibility to Protect." *The International Studies Encyclopedia*. R.A. Denemark. Blackwell Reference Online, www.

isacompendium.com/subscriber/tocnode?id=g9781444336597_chunk_
g978144433659711_ss1–32.

Kaplan, H. and K. Hill (1985) "Food Sharing among Ache Foragers: Tests of
Explantory Hypotheses." *Current Anthropology,* 26(2): 223–239.

Kelman, H.C. (1992) "Informal Mediation by the Scholar Practitioner." *Mediation
in International Relations.* J. Bercovitch and J.Z. Rubin. New York, St. Martin's.

Krasner, S.D. (1983) *International Regimes.* Ithaca, NY, Cornell University Press.

Kriesberg, L. (1980) "Interlocking Conflicts in the Middle East." *Research in Social
Movements, Conflicts, and Change.* L. Kriesberg. Greenwich, CT, JAI Press. 3:
99–118.

Kriesberg, L. (1999) "On Advancing Truth and Morality in Conflict Resolution."
Peace and Conflict Studies, 6(1): 7–19.

Kriesberg, L. (2011) "The Conflict Transformation Field's Current State of the
Art." *Berghof Handbook for Conflict Transformation.* M. Fischer, J. Giessmann and B.
Schmelzle. Farmington Hills, MI, Barbara Budrich Publishers.

Kriesberg, L. and B.W. Dayton (2012) *Constructive Conflicts: From Escalation to Resolution,* 4th edn. Lanham, MD, Rowman & Littlefield.

Laue, J. (1982) "Ethical Considerations in Choosing Intervention Roles." *Peace and
Change,* 8 (Summer 1982): 34.

Laue, J. and G. Cormick (1978) "The Ethics of Intervention in Community Disputes." *The Ethics of Social Intervention.* G. Bermant, H.C. Kelman and D.P.
Warwick. Washington, D.C., Halstead Press.

Lederach, J.P. (1997) *Building Peace: Sustainable Reconciliation in Divided Societies.*
Washington, D.C., United States Institute of Peace Press.

Maslow, A.M. (1970) *Motivation and Personality,* 3rd edn. New York, Harper & Row.

Mills, K. and C. O'Driscoll (2010) "From Humanitarian Intervention to the
Responsibility to Protect." *The International Studies Encyclopedia.* R.A. Denemark.
Blackwell   Reference   Online   www.isacompendium.com/subscriber/
tocnode?id=g9781444336597_chunk_g97814443365978_ss1–28.

Mitchell, C. (2005) "Ending Confrontation between Indonesia and Malaysia: A Pioneering Contribution to International Problem Solving." *Paving the Way.* R.A.
Fisher. Lanhan, Lexington: 19–40.

Mueller, J. (1983) *The Retreat from Doomsday: The Obsolescence of Major Wars.* New
York, Basic Books.

Nader, L. (1991) "Harmony Models and the Construction of Law." *Conflict Resolution: Cross-Cultural Perspectives.* K. Avruch, P.W. Black and J.A. Scimecca. New
York, Greenwood Press: 41–59.

Pentz, M.J. and G. Slovo (1981) "The Political Significance of Pugwash." *Knowledge
and Power in a Global Society.* W.M. Evan. Beverly Hills/London/New Delhi, Sage:
175–203.

Pinker, S. (2011) *The Better Angels of Our Nature: Why Violence has Declined.* New York,
Viking.

Putnam, H. (1987) *The Many Faces of Realism.* LaSalle, Illinois, Open Court.

Rotblat, J. (1972) *Scientists in the Quest for Peace: A History of the Pugwash Conferences.*
Cambridge, MA, MIT Press.

Rouhana, N.N. (1995) "The Dynamics of Joint Thinking between Adversaries in
International Conflict: Phases of the Continuing Problem-Solving Workshop."
Political Psychology, 16(2): 321–345.

Rouhana, N.N. and H.C. Kelman (1994) "Non-official Interaction Processes in the

Resolution of International Conflicts: Promoting Joint Israeli-Palestinian Thinking Through a Continuing Workshop." *Journal of Social Issues*, 50(1): 157–178.

Rubinstein, R.A., C.D. Laughlin and J. McManus (1984) *Science as Cognitive Process: Toward an Empirical Philosophy of Science.* Philadelphia, University of Pennsylvania Press.

Saunders, H.H. (1995) "Sustained Dialogue on Tajikistan." *Mind and Human Interaction*, 6 (August 1995): 123–135.

Sites, P. (1973) *Control: The Basis of Social Order.* New York, London, Dunellen.

Sober, E. and D.S. Wilson (1998) *Unto Others: The Evolution and Psychology of Unselfish Behavior.* Cambridge, MA, Harvard University Press.

Väyrynen, T. (2001) *Culture and International Conflict Resolution: A Critical Analysis of the Work of John Burton.* Manchester and New York, Manchester University Press.

von Schorlemer, S. (2007) *The Responsibility to Protect as an Element of Peace.* Policy Paper 28. Bonn, Development and Peace Foundation: 1–12.

Waltzer, M. (1997) *Just and Unjust Wars: A Moral Argument with Historical Illustrations*, 4th edn. New York, Basic Books.

Weber, M. (1946) "Politics as a Vocation." *From Max Weber: Essays in Sociology.* H.H. Gerth and C.W. Mills. New York, Oxford University Press.

Welch, D.A. (1994) "Can We Think Systematically about Ethics and Statecraft?" *Ethics and International Affairs*, 8: 23–37.

Wiseman, G. (2002) *Concepts of Non-Provocative Defence: Ideas and Practices in International Security.* New York, Palgrave, in association with St. Antony's College, Oxford.

Yarrow, C.H.M. (1978) *Quaker Experiences in International Conciliation.* New Haven, CT, Yale University Press.

5 Ethics of the conflict resolution mediator

From scientific gaze to sensitive and skillful action

Tarja Väyrynen

Introduction

For many peace theorists and practitioners, the third party's commitment to peace is analogous to the commitment of the medical profession to the value of health. Johan Galtung enforces the medical analogue by suggesting that a conflict resolution theorist-practitioner should be able to present a triangle that includes the diagnosis of the causes of the conflict, the prognosis of its development and the therapy through which conflict resolution can be sought. He argues that the triangle forms a solid foundation for conflict resolution (Galtung 1996; see also Dunn 2005; Jutila *et al.* 2008; Lawler 1995). For John Burton (1990, 1997), a conflict resolution practitioner works on the basis of his scientific knowledge, brings this knowledge into practice and theorizes on the bases of his practical experiences. According to Burton, there are natural law-like regularities, i.e. human needs, that determine human behavior and that can be known and brought to the field of conflict resolution. Hence conflict resolution resembles the medical profession with its solid scientific foundation and practical orientation. In this frame of thought that equates the work of the theorist-practitioner with the work of the medical practitioner, the idea of impartiality and neutrality of the mediator forms a cornerstone for good and ethical facilitative conduct. In short, impartial and neutral behavior, and thereby professional conduct, is thought to be ethical behavior on the part of the mediator (for summaries see Bolger *et al.* 2010; Fisher 1991).

I argue in this chapter that the medical analogy that is often used to describe the work of the conflict resolution theorists and practitioners is insufficient as it leaves a large part of the contextual sensitivity of conflict resolution unnoticed. It follows that the view is bound to offer a limited understanding of mediation ethics. I derive inspiration from anthropology and ethnography and argue that conflict resolution mediators deal with violent political formations that call for situational ethics. In the first part of the chapter, a critique of the medical analogy is presented. In the second part, the rule ethics which are embedded in the medical analogy is discussed. The third and fourth sections introduce an alternative analogy for third-party involvement based on medical anthropology and ethnography and pointing towards skill ethics. I argue that the analogies are important since they frame the world to us in a certain way and guide our action.

Revisiting the medical analogy

The peace researchers' ideal that the field could fulfill the scientific criteria of objectivity and universality, and yet contribute to practice, characterizes peace research from its very beginning. It is thought that scientific – which is seen to imply objectivity and universality – and non-ideological models will help to improve the human condition plagued by war and violence (for a summary see Jutila *et al.* 2008). Galtung's triangular model of diagnosis-prognosis-therapy and his work on structural violence, as well as Burton's Human Needs theory, echo this tradition, where the objectivity and universality form the ideal for peace research and conflict resolution practices (Burton 1979, 1982, 1997; Galtung 1969, 1971, 1985).

When a conflict theory is founded on human needs, the third party is needed to increase the ability of the participants to understand the development of a particular conflict, the conflict's origins in universal human needs and the relationships as they relate to the conflict. The subject's own interpretation of a conflict situation is important, but the third party is needed to refer to human needs as the navigation points, ontological principles and goals of conflict resolution. Human needs are employed by the conflict resolution facilitator in the same way as metapsychological principles are used by the psychoanalyst. Needs are depth metaphors of which the facilitator is aware, but the participants are not. The facilitator can help the participants to interpret the situation by referring to these ontological principles. Burton argues that the conflict resolution facilitator is an outside observer in a scientific role. He writes that he is an "observer in a scientific role" who "makes no assessments, judgments or value interventions" (Burton 1979: 37, 1982: 121, 1990: 204). When conflict resolution is, on the other hand, seen to go through the process of diagnosis-prognosis-therapy, the role of the peace researcher is important too as he is thought to be able to conduct an objective analysis of the conflict and guide the parties through the conflict resolution process successfully. The parties in conflict may not be able to see the root causes, namely structures, of their conflict and thereby a third party is needed to assist them to see the violence embedded in unjust structures (Galtung 1996).

In both frameworks, the work of the third party comes close to that of the medical practitioner. The third party has theoretical knowledge of the root causes of the conflict in question, is able to apply the knowledge to the practical conflict resolution process and helps the parties in conflict to restructure their conflictual relationship. Furthermore, the medical analogy insinuates that dysfunctional conflicts and deviant behaviour are signs, like physical symptoms, of something else, of diseases. Conflict, like symptoms of a disease, as such is not malign since it is merely a sign of structural failings or failures in basic human needs satisfaction which cause violent political behaviour.

This approach is, in my view, highly problematic. As Hanna Arendt writes in the context of the Black Power movement in the USA and the riots in the 1970s:

> Nothing, in my opinion, could be theoretically more dangerous than the tradition of organic thought in political matters by which power and violence are interpreted in biological terms. [...] The organic metaphors with which our entire present discussion of these matters, especially of the riots, is permeated – the notion of a "sick society," of which riots are symptom of a disease – can only promote violence.
>
> (Arendt 1970: 75)

According to Arendt, biological metaphors and explanations, including medical analogies, of violence strip conflicts and violence of their political (humans acting in concert in a means-ends manner) dimensions. When, for example, people fight for their homeland, the explanations should not be searched from among drives, instinct-like behavior or needs, but from the political realm of human affairs where the means sometimes overcome the ends which, however, remain in the domains of the human and the rational. Furthermore, and even more dangerously, argues Arendt, the use of the biological metaphors naturalizes violence by making it a natural reaction for a human-being in constraining situations (Arendt 1970: 59–87).

Seeing society in organic and biological terms and using medical metaphors in conflict resolution increases the role of expertise knowledge and power in political and societal matters. Whenever there is a need for a surgical treatment of the patient, the greater the power of the surgeon, argues Arendt (1970: 75). In a similar fashion, it is only through professional, scientific and universally applicable knowledge, and even social engineering, that "sick" societies can be dealt with. Little space is left for other forms of knowledge (e.g. everyday and situational knowledge) when an expert intervention is planned and executed. When this view is applied to conflict resolution it follows that the more the conflict is theorized in biological terms, the greater the influence of the expertise knowledge in resolving conflicts. At the center of Arendt's critique is a concern that organic thought dismisses power in human affairs and naturalizes violent political events by turning them into something intrinsic to human society.

Rule ethics and the professionalization of mediation

The organic thought and its counterpart, namely expertise knowledge, reflect the need to professionalize the field of conflict mediation and establish a universally applicable code of conduct for mediators. As in the medical professions, there is a call for a mediation ethics that guarantees professional conduct on the part of the mediator. The study of conflict and the practices of conflict resolution are seen to be professions in the same way that medicine is a profession. They are thought to be universal ways of life in the sense that the basic principles of those fields do not vary across time and space. It is argued that, as with many other occupations, the profession of the mediator needs a universal ethical code which guides mediation behaviour and guarantees its quality.

Burton's *Resolving Deep-Rooted Conflict: A Handbook* (1987) is one of the early attempts to establish a clear set of rules for mediators and facilitators. He notes the lack of a code of conduct in facilitative behavior and justifies the need for the rules by claiming that:

> Ethics used in this context has more of a function connotation than a moral one. There are rules to be observed that are designed to ensure success. It is the possibilities of failure because rules were inadequate or were not observed that draws attention to the ethics of intervention.
>
> (Burton 1987: 27)

Burton (1984: 149, 162–163) derives three general rules from medicine and suggests professionalism, secrecy and perceived neutrality for the third party that would guarantee the ethicality of his action.

Many scholars and practitioners concur with Burton and feel that there is a need for a single code of mediator's conduct because it would imply ethicality of mediation behavior. Very strict guidelines are, however, seen to limit the multiple ways mediation can be conducted and non-binding guidelines are preferred over strict hand-book type lists for ethical behavior. Neutrality and impartiality are seen to form the cornerstone of good conduct and therefore mediation ethics. It is argued that by remaining neutral, a mediator will not agree with or condone any of the political goals or ideologies of the conflicting parties, and by remaining impartial the mediator will treat all conflicting parties equally regardless of their background. Neutrality is sometimes disputed in this discussion when it is openly declared that the third party has his principles and values to adhere to, and this can be seen to imply non-neutrality (see, for example, *Humanitarian Negotiations with Armed Groups* 2006; *International Alert, Code of Conduct* 1998; for the EU see http://ec.europa.eu/civiljustice/adr/adr_ec_code_conduct_en.pdf; for summaries see Bolger *et al.* 2010; Fisher 1991; and for classical discussion see Touval 1975; Young 1967).

The emphasis on neutrality and impartiality coincides with the quest for professionalism that is expressed by many conflict resolution scholars and practitioners. Bolger and his colleagues (Bolger *et al.* 2010) conducted a survey among mediation scholars and practitioners; the outcome was that the scholars and practitioners think that the codes of conduct can be effective for all types of mediation if they are applied with flexibility. The codes of conduct would provide guidance for the mediator and, as one of their interviewees put it, "ensure the conscientious application of professional practice" while still allowing for creativity and ingenuity should the need arise. The survey demonstrated that many scholars and practitioners believe that the credibility of the mediator is paramount to the success of any mediation process and flexible guidelines would ensure credibility by ensuring a professional, uniform approach while allowing the mediator to utilize creativity and spontaneity when faced with challenging situations.

Why not anthropology?

The quests for professionalization and for the flexibility of the third-party code of conduct might suggest an alternative occupational analogy. Anthropology with its sub-field, namely medical anthropology, offers a rich source for alternatives analogies that do not rely on organic thought. The conventional version of the medical analogy leaves the contextual sensitivities of mediation and mediation ethics unnoticed, and is therefore vulnerable in subsequent critique. Merton Benvenisti (1986: 118–119) writes on a conflict resolution workshop he took part:

> One winter not long ago I participated in a workshop for resolving the Israeli–Palestinian conflict held at a distinguished American university. Our workshop was squeezed between similar workshops dealing with the "Northern Ireland conflict" and the "Cyprus conflict." My frustration grew slowly until at a formal dinner I had one glass too many. I stood up and said to the organiser, a "resolver" par excellence, "I wonder if you know who we are at all. For all you care, we can be Zimbabweans, Basques, Arabs, Jews, Catholics, Protestants, Greeks, Turks. To you we are just guinea pigs to be tested, or at least best to be engineered."

Benveniste's critique reflects his frustration from the perspective of the participant on the universalizing tendencies in the field of third-party conflict resolution. Unlike organic thought and its medical analogy, medical anthropology demonstrates how the sense of illness, disease and even physical symptoms vary across time and space and leaves no space for "conflict resolution engineering." Anthropologists have shown the "shifting historical meanings of pain, the local elaboration of salient symptoms, and the ethnomethodological categories through which healing is evaluated in political as much as personal terms" (Kleinman and Kleinman 1994: 710). The simplified cause-symptom causal chain does not hold since the meaning of illnesses and diseases vary across cultures. It follows that the cure is also context-dependent. There is hence a shift from universalist to contextual thought where the underlying analogies that structure our thought and action change radically.

In addition to the cultural understanding of illness and cure, for medical anthropology such a basic concept as the human body is by no means neutral. Nor should the concept of conflict be neutral for conflict theorists and practitioners. Medical anthropology argues that there is an intimate connection between the body and the social, and the subject matter is not just how culture influences corporeal experiences but, rather, how the body is a nexus where social relations, institutions and bodily processes meet. The questions to be asked are more concerned with what the body's cultural form means and why its representation differs in different epochs and among different groups. Medical anthropology recognizes the role of power that writes its scripts on the human body, and examines how the body acts out the power, often in the form of socially recognizable, acceptable and curable illnesses (Kleinman and Kleinman 1994). When this insight is applied to conflict theory, it is possible to argue that conflict is a violent political formation, a "political form" that is structured by constellations of power. Ultimately, there is an intimate connection between power, institutions, violent practices and human agency and action (cf. Avruch 1998; Avruch and Black 1991, 1993; Avruch *et al.* 1991; Bleiker and Brigg 2011; Jabri 2007; Väyrynen 2001, 2011).

Arendt uses the notion of "violence" when she speaks about violent political events. Arendt's thinking calls forth conceptualizations where violence is seen to be a multi-faceted phenomenon without clear-cut boundaries. For example, Veena Das (1995: 79) follows the Arendtian line of thought when she studies violence in her native country of India. What is notable in her and many other anthropologists' works that study violence (see, for example, Aretxaga 1997; Butalia 1998; Das *et al.* 2002; Feldman 1991; Nordstrom 1997) is that they always discuss the notion of violence in the context of the "local," and the local is seen to be partly constructed through the violence. Furthermore, violence is examined within the context of the local in reference to the global processes that intertwine and take part in producing the local. These scholars challenge the universalist frame of thought as well as organic thinking by locating violence in a specific time and space continuum. For them, the analysis of conflict means a detailed documenting and understanding of the violent local processes that require time- and space-specific solutions.

Given the evolving dynamics of violent political forms, they are something where clear-cut interventions are impossible. Their limits and boundaries are shifting as the violent formation mutates, and thereby a scientific gaze that is static and distant seldom offers a sufficient tool to approach them. If there is a structure in violence it is a more rhizome-like non-hierarchical and non-linear type of structure than a strict recognizable and observable form. Although the rhizome metaphor could bring us back to organic thought, the way Gilles Deleuze and Felix Guattari describe it places it firmly in the domain of the political and social. Deleuze and Guattari (1980: 7) describe the rhizome as "ceaselessly established connections between semiotic chains, organizations of power, and circumstances relative to the arts, sciences, and social struggles." It has no specific origin or genesis, for a "rhizome has no beginning or end; it is always in the middle, between things, interbeing, intermezzo." When this is applied to conflict there is no easily traceable linear development (beginnings and ends) in the history of violence. Its local expressions vary and it is difficult to form a general view of the violent political formation. Violence eventually resists attempts to grasp it in its entirety. Violence and its rhizome-like quality escape attempts to conceptualize it in the form of a medical report and produce the triangle of diagnosis-prognosis-therapy since there are no indivisible symptoms to be observed, no simple causal connections to be established and no universally applicable treatments to be administered.

If the conflict is seen as a rhizome-like violent formation, the role of the mediator needs to be reconceptualized too. The ethical conduct of the mediator is no longer reducible to neutrality, ability to use theoretical models that are thought to be universal or to the mediator's independence from the case at hand. Rather, his ethicality finds other sources. As much as medical anthropology has added to our understanding of the variety of curative and healing practices in different local contexts, new ways of understanding conflict might do the same and add a new layer to our practices of conflict resolution.

Skill ethics and mediator moral neutrality

Anthropologist Ruth Behar describes in *The Vulnerable Observer: Anthropology that Breaks Your Heart* (1996) her journey in the academic world of anthropology. She writes how she was first keen to obey the rules of the profession and withdraw her personal voice and self from her scientific writing. Although there had been openings in the direction of the questioning of the status of the disinterested observer in anthropology, notably in the works of George Devereux and Clifford Geertz, it took some time for Behar to allow herself to follow that path. For Devereux, writes Behar, if the phenomenon to be observed is to be understood, it is worth inquiring what happens with the subjectivity of the observer. The subjectivity of the observer influences the course of the observed event in human and social matters as inspection disturbs the behavior of an electron in the laboratory. Geertz, on the other hand, argues that anthropologists' truths are "person-specific," in the sense that different sorts of minds take hold of different elements of the phenomenon. Behar writes how her acknowledging the subjective nature of social knowledge, her growing more skillful in her anthropological practices, as well as some personal events in her life, made her vulnerable in her professional practices, including the field-work and writing. After this process of growing more sensitive in her profession and questioning the universal foundations of knowledge, her anthropologist's ethics started to change and emerge from the skillful and situational practices that she uses when she locates herself in the midst of the world she seeks to examine, interact with and write about (Behar 1996).

Instead of relying on rule ethics, Behar's work suggests situational ethics. In a similar vein, tackling violence and rhizome-like violent political formations calls for situational ethics. Unlike rule ethics, that believes in rules that tell us what is right and where the morality of action is judged by the mediator's adherence to rules, such as those of impartiality and neutrality, situational ethics urges us to engage with a tradition that defines what is good. Situational ethics is a variation of virtue ethics, which emphasizes practical wisdom and the development of traits that lead to ethical action. Instead of seeking to define the universally applicable rules for mediation, virtue ethics invites us to reflect what it means to be a human being and act according to the situation. In Hubert and Stuart Dreyfus' virtue ethics model developed in their *Towards a Phenomenology of Ethical Expertise* (1991), good and ethical conduct is derived from skill acquisition, and ultimately from sensitivity and intuition. When the model is applied to mediation, mediation comes to be understood as a historical and societal thing: what is considered to be right and ethical in mediation is considered right and ethical given our history of mediation practices (cf. Flyvbjerg 1991).

According to Dreyfus and Dreyfus, skill acquisition, and thereby the maturing of ethical conduct, consists of five stages: novice, advanced beginner, competence, proficiency and expertise. At the stage of the novice, skill acquisition is based on recognizing context-free rules for determining actions. This level is characterized by a handbook type of knowledge that relies on rules and action that follows the rules. The stage of the advanced beginner includes incorporating situational aspects into instructional maxims. With increasing competence at the third stage, the performer learns to choose a "plan, goal or perspective which organizes the situation and by examining the small set of features and aspects that he has learned are relevant given that plan, the performer can simplify and improve his performance" (Dreyfus and Dreyfus 1991: 233). This stage consists also of an "emotionally involved experience of the outcome," because the choice and successful completion of a goal can be frustrating. Proficiency at the fourth stage is characterized by stopping reflecting on problematic situations. At this stage, a plan, goal or perspective is noticed rather than looked for. A proficient performer sees what needs to be done, but must decide how to do it.

An expert performer, on the other hand, knows how to perform the action without calculating and comparing alternatives. This stage of expertise is largely based on intuition, not on analysis or deliberative comparison of alternatives. The expert does not solve problems. Neither does he reason. Rather, he spontaneously does what has normally worked as he has grown more sensitive to the qualities of a variety of situations, and is intuitively able to detect similarities and differences between the situation at hand and his earlier experiences. There is no need for certainty since skillful performances and sensitivity help the expert to grasp the contextual properties that characterize that particular situation.

When this five-stage model is applied to the skill acquisition of the mediation work – which implies the maturing of the mediator's ethical conduct – it is possible to see how a beginner tries to follow the rules available, whereas an expert performs the actions needed without deliberation of either rules or a plan, goal or perspective. Learning through experience is a basis of the expertise of the mediator. Hence the expertise, in this view, does not arise from superior scientific knowledge, it rather arises from learning and acquiring skills by performing, i.e. from practical wisdom. Ethical comportment is a form of expertise and follows the path of skill acquisition. An ethical expert behaves according to the situation without appealing to rules and maxims. The greater the expertise, the rarer the need for deliberation. Principles and theories serve only for early stages of learning and an expert ethical response to a situation is not grounded in them. In problematic situations, the expert deliberates rather about the appropriateness of his intuitions than abstract principles. Dreyfus and Dreyfus (1991: 244) write about principles and intuition:

> Yet, as we have seen, principles can never capture the know-how an expert acquires by dealing with, and seeing the outcome of a large number of concrete situations. Thus, when faced with a dilemma, the expert does not seek principles but, rather, reflects on and tries to sharpen his or her spontaneous intuitions by getting more information until one decision emerges as obvious.

Expert performance in ethics is doing what those who already are accepted as ethical experts do and approve. There is thus an element of convention which derives from the community of the ethical experts. Being a master means also responding to the unique situation out of a fund of experience in the context. Reaching a stage of maturity does not mean transcending a tradition: it implies leaving behind the rules of conventional morality for a new contextualization, for being more open to the contextual properties of moral dilemmas. In a case of ethical disagreement, two experts should be "able to understand and appreciate each other's decisions. This is as near as expert ethical judgments can or need come to impartiality and universality" (Dreyfus and Dreyfus 1991: 242).

Ultimately, "there is no final answer as to what the appropriate response in a particular situation should be" (Dreyfus and Dreyfus 1991: 246). The situations the expert responds to are constantly changing, and his responses become constantly more refined. A sign of maturity is not reflective detachment from a unique situation to universal principles as the codes of conduct for mediation that seek to list universally applicable rules suggest. On the contrary, in Dreyfus and Dreyfus' model, maturity means being able to learn from experiences, use what one has learned, stay involved and refine one's intuitions. In Seyla Benhabib's (1992: 54) words, "the more we can identify the different viewpoints from which a situation can be interpreted and construed, the more will we have sensitivity to the particularities of the perspectives involved" and the more mature our ethical conduct grows.

Concluding remarks

I have argued in this chapter that the ethical conduct of the mediator does not need to rely on the maxim of impartiality or a set of universally applicable rules. Instead, virtue ethics can provide a source for ethical conduct for conflict resolution mediators too. The quest for professionalization in the field of peace mediation enforces the attempts to establish rule-based ethics for third-party action. The medical analogy that equates the work of conflict resolution theorist-practitioners with medical professionals and their universal ethics distances the mediator from the contextual qualities of political violence. "Peace science" and its counterpart, expertise knowledge, do not provide a sufficient foundation for practical conflict resolution. The Arendtian critique of organic thought points out the dangers of using medical analogies in human political affairs and suggests alternative ways of conceptualizing conflicts, their resolution and the roles and ethics of the third party.

If our understanding of conflict includes conflict's rhizome-like qualities and its political nature, the role of the mediator and the foundations of his ethical conduct can rely on an openness to different and variable contexts, on an openness to relativize each situation. In this line of thought, sensitivity to uniqueness and difference come to imply ethical expertise. This is not to say that rules and maxims may not be needed in the context of mediation. They may be needed, for example, to clarify the idea of third-party involvement for the participants and to offer instructive advice for an inexperienced mediator. However, rules should not be understood to be universal maxims according to which the mediator should guide his conduct independent on the situation.

In other words, the crux of this chapter is that the expertise of the mediator does not require a scientific gaze (attitude), but it requires skill acquisition where the mediator has been in similar situations earlier and he has become a skillful performer. His ethical conduct matures in a similar fashion as skills are acquired. The mediator responds to situations in a manner that involves ethical participation, not scientific detachment. Ethical expertise is a desired quality, a desired way of behaving that has evolved when the mediator has learned his skills through action, namely mediation. This would mean in practical terms establishing mediation teams where less experienced mediators can learn the skills of mediation from expert mediators and thereby mature ethically to use their intuition instead of rules. Since ethical maturity includes the cultural tradition of mediation, mediators should have platforms where they could reflect their action among peers. Mediation does not take place in a vacuum or laboratory, but it is a highly context-dependent form of human action which is tied to a specific time and place.

References

Arendt, H. (1970) *On Violence*, San Diego, New York and London: A Harvest Book.

Aretxaga, B. (1997) *Shattering Silences: Women, Nationalism and Political Subjectivity in Northern Ireland*, Princeton: Princeton University Press.

Avruch, K. (1998) *Culture and Conflict Resolution*, Washington, D.C.: United States Institute of Peace Press.

Avruch, K. and Black, P. (1991) "The Culture Question and Conflict Resolution," *Peace and Change*, 16(1): 22–45.

Avruch, K. and Black, P. (1993) "Conflict Resolution in Intercultural Settings: Problems and Prospects," in D. Sandole and H. van der Merwe (eds) *Conflict Resolution Theory and Practice: Integration and Application*, Manchester: Manchester University Press.

Avruch, K., Black, P. and Scimecca, J. (eds) (1991) *Conflict Resolution: Cross-Cultural Perspectives*, New York, Westport and London: Greenwood Press.

Behar, R. (1996) *The Vulnerable Observer: Anthropology that Breaks Your Heart*, Boston: Beacon Press.

Benhabib, S. (1992) *Situating the Self*, Cambridge: Polity Press.

Benvenisti, M. (1986) *Conflicts and Contradictions*, New York: Random House.

Bleiker, R. and Brigg, M. (eds) (2011) *Culture and Conflict Resolution*, Hawaii: Hawaii University Press.

Bolger, S., Daly, B. and Higgins, N. (2010) "International Peace Mediators and Codes of Conduct: An Analysis," *The Journal of Humanitarian Assistance*. Online. Available: http://jha.ac/2010/08/04/international-peace-mediators-and-codes-of-conduct-an-analysis/ (accessed June 28, 2012).

Burton, J. (1979) *Deviance, Terrorism and War*, New York: St. Martin's.

Burton, J. (1982) *Dear Survivors*, Boulder, Colorado: Westview Press.

Burton, J. (1984) *Global Conflict: The Domestic Sources of International Crisis*, Brighton: Wheatsheaf.

Burton, J. (1987) *Resolving Deep-Rooted Conflict: A Handbook*, London and New York: University Press of America.

Burton, J. (1990) *Conflict: Resolution and Provention*, London: Macmillan.

Burton, J. (1997) *Violence Explained: The Sources of Conflict, Violence and Crime and Their Provention*, Manchester and New York: Manchester University Press.

Butalia, U. (1998) *The Other Side of Silence, Voices from the Partition of India*, New Delhi: Penguin Books.

Das, V. (1995) *Critical Events: An Anthropological Perspective on Contemporary India*, Delhi: Oxford University Press.

Das V., Kleinman, A., Lock, M., Ramphele, M. and Reynolds, P. (eds) (2002) *Remaking a World: Violence, Social Suffering, and Recovery*, Berkeley: University of California Press.

Deleuze G. and Guattari F. (1980) *A Thousand Plateaus: Capitalism and Schizophrenia*, London and New York: Continuum.

Dunn, D. (2005) *The First Fifty Years of Peace Research*, Aldershot: Ashgate Publishing.

Dreyfus, H. and Dreyfus, S. (1991) "Towards a Phenomenology of Ethical Expertise," *Human Studies*, 14(4): 229–250.

European Code of Conduct for Mediators. Online. Available: http://ec.europa.eu/civiljustice/adr/adr_ec_code_conduct_en.pdf (accessed June 28, 2012).

Feldman, A. (1991) *Formations of Violence: The Narrative of the Body and Political Terror in Northern Ireland*, Chicago: University of Chicago Press.

Fisher, R.J. (1991) "Developing the Field of Interactive Conflict Resolution: Issues in Training, Funding and Institutionalization," paper presented at 14th Annual Scientific Meeting of the International Society of Political Psychologists, Helsinki, Finland, July 1–5, 1991.

Flyvbjerg, B. (1991) "Sustaining Non-rationalized Practices: Body-Mind, Power and Situational Ethics. An Interview with Hubert and Stuart Dreyfus," *Praxis International*, 1: 92–113.

Galtung, J. (1969) "Violence, Peace and Peace Research," *Journal of Peace Research*, 6(3): 167–191.

Galtung, J. (1971) "A Structural Theory of Imperialism," *Journal of Peace Research*, 8(2): 81–117.

Galtung, J. (1985) "Twenty-Five Years of Peace Research: Ten Challenges and Some Responses," *Journal of Peace Research*, 22(2): 141–158.

Galtung, J. (1996) *Peace by Peaceful Means: Peace and Conflict, Development and Civilization*, Oslo: International Peace Research Institute.

Humanitarian Negotiations with Armed Groups: A Manual and Guidelines for Practitioners (2006) New York: United Nations. Online. Available: www.unicef.org/emerg/files/guidelines_negotiations_armed_groups.pdf (accessed June 28, 2012).

International Alert, Code of Conduct: International Transformation Work (1998). Online. Available: www.humanitarianinfo.org/imtoolbox/10_Reference/Humanitarian_General/1998_Code_Of_Conduct_Intl_Alert.pdf (accessed June 28, 2012).

Jabri, V. (2007) *War and the Transformation of Global Politics*, London and New York: Palgrave.

Jutila, M., Pehkonen, S. and Väyrynen, T. (2008) "Resuscitating a Discipline: An Agenda for Critical Peace Research," *Millennium: Journal of International Studies*, 36(3): 623–640.

Kleinman, A. and Kleinman, J. (1994) "How Bodies Remember: Social Memory and Bodily Experience of Criticism, Resistance, and Delegitimation Following China's Cultural Revolution," *New Literary History*, 24: 707–723.

Lawler, P. (1995) *The Question of Values: Johan Galtung's Peace Research*, Boulder and London: Lynne Rienner.

Mitchell, C. (1981) *Peacemaking and the Consultant's Role*, Farnborough: Gower.

Nordstrom, C. (1997) *A Different Kind of War Story, Ethnography of Political Violence*, Pennsylvania: University of Pennsylvania Press.

Touval, S. (1975) "Biased Intermediaries: Theoretical and Historical Considerations," *Jerusalem Journal of International Relations*, 1(1): 51–69.

Väyrynen, T. (1998) "Medical Metaphors in Peace Studies," *International Journal of Peace Studies*, 3(1): 3–18.

Väyrynen, T. (2001) *Culture and International Conflict Resolution*, Manchester and New York: Manchester University Press.

Väyrynen, T. (2011) "Silence and Conflict Resolution," in R. Bleiker and M. Brigg (eds) *Culture and Conflict Resolution*, Hawaii: Hawaii University Press.

Young, O. (1967) *The Intermediaries: Third Parties in International Crisis*, Princeton, NJ: Princeton University Press.

6 Explaining human conflict

Human Needs theory and the Insight approach

Jamie Price

My purpose in this chapter is to advance the foundational theoretical project in the field of conflict analysis and resolution; that is: the development of an explanatory account of conflict that makes it possible for scholars, practitioners, policy-makers and leaders of all sorts to understand conflict in its various manifestations, and to carry out targeted, effective strategies to ameliorate it. Of course, any such attempt must acknowledge its debt to the pioneering efforts of John Burton and his Human Needs theory of conflict. For as Vivian Jabri points out, Burton's "self-conscious integration of theory and practice" is the intellectual contribution "which has had most influence in the field of Conflict Studies and which has placed Burton at the heart of debates around the question of responses to conflict" (Jabri 1997: xii).

To my mind, there are two elements of Burton's thought that constitute permanently valid contributions to the field. The first is his insistence upon the foundational importance of an explanatory account of conflict. For as Burton puts it: "It is only on the basis of an adequate explanation of the problem that we can evolve a constructive approach to solving it" (Burton 1990: 1). Or more pointedly: "One of the major obstacles in dealing with basic problems [of] conflict has been the absence of an adequate theoretical framework and, even more serious, the absence of a realization that such a framework is necessary for solving a problem" (Burton 1990: 25). The second contribution is related to the first, and lies in Burton's identification of the key terms and relations of that foundational project. He explicitly identified "the human dimension of conflict" as the locus of explanatory efforts in the field, and called in particular for an explanation of the functional relationship of human behavior, social structures and conflict (Burton 1990: 25–33).

That said, Burton's own effort to meet the explanatory exigence of the field has proven to be less enduring than his framing of the foundational task itself. He dubbed the fruit of his effort "Human Needs theory," and explained the link between conflict behavior and social structures as follows: "There are certain ontological and genetic needs that *will* be pursued, and socialization processes, if not compatible with such human needs, far from socializing, will lead to frustrations, and to disturbed and anti-social personal and group behaviors" (Burton 1990: 33). Burton went on to argue that his analysis paved the way to resolving conflict, because it provided analysts with an "explanation of conflict from which to deduce the principles of its treatment" (Burton 1990: 1).

Over the years, a variety of objections to Burton's Human Needs theory have emerged. On the level of analysis, scholars have argued that it fails to account adequately for key elements of the relationship between social structures and conflict behaviors – notably the role of culture (see, for example, Avruch and Black: 1987; Avruch 2012: 21–23). Others have pointed out that, as formulated by Burton, Human Needs theory fails to adequately explain the conflict behaviors of key protagonists in specific conflicts – especially those in power (see, for example, Rubenstein 2001). On the level of practice, scholars and practitioners have identified both conceptual and practical limitations in the problem-solving approach to conflict resolution that Burton extrapolated from his theory (see, for example, Mitchell 1990; Jabri 1997: xii). Although these critiques of Human Needs theory seem to me on point, it is not my purpose in this chapter either to rehearse or to add to them. Instead, I will follow a differ-ent line of questioning. Not: how relatively adequate is Burton's *explana-tion* of conflict? But rather: what is Burton doing when he is *explaining* conflict, and how relatively adequate is this approach?

This line of questioning picks up the thread of Burton's foundational, theoretical aspirations for the field. It also seems to me appropriately Bur-tonian in a second sense, for Burton regularly argued that the social and political problems generated by conflict behavior are symptomatic of deeper, causal factors that must be attended to, clarified and explained if those problems are to be solved. In similar fashion, I will argue that the conceptual and practical anomalies generated by Burton's Human Needs theory are symptomatic of deeper, analytical issues that must to be attended to, clarified and explained if those problems are to be resolved. More specifically, I will go on to argue that the Insight approach to con-flict analysis offers a way of overcoming the shortcomings of Burton's approach to explaining conflict and of advancing his permanently valid contributions to the field. First, however, I will clarify the approach to explaining conflict employed by Burton and his formulation of Human Needs theory.

Explaining conflict: Burton and Human Needs theory

Burton was an astute observer of human affairs, and the power of his authorial voice is evident on virtually every page of his writings. He com-bined a bracing forthrightness with a common-sense practicality powered by a rigorous logical argument for a self-consciously revolutionary goal: the overthrow of authoritative power and coercive force as the dominant paradigm for dealing with conflict. In Burton's words: "There will be a major shift in thought, a genuine paradigm shift only when there is a movement away from authoritative power as the main focus, for it is this that is the essence of traditional thinking" (Burton 1990: 114). As Kevin Avruch points out, Burton packaged the social and political ideals of the peace studies movement into an intellectual argument Burton described as "a reconstructed sense of political realism" (Burton 1990: 3; Avruch 2012: 23–26, 141–142). Burton's de-facto motto was: If we can explain conflict, we can solve the problems it causes. It is little wonder that these hard-nosed intellectual and political ideals would rally scholars and practitioners to the development of a new academic field.

Over the years, however, the various critiques of Human Needs theory have steadily gained purchase, the intellectual winds have come out of the Burtonian sails, and the collaborative, explanatory effort that Burton championed in the field has increasingly lost its bearings. But as I will endeavor to show, Burton's foundational effort is not becalmed because he was wrong about the limits of authoritative power, or because his ideals for the field of conflict analysis and resolution proved too good to be true. It is because the approach to explaining conflict that Burton used to carry out his analysis could not handle the freight he wanted it to bear.

What was Burton's approach to explaining conflict? In a word, I contend that he was "Aristotelian" in his approach to explaining conflict. But I must also hasten to clarify and qualify what I mean by this. For Burton never explicitly cited Aristotle as an authoritative source for his approach to explaining conflict; he was a student of international relations, not Aristotle. Moreover, as Patrick Byrne argues, Aristotle's understanding of science, scientific truth and scientific investigation was much more nuanced and acute than his interpreters and followers typically acknowledge (Byrne 1997). It is therefore important to distinguish Aristotle from "Aristotelian," and to clarify that I am not equating Burton and Aristotle per se. It remains, however, that Aristotle's name has for centuries been attached to an approach to scientific reasoning that appeals to the criteria of deductive logic to establish its truth claims. And since (as I will show) Burton's efforts to explain conflict are representative of that approach, I am adopting the time-honored convention of referring to Burton's effort as Aristotelian.

For as Richard McKirahan explains, when Aristotle was seeking to develop a model for scientific investigation and explanation in the fifth century BCE, he turned to the most successful area of intellectual thought in his day: geometry. What particularly appealed to Aristotle was the way that geometers were able to convincingly demonstrate the necessity of their conclusions by reasoning deductively from previously defined principles. Thus, in his *Posterior Analytics*, Aristotle adapted the analytical approach geometers used to construct their geometric proofs to solve the problem of how best to conduct scientific investigations of natural phenomena (McKirahan 1992: 7–20). Broadly speaking, Aristotle argued that if an investigator could rationally identify the cause of a thing, the investigator would then be in a position to offer an explanatory account of this thing by deducing its reality from its cause (see Irwin 1988: 117–120; Byrne 1997: 81–91).

For my purposes, the significance of Aristotelian science is this: as an analytical framework, it leads investigators to structure their analysis of a particular phenomena by asking the question, "What is the cause of this?" It then leads them to explain the reality of what they are investigating by making logical deductions from the cause they have identified. My first claim is that in formulating Human Needs theory to explain what he called "the human dimension of conflict," Burton employed a model of scientific knowing that is strikingly Aristotelian. My second claim is that the collaborative, explanatory project Burton championed for the field could regain its bearings if it were transposed to a relatively more adequate framework for explaining conflict – an approach that seeks empirical rather than logical controls for its truth claims; an approach that deals more concretely with the human dimension of conflict; an approach that could help us critically ground our explanation of what we are doing when we lock ourselves intractably into conflict with each other – and what we are doing when we move beyond these intractable situations. I will explore one such framework in the next section of this chapter.

First, then, Burton was clear about the phenomenon he wanted to explain. He was especially intrigued by what he called "deep-rooted conflict," by which he meant: "intractable opposition to authorities at one social level or another" (Burton 1990: 15). As Burton noted: "We are becoming increasingly aware of the many complex conflicts, within societies and internationally, that are not contained when treated by the enforcement of legal norms or by coercive power means" (Burton 1990: 13). Why was Burton specifically interested in incidents of conflict "already outside the bounds of authoritative containment"? Because, as he put it: "This reality forces a reconsideration of the basic hypothesis on which coercive policies were, and are, based" (Burton 1990: 4). In other words, Burton thought that if he could explain the reality of intractable resistance to coercive force, he could both invalidate the justification for coercive power animating the policies and political systems based on so-called "political realism." In its stead, Burton envisioned "conflict resolution as a political system" (Burton 1990: 260–269). He thought an adequate explanation of intractable conflict could lay the foundations for a new approach to social order from the family to the international system (Burton 1997: 48–110).

So what approach did Burton take to explaining intractable resistance? In recognizably Aristotelian fashion, he sought to identify its cause. As Burton put it, concern for the problem of conflict "implies a concern with the causes that lead to conflict – for example, the underlying and causal sources of gang warfare and of terrorism, or the institutional and human origins of ethnic conflict" (Burton 1990: 5). And in the manner character-istic of Aristotelian science, Burton pursued his concern to identify these causes through a process of logical argumentation and rational specula-tion, which I will endeavor to illustrate in what follows.

Burton summarized his basic argument for the cause of conflict in the following words: "If there is great ferment in the home, the school, indus-try, society, and world society that cannot be curbed by authoritative coer-cion, we can deduce that there are some non-random human behaviors at work" (Burton 1990: 117). In other words, if people are responding with intractable resistance to authoritative coercion at all levels of society and institutional form, it follows that the cause of this recurring phenomenon is not to be explained by appealing to social context, but rather to the factor that is common to all these situations: human behavior.

But the question remains: what is the cause of this "non-random" behav-ior? According to Burton, "it would appear that in all these cases there are frustrations and concerns under the surface that are not negotiable and cannot be repressed" (Burton 1990: 13). Burton readily admitted that he had not yet pinned down these causal factors with precision. "What these human drives are is still far from clear. They seem to relate to the individ-ual's need for identity and recognition, and these relate to the need for security, and perhaps, ultimately for development" (Burton 1990: 33). But Burton's argument does not turn on empirically verifying these basic human needs; it turns on making a rationally compelling case that such needs are the cause of conflict. "From the perspective of conflict studies, the important observation is that these needs *will* be pursued by all means available" (Burton: 1990: 36).

To Burton, the idea that "needs *will* be pursued" was important to con-flict studies for both theoretical and political reasons. First, since it identi-fies the cause of conflict, it is the foundation of valid theory making in the field. In good Aristotelian fashion, Burton regarded Human Needs theory as the first principle from which to deduce the remedies to conflict. As he put it: "It is from theory that conflict resolution processes and provention policies must be deduced," and it is by means of theory that it becomes possible "to avoid policies that could lead to dysfunctional outcomes immediately or at a later date" (Burton 1990: 26, 27).

Second, the idea that "needs *will* be pursued" was also important to Burton because it served as the lynchpin of his argument against political realism. Hans Morgenthau made the case for political realism in inter-national relations in its modern form (Morgenthau 1948). Moreover, Mor-genthau formulated his argument in the manner of Aristotelian scientific analysis (see Price and Bartoli 2012: 161–162). To my mind, this goes a long way in accounting for Burton's apparent disregard for explicitly empirical approaches to explaining conflict. His larger goal was to refute the theory of political realism on its own terms.

Thus, Burton challenged the premise upon which the argument for political realism is based: the premise that human nature being what it is, only coercive force can bring balance to the conflict of competing interests that indelibly and unavoidably mark the relationships of individuals and groups (see Morgenthau 1948: 3–4). As Burton put it: "There has been a fundamental error in the traditional assessment of the human dimension involved in conflict and its management" (Burton 1990: 4). And his argument consisted in a straightforward appeal to the canons of deductive logic: "If it is a valid perspective that there are some behaviors that cannot be altered by socialization processes or deterred by coercion, it follows that there are effective limits to the use of coercion by authorities over citizens" (Burton 1990: 4). Moreover, in making his argument, Burton went on to unmask the social and political motives legitimated by the logic of political realism: "It is a mistake not only in theory, but also pragmatically when coercive and authoritative processes of control are used in an attempt to preserve existing interests and institutions" (Burton 1990: 4).

A final clarification may be in order. To say that Burton was Aristotelian in his approach to explaining conflict (and refuting political realism) is not to say that he completely eschewed empirical observation or that he was inattentive to the facts on the ground. Neither is true. It is to say, however, that for Burton – as for Aristotelian science in general – the purpose of deductive logic was to illuminate and explain empirical observation, not the reverse. For instance, Burton explicitly acknowledged the importance of empirical data in the conflict resolution process. He called for "an accurate costing of the consequences of actions and policies" and for analyses that concretely "reveal the experienced deprivations" of the parties engaged in conflict behavior (Burton 1990: 27). Nevertheless, it is clear that the questions behind Burton's call for these particular empirical answers – What is the cost of intractable resistance? What are the derivations that trigger this resistance? – are driven by the logic of Human Needs theory and not by empirical inquiry into the concrete exigencies of the situation. Burton himself was impressively consistent on this point: "Conflict resolution and provention processes are not pragmatic responses to situations, but are deduced from a generic theory of conflict" (Burton 1990: 27).

The importance of dwelling at such length and in such detail on the Aristotelian character of Burton's approach is that it enables us to differentiate both his explanation of conflict and his approach to explaining it. This in turn enables us to avoid the mistake of presuming that Burton's Human Needs theory is an empirical hypothesis rather than a logical construct. For down that path lies the temptation of seeking to verify or refute Burton's Human Needs theory on empirical grounds – of seeking to identify the nature, number and existence of basic human needs. And to do this is to commit what Whitehead called a fallacy of misplaced concreteness: the fallacy of mistaking an abstract concept for a concrete reality. Ultimately, however, the importance of differentiating Burton's explanation of conflict (Human Needs theory) from his approach to explaining it (Aristotelian) enables us both to retrieve the collaborative, explanatory effort that Burton championed for the field, and to establish it explicitly on the basis of empirical principles rather than logical controls. To that task we now turn.

Explaining conflict: the Insight approach

To my mind, the transposition of Burton's foundational project from an Aristotelian approach to explaining conflict to a properly empirical approach would require at least four elements. First, it would acknowledge the foundational need for an explanatory account of conflict. Second, it would recognize the human dimension of conflict as the key variable in that explanation – as the data to be explained. Third, it would explain conflict behaviors that manifest as seemingly intractable resistance to the coercive exercise of power. Fourth, it would explain the functional relationship of these behaviors to the social, political and cultural institutions and contexts in which they occur. Above all, these findings would take the form of hypotheses that could in principle be verified, refined, or refuted by appeals to the relevant data. And as such – as with any successful science – it would serve it as a framework for collaboration that yielded "progressive and cumulative results" (Lonergan 1985: 15; see also Price 2011).

First, then, there is the foundational need for an explanatory account of conflict, an account based on a properly empirical approach. But what is an empirical approach, let alone a proper one? As we have seen, an empirical approach involves more than paying close attention to empirical data, because Human Needs theory calls for that too. In this regard, the example of Galileo Galilei (1564–1642) is useful, because his experiments with falling objects illustrate the shift from an Aristotelian approach to scientific investigation to an empirical approach. Galileo is known as the father of modern physical science because he stopped asking the traditional Aristotelian question – What is the *cause* of falling objects? – and began to explore an entirely different line of inquiry: What are objects doing when they fall? (See Butterfield 1957.) Thus, if we transpose Galileo's line of inquiry to the conflict behavior that Burton sought to explain, we would shift from the Aristotelian question Burton asked – What is the *cause* of intractable resistance to authoritative coercion? – to a line of inquiry that asks instead: What are people doing when they are intractably resisting the efforts of authorities to coerce them? But this in turn gives rise to a more fundamental question: How would we go about answering the new line of inquiry?

Of course, Galileo sought to answer his new line of inquiry by using mathematical reasoning as an analytical framework. As a consequence, he asked such questions as: How far did the object fall? How much time did it take? These were new questions at the time, and they led him to pay attention to a new set of data. The empirical reality of falling objects remained the same, but his analytical framework enabled him to attend to a new dimension of that reality. Indeed, Galileo's inquiries led to the discovery that the natural world is in fact mathematically intelligible, and over the last four centuries, this has proved to be an exceedingly useful discovery. Clearly, however, it is here that Galileo's example begins to reach its limits for foundational theory in conflict analysis. For whereas Galileo's project was geared to seek explanation of the physical world, Burton's project was geared to seek explanation of the human world; in particular the human dimension of conflict, and more specifically the way people lock themselves into seemingly intractable conflict with each other. Thus, the relevant question is: What analytical framework could help us explain what people are doing when they are doing that? And what set of data would we attend to?

My suggestion – my hypothesis – is that an analytical framework based on Bernard Lonergan's Insight theory offers a promising way of explaining the human dimension of conflict and of recovering Burton's foundational project for the field. In framing this hypothesis, I build upon the seminal work of Kenneth Melchin and Cheryl Picard, who first introduced Lonergan's Insight theory to the field of conflict analysis and resolution, and who used it as a way of explaining the transformation of conflict that takes place in interpersonal and small group mediation (Melchin and Picard 2008). For reasons that will become clear in what follows, I call this analytical framework "critical reflexivity," and the approach to analyzing and resolving conflict that follows from it, the Insight approach.

The best way to clarify the Insight approach is to take it out, give it a spin and see how it works. Burton identified intractable resistance to authoritative control as the paradigmatic instance of conflict behavior, and he observed that such behavior is in evidence around the world and across the entire spectrum of institutional forms. In Burton's words: "There is great ferment in the home, the school, industry, society, and world society that cannot be curbed by authoritative coercion" (Burton 1990: 117). To explain the empirical basis of the Insight approach, it is necessary to begin with a concrete example, so I offer an example that I take to be illustrative of the "great ferment" that Burton observed.

Not long ago, I had a meeting with the Vice Principal of a high school. It was the second week of classes, the beginning of a new school year. I had arrived a bit early for the meeting, so I was waiting for the Vice Principal in her office when she suddenly swept in with six students in tow, all of them freshmen, three men and three women. It was immediately evident that nobody was happy, especially the Vice Principal. As it turned out, none of these students had gone to their assigned classes. Instead, they had all gone to a different class – the same different class – and they were in trouble. The Vice Principle questioned each of the students in my presence, and every exchange went something very much like this:

VP: Why were you in that class?
S: I don't know.
VP: But you went into that class?
S: Yes.
VP: And you don't know why?
S: No.
VP: Why didn't you go to your assigned class?
S: I didn't know where it was.
VP: Why didn't you know where it was?
S: I lost my schedule.
VP: Why didn't you go to the school office to find out?
S: I don't know.
VP: But you went into that class instead?
S: Yes.
VP: Why?
S: I don't know.

The Vice Principal got no further information from these students. She suspended all six.

As Burton put it:

> Conflict can meaningfully be defined as a situation in which authority or power is being exercised without the sanction or approval of those over whom it is being exercised. This definition applies to all social levels, parental authority, industrial authority, religious authority, communal authority and state authority.
>
> (Burton 1990: 26)

In its function as an analytical framework, Burton's theory would lead us to ask whether the exchange between the Vice Principal and the students qualifies as an example of deep-rooted conflict. And if we determined that it did so, Burton's theory would lead us to wonder how the administrative policies and procedures of the school were suppressing the basic human needs of the students. In contrast, the Insight approach would lead us to inquire: "What were the students and the Vice Principal doing in that conflicted encounter with each other?"

The distinguishing feature of Lonergan's Insight theory is that it takes its bearings from the common-sense observation that as human beings, we have minds and we use them. To put it another way, Insight theory is Lonergan's answer to the question: What are we doing when we use our minds? And when applied to the realm of conflict studies, the basic question of the Insight approach becomes: What are we doing when we use our minds to lock ourselves into conflict with each other? This question reveals what the Insight approach would mean by the phrase, "the human dimension of conflict," and in this connection, it is important to note the object that this basic question intends. It is not asking: What is this conflict about? Or, what do we have in mind? But rather: What are we doing when we use our minds? This is not to say that the content of our thoughts is not important. Obviously, it is. But as I will show, the explanatory purchase of the Insight approach comes from its focus on the operations of the mind, rather than its content.

More technically put, Insight theory consists in the phenomenological apprehension and objectification of what Lonergan calls "the data of consciousness," that is, the inner flow of conscious activity operative when we are using our minds (Lonergan 1972: 201, 206–213; 2001: 234–242). Insight theory is *reflexive* in the sense that it calls for analysts and practitioners to pay explicit attention to the cognitive and affective states, operations, levels and norms that pattern the flow of our consciousness. Insight theory is *critical* in the sense that it commits analysts and practitioners to the empirical principle of grounding any phenomenological or explanatory claims they might make in the relevant data of consciousness. Returning then to the encounter between the Vice Principal and the students, the Insight approach would lead us to attend explicitly to the way both parties are using their minds in this encounter. But for the sake of illustration, I will focus only the students' response to the Vice Principal's inquiries, and I will do so in two steps: the first is their response in terms of the general pattern of human consciousness as objectified by Insight theory, and the second is their response as specified more precisely by the analysis of conflict presented by the Insight approach.

Broadly speaking, the Insight approach to conflict analysis would lead us to pay attention to the way the students were using their minds when they were stonewalling the Vice Principal. It would lead us to adopt the working hypothesis that the students were using their minds in a manner that was neither singular nor unique to themselves, but representative of the cognitive and affective pattern of states, acts and levels that mark the operation of human consciousness in general. I have sought to represent this patterned flow of conscious operations in Figure 6.1.[1] And in this regard I must add a clarification. Both the working hypothesis provided by the Insight approach and the diagram I constructed to objectify it should be understood as empirically rebuttable presumptions. Every element on the diagram – the questions, the operations and their sequences – is open to verification, clarification, rejection and correction by an appeal to the data of consciousness.

Thus, functioning as an analytical framework, the Insight approach would leads us to recognize that the stonewalling behavior of the students did not spontaneously manifest itself in the realm of sense data: sound, sight, touch. Indeed, it would lead us to differentiate the data of sense and

Figure 6.1 Patterned flow of human consciousness.

the data of consciousness. In analyzing the situation, it would lead us to account for the fact that the conflict behavior manifested in the words "I don't know" was constituted by a complex but intelligible pattern of conscious operations. Moreover, to sketch this analysis in the terms of pattern traced on the upper loop in Figure 6.1, it would lead us to recognize that the observable act of saying "I don't know" to the Vice Principal was for each student a function of an inner, conscious performance of deciding. For if the students hadn't decided to act by saying these particular words, they would have decided to do something different: to remain silent, to say something else, to make a run for it, or perhaps to cooperate with the Vice Principle. And once we differentiate the conscious act of deciding from the act decided upon, it becomes possible to attend explicitly to the fact that deciding (*What will I do?*) is a function of an inner performance of evaluating (*What should I do? What is best here?*), which is a function of an inner performance of deliberating (*What could I do?*) and which is a function of the students' conscious valuing of their concrete circumstances: their apprehension of the value (or in this case, disvalue) of being caught in the wrong class at the wrong time and hauled off to the Vice Principal's Office (*So what? How does this matter to me?*)

The sequence of conscious operations I just described is logical, which is to say that it is intelligible and coherent. But if in fact this sequence accounts for the general pattern of the flow of human conscious (which I obviously think it does), this sequence isn't true because it's logical. It is true because this pattern can be verified in the data of consciousness and the path to verifying it is critical reflexivity. Indeed, the practice of critical reflexivity is an inherently collaborative and self-correcting exercise (see Lonergan 2004: 10–29) and I have had the privilege and pleasure of engaging in a series of experiments in critical reflexivity with colleagues and students at George Mason University, Carleton University, and the University of Malta.[2] The fruit of this exercise is increasing precision in the functional analysis of conflict offered by the Insight approach, which I will present here as a way of explaining what Burton might characterize as the seemingly intractable resistance of the students to the authoritative coercion of the Vice Principal.

What are we doing when we lock ourselves into conflict with each other? When the analytical framework one is using to analyze conflict explicitly enjoins inquiry into the data of consciousness, one tends to ask a related set of questions: What is the performance of valuing in conflict situations? What is the performance of deciding? What is the quality of these performances? What is the relationship between the two? What conditions them? How? Note that these questions are concrete, not abstract, and that the answers are to be found through the exercise of critical reflexivity. I have asked questions like these, and in the company of colleagues and students I have wrestled with their answers. Many questions remain, but to my mind, the evidence seems compelling enough to suggest that concrete instances of conflict behavior are a function of at least four variables and their relationships: valuing, deciding, narrative and institution.

The first variable specifies the function of *valuing* in conflict behavior. My contention is that whenever there is conflict behavior, there is also a performance of valuing constituted by the apprehension of threat, a cover term for the wide range of feelings – including trepidation, dread, angst and panic – that constitutes the recognition that something important is both at stake and in jeopardy. (Let conflict behavior be represented by the symbol CB, "C" stands for conflict and "B" stands for behavior. And let this first variable be represented by the symbol Vt, where "V" stands for valuing and "t" stands for threat.)

The second variable specifies the function of *deciding* in conflict behavior. My contention is that wherever there is conflict behavior, there is also a performance of deciding constituted by the decision to defend what is at stake or in jeopardy in the situation, whether through fight, flight, or freeze. (Let this variable be represented by the symbol Dd, where "D" stands for deciding and "d" stands for defended.)

The third variable specifies the *narrative* relationship between valuing and deciding. As traced in Figure 6.1, there is a functional relationship between valuing and deciding in the normal flow of human consciousness. My contention is that whenever there is conflict behavior, the relationship between valuing and deciding tends to be very compact, and the flow of consciousness tends to be constrained by a performance horizon characterized by a sense of certainty about the possibility for loss, and the necessity for defensive action. My contention is also that whenever there is conflict behavior, there is a narrative carrying and constituting the compact relationship between valuing and deciding – a narrative that simultaneously legitimates the apprehensions of threat and reinforces the sense of certainty that drives the performance of deciding (see Melchin and Picard 2008: 84–90). (Let this variable be represented by the symbol N, where "N" stands for narrative.)

The fourth variable specifies the *institutional* context of the performance of valuing and deciding, as well as the narrative(s) that carry and shape that performance. My contention is that whenever there is conflict behavior, there are institutional patterns of roles, tasks and relationships that constitute the social, political and cultural horizon of valuing and deciding, and that legitimate of the narrative(s) that carry those performances. (Let this variable be represented by the symbol I, where "I" stands for institution.)

Having distinguished and related the four variables that are constitutive of conflict behavior (CB) – namely valuing (Vt), deciding (Dd), narrative (N) and institution (I) – I seek now to suggest the explanatory power of this hypothesis by formulating the functional relationship of these variables in form of the following equation:

$$CB \sim \frac{[Vt\,Dd]N}{I}$$

Broadly speaking, the implication of this explanatory perspective for conflict analysis and resolution is as follows. At the level of prediction, if conflict behavior is indeed a function of valuing, deciding, narrative and institution, then were any of the variables that constitute a particular conflict behavior to be changed, the conflict behavior would change too. This would make it possible to devise targeted conflict resolution strategies. For example, were the valuing of the threat apprehended in a particular situation to change, the performance of deciding related to that apprehension would change too – as would the conflict behavior. Or again, if the narrative carrying a compact performance of valuing and deciding were to change for a narrative with a broader performance horizon, options foreclosed or unimagined within the previous narrative would become available. Deciding would be different. The conflict behavior would change. The same is true of institutional context. Change the roles, the tasks, or the relationships and you change the institution pattern. This in turn sets a different horizon for valuing, deciding, and for narrative. Above all, this analytical framework leads analysts and practitioners to shift the focus of their inquiry from the conflict behavior in question to the concrete relations of the precipitating variable. I illustrate this approach briefly in what follows.

In seeking to understand a particular instance of conflict behavior (the stonewalling of the Vice Principal by the students, for example) an Insight analyst would be curious about what the students were doing when they were using their minds to make that particular decision. The analyst would bring focus to this line of inquiry by seeking to understand the concrete relations among the four precipitating variables operative in the conflict. In carrying out this analysis, the Insight analyst would explicitly differentiate the patterned flow of the students' consciousness from the content of their consciousness, the working of their minds from what was on their minds. As a practical matter, of course, the mind and what's on it travel together, so it is easy to conflate the two. It is easy to be unmindful, so to speak: to overlook the fact that we have minds, that we use them, and that others (like the students) do too. But given this differentiation, the Insight analyst would ask a targeted set questions about what was on the students' minds in order to foster insight into the way they were using them.

With regarding the students' valuing, then, the Insight analyst would wonder: What was at stake for any one or another of them in their encounter with the Vice Principal? What were they concerned about? What were they worried they might lose? Note that this line of questioning is not pursued for the benefit of the Insight analyst as much as it is for the student (or for the Vice Principal). The goal is to release the flow of curiosity within the student, so that she becomes critically reflexive about her own sense of threat. Nothing locks in certainty and shuts off curiosity like the apprehension of a threat. So it may be that a student could realize that her sense of threat was misplaced. If so, her evaluation of the situation would change. Her deciding would therefore change too, and her conflict behavior would disappear. Of course, these changes would only happen if the student herself grasps the relevant insight. Nothing will change if the analyst is the only one who gets it.

The Insight analyst would take the same kind of approach to the other variables. With regard to the students' deciding, the analyst would wonder:

What did they hope to accomplish by stonewalling the Vice Principal? What did the students think might happen? What undesirable future were they trying to avoid? Regarding the narrative(s) operative in the incident, the Insight analyst would explicitly differentiate the inherently dramatic pattern of the flow of the students' consciousness from the objective narrative carrying that flow and setting the horizon of its performance. The analyst would wonder: What's the story here? How does this story link the student's valuing and deciding? How does it legitimate the decision to stonewall the Vice Principal? What other possibilities for decision and action might this story make available? Are there other narratives available to the student? Finally, regarding the institutional context of the event, the Insight analyst would wonder: How does the functional structure of the school – the roles, tasks, responsibilities and patterns of cooperation that constitute this particular institution – legitimate and shape the narrative that carries the valuing and deciding of the students? Obviously, none of the answers to these questions can be logically deduced. They can only be discovered and verified by inquiry into the relevant data of sense and consciousness.

To my mind, the permanent contributions of John Burton to conflict studies lie in his identification of the need for an adequate explanation of conflict, and the emphasis he gave to the human dimension of conflict in the process. I argue, however, that because he pursued a deductive, Aristotelian-style approach to explaining conflict, Burton's formulation of Human Needs theory does not meet the explanatory exigence he identified for the field. With that said, a final precision about the meaning of my argument is in order. First, I am not saying that Burton's theory of Human Needs is untrue. For human beings do have needs, and it is perfectly sensible to point out that if human needs go unmet, conflict logically ensues. Second, I am not denying the ongoing relevance and importance of Burton's argument in the field. On the one hand, his argument remains as rhetorically powerful and logically valid as the day he first argued it,[3] and on the other hand, it focuses our attention analytically in the right direction: toward the human dimension of conflict. However, once we direct our attention this way, Human Needs theory does not adequately explain what is going on or what to do about it. This is because Burton's theory is a logical construct, not an explanatory set of terms and relations. Thus, to fulfill Burton's foundational call for an explanatory account of conflict, I contend we would do better to pursue – and to work together to develop – the Insight approach to conflict analysis and resolution.

Notes

1 I am grateful to Michael Stebbins for the inspiration to represent the patterned flow of human consciousness as a combination of interconnected loops.
2 I am especially indebted to colleagues Marnie Jull, Radha Kramer, Megan Price, Cheryl Picard and Ken Melchin.

3 For evidence of that this is so, we need only pay attention to the op-ed pages of the major newspapers of the world, such as the recent opinion piece on the bullying epidemic in the United States by Joaquin Phoenix and US Representative Michael Honda (Phoenix and Honda 2012).

References

Avruch, K. (2012) *Context and Pretext in Conflict Resolution: Culture, Identity, Power, and Practice*, Boulder: Paradigm.

Avruch, K. and Black, P.W. (1987) "A Generic Theory of Conflict Resolution: A Critique," *Negotiation Journal*, 3: 87–96, 99–100.

Burton, J. (1990) *Conflict: Resolution and Provention*, New York: St. Martin's.

Burton, J. (1997) *Violence Explained*, Manchester: Manchester University Press.

Butterfield, H. (1957) *The Origins of Modern Science*, New York: Macmillan/Free Press.

Byrne, P.H. (1997) *Analysis and Science in Aristotle*, Albany: State University of New York Press.

Irwin, T. (1988) *Aristotle's First Principles*, Oxford: Clarendon Press.

Jabri, V. (1997) "Foreword," in J. Burton, *Violence Explained*, Manchester: Manchester University Press.

Lonergan, B. (1972) *Method in Theology*, New York: Herder and Herder.

Lonergan, B.(1985) "Method: Trends and Variations," in *A Third Collection: Chapters by Bernard J.F. Lonergan*, ed. F.E. Crowe, New York: Paulist Press: 13–22.

Lonergan, B. (2001) *Phenomenology and Logic: Collected Works of Bernard Lonergan*, Vol. 18, ed. P. McShane, Toronto: University of Toronto.

Lonergan, B. (2004) *Theological and Philosophical Chapters 1965–1980: Collected Works of Bernard Lonergan*, Vol. 17, ed. R.M. Doran and R.C. Croaken, Toronto: University of Toronto Press.

McKirahan, R.D. (1992) *Principles and Proofs: Aristotle's Theory of Demonstrative Science*, Princeton: Princeton University Press.

Melchin, K. and Picard C. (2008) *Transforming Conflict through Insight*, Toronto: University of Toronto Press.

Mitchell, C.R. (1990) "Necessitous Man and Conflict Resolution: More Basic Questions about Basic Human Needs Theory," in J. Burton, *Conflict: Basic Human Needs*, New York: St. Martins: 149–176.

Morganthau, H.J. (1948) *Politics among Nations: The Struggle for Power and Peace*, Boston: McGraw-Hill.

Phoenix, J. and Honda, M. (2012) "Our Children Face a Bullying Epidemic," *USA Today*, August 28. Online: www.usatoday.com/news/opinion/forum/story/2012–08–28/joaquin-phoenix-bullying-epidemic/57379318/1 (accessed October 4, 2012).

Price, J. (2011) "Method in Peacemaking," in S.A. Nan, Z.C. Mampilly and A. Bartoli (eds) *Peacemaking: From Practice to Theory*, Vol. 2, Santa Barbara: Praeger: 610–621.

Price, J. and Bartoli, A. (2012) "Spiritual Values, Sustainable Security, and Conflict Resolution," in C. Seiple, D. Hoover and P. Otis (eds) *The Routledge Handbook of Religion and Security*, New York: Routledge: 160–170.

Rubenstein, R.E. (2001) "Basic Human Needs: The Next Steps in Theory Development," *International Journal of Peace Studies*, 6: 151–158.

7 From human needs to the moral imagination

The promise of post-Burtonian conflict resolution

Solon Simmons

The basic needs paradigm has not been exhausted, neither intellectually, nor politically.

Johan Galtung

Every so often, HN theory needs to be revisited, if for no other reason than to reground practitioners.

Wallace Warfield

In a recent tribute to John Burton in Arlington, Virginia, both Kevin Avruch and Dennis Sandole agreed that it was John Burton's concept of Basic Human Needs that served as the central problematic for the approach to Conflict Resolution that shaped the George Mason School. Central as the concept remains, there is little consensus about what needs really are and how they fit into larger interpretations of self and society. Among younger scholars today, the concept of human needs is largely displaced and relegated to little more than a heuristic device. Burton's needs confront the new generation as a challenge which they feel unprepared to meet. I propose to revisit the concept of basic human needs in order to chart a new way to fuse its central concerns with the cultural particularity made salient by Avruch and Black (1987, 1990; Avruch 1998).

Progress in the development of ideas is never a simple business. In order to move forward, it is often necessary to look backward, and in order to initiate a spirit of intellectual innovation it is often necessary to dwell on the power and failings of previous paradigms and points of departure. The most famous example in this regard was Joseph Schumpeter's devastating critique/celebration of Karl Marx when he wrote in his *Capitalism, Socialism and Democracy*:

> Marxism is a religion. To the believer it presents, first, a system of ultimate ends that embody the meaning of life and are absolute standards by which to judge events and actions; and, secondly, a guide to those

ends which implies a plan of salvation and the indication of the evil from which mankind, or a chosen section of mankind, is to be saved.

(Schumpeter 1950)

Like Marx, Burton sought to fill an almost spiritual gap in his time with "scientific" ideas which compelled action with necessary conclusions about the immediacy of human needs. Like Marx, his efforts were doomed to a kind of failure while revealing an essential truth. Burton's ideas sprang from the denuded soil of power politics and strategic realism in international relations, and flowered in a theory of how irrepressible humanity would either be recognized in human affairs or would fester, producing deviance terrorism and war (Burton 1979). In this Burton was profoundly right; when the needs of humanity are thwarted, there will be perversion of the sort and on the scale that he predicted. Where he was wrong was to imagine that the source of these needs was in "the hidden behavioral realities" of individuals. In short, Burtonianism failed because his was a psycho-social theory where it should have been a socio-cultural one. As theorists from Robert Merton to Ted Gurr have recognized, it is not the absolute deprivation of needs that drives (wo)men to rebel, it is the test of this state of suffering relative to some standard set by the political culture (Merton 1968; Gurr 1971).

In the end, Schumpeter's critique of Marx holds for John Burton as well. Burton served more as the prophet than the sociologist of conflict resolution. Like Marx, his ideas were powerful, transformative and grounded in language with a scientific and objectivist feel, but like Marx's labor theory of value, Burton's specific formulation of basic human needs ultimately failed. It failed because it reified human nature at the very moment that social science was rediscovering the science of meaning, and because it crammed phenomena that can only be discovered in socio-cultural context of the battle for hearts and minds into the seemingly firm container of nativist psychology. Burton had a vision of the human universal, but in resorting to long-since rejected sociological concepts he failed to carry his quest for a general theory of conflict through the rough waters of the interpretive turn in social science and the clashing rocks of the post-modern moment.

Burton recognized that a sound science of politics would demand a theory of shared humanity, and where his basic human needs solution has often led adherents down productive paths, fatal flaws in his formulation have hamstrung the field and impeded theory development. At the heart of the field today, we find visionaries like John Paul Lederach who suggest that the future of the field lies in pursuit of the art and soul of conflict transformation (Lederach 2010), not a stale science of conflict resolution. Although he is right in this, he fails to articulate how much he and John Burton had in common and what his true debt to Burton is, for John was proposing categories through which we could analyze and depict the moral imagination of whomever we encounter anywhere in the world.

Like Johan Galtung's theories of violence, Burton's Human Needs theory not only captures the spirit of the enterprise of conflict resolution, but if properly reformulated, holds the promise of contributing something truly new in the world of political philosophy and practical action – something hinted at but less well portrayed in both Joseph Nye's theory of "soft power" and Michel Foucault's theory of discourse and episteme (Lukes 2005). Moreover, if purged of its distracting and millenarian overtones, Basic Human Needs (BHN) theory might serve as a way to re-imagine civility in politics. Taken to its limit, Burton's efforts, reformulated in post-Burtonian terms, amount to nothing less than a new theory of civilization suitable for bringing both peace and prosperity to a diverse but shrinking planet – no small task (Burton 1991). We might think of this as the Burtonian challenge and, given the ambition of the project, not fault John for having fallen short in his pursuit. It will be my task here to begin to make the case that John was on to something big that we might profit in pursuing.

John Burton's Basic Human Needs theory

The ideas and focus on John Burton's Human Needs theory are well enough known that they need not be reviewed in any detail here. The allure of the idea lies in an optimistic prediction that human nature is not as pliable as many despots imagine it to be. When denied fulfillment of needs that all people share, like identity, security and recognition (other lists were proposed with different items), all people will rebel, rising up to cause problems for those who manage the offending institutions of society. Power politics therefore has limits beyond which it must not go. The mechanism in Burton's needs theory is a mismatch between the psychology or behavioral realities of human nature and the artificial designs of social institutions. For his cohort of thinkers BHN theory was probably appealing as well because socialist systems were seen as just as likely to fail to meet these core needs as were capitalistic ones. The central insight was that individual people need to respected in their ontological (if not biological) complexity, which power-drunk political leaders of every ideological stripe imagine they can ignore. The inherent dignity of individual experience could then be trusted to oppose oppression always and everywhere, even if it could only manifest in occasionally perverse forms.

In this John was following unknowingly in the footsteps of the Chicago school of sociology and the discarded ideas of one of that school's leading lights. W.I. Thomas was once famous for his theory of the "four wishes," which he understood to be human universals that would either find satisfaction or manifest in deviant and unproductive social pathologies. Thomas' work on prostitutes and other struggling cast-offs of the Polish immigration to Chicago in the early twentieth century provided the model for the Burtonian Human Needs paradigm, even though this origin was largely forgotten because Thomas' ideas had fallen out of favor with the rise of Parsonian conceptions of social structure and a turn away from a microfoundational approach in sociology in the 1930s.

But, as John Stuart Mill once argued, good ideas have a way of resurfacing. The sociological retreat from the vivid conception of human universality that Thomas had been developing in his immigrant deviance studies constituted a kind of truth that we would be forced to rediscover.[1]

> The real advantage that truth has, consists in this, that when an opinion is true, it may be extinguished once, twice or many times, but in the course of ages there will be found persons to rediscover it, until some one of its reappearances falls upon a time when from favorable circumstances it escapes persecution until it has made such head as to withstand all subsequent attempts to suppress it.
>
> (Mill 1993)

It may be that Thomas' theory of wishes and therefore Burton's needs theory speaks to the kind of truth that Mill imagined was awaiting favorable circumstances for its revival. But as these ideas traveled through the back channels of the sociological imagination from Thomas to Paul Sites, to John Burton and down to us, something was lost. W.I. Thomas's sociology was deeply immersed in the spirit of pragmatism represented by figures such as leading Chicago intellectuals John Dewey and George Herbert Mead. This left a profound impression on his thought. Although Thomas' "four wishes" theory is now something remembered only by specialists, his "Thomas Theorem" is more recognizable and points the way forward for a living and vibrant needs theory: "If men define situations as real, they are real in their consequences." Thomas' theory was a deeply constructivist one long before these ideas became fashionable. From this baseline, the power of what Thomas called "the definition of the situation" became standard tools within sociological kit, while his universalistic interpretations were lost and forgotten. The Burtonian challenge is then to take human needs seriously while preserving the interpretive and constitutive role of culture that was always a part of Thomas' definition of the situation.

One place to begin what I will call a post-Burtonian reconstruction is with Burton's more lasting contribution, the distinction between a dispute and a conflict. He used this device to demonstrate how interest-based bargaining and negotiation were doomed to fail in many circumstances and to point to the deeper roots of conflict that public choice theorists failed to recognize. He described his method in a reflective essay in 1993:

> Disputes were those confrontations that could be settled by traditional means of negotiation or arbitration, while conflicts had to be resolved

by analytical processes. These required a facilitator who could help the parties to reveal the hidden behavioral realities of a complex conflict situation. They were still searching for an explanation of the empirical evidence that had led them to make this distinction between conflicts and disputes.... The task then was to deduce an alternative, and to test and spell out relevant processes. In practice it was soon found that in a facilitated conflict analysis the more "powerful" party was helped to perceive behavioral realities, in respect of which there cannot be compromise, and was able to reassess the costs of the employment of power and its likely failure. Other options could then be explored.

Much of the work that has developed in the Burtonian mold has followed on this journey to find the hidden behavioral realities John adverted to in passages like this. There is no agreement on what precisely distinguishes a conflict from a dispute, but some of those features can be found in Table 7.1.

This simple set of distinctions (which Burton himself would not have fully recognized) points to the enduring contribution of Burtonian conflict analysis. Our folk image of conflict places us on the left-hand column. Conflicts are rendered as disputes between self-interested parties who use what mechanism of power they have to struggle for concrete results. We can think of the problem in a dispute as a breach of a kind of contract that can be resolved on the basis of rational debate in a negotiation of specific content that will inform the agreement. This folk image is not only common in the way many people talk about disputes in their daily lives, but it also informs very sophisticated understandings of international politics, like those that scholars like Kenneth Waltz have developed in the tradition of strategic realism (Waltz 1979, 2000). What matters in a dispute are interests, power, results, specific wrongs, reason, negotiation and content.

Students of conflict will quickly see through this kind of approach to complex conflict, while perhaps failing to recognize their debt to John

Table 7.1 Disputes and conflicts

Dispute	Conflict
Strategic interests	Human needs
Power politics	Civil forces
Concrete results	Moral order
Breach of contract	Abuse of power
Rational debate	Emotional processing
Negotiation	Reconciliation
Content	Code

Burton for developing an alternative model for analyzing deep-rooted conflict at the very moment that the realist paradigm was consolidating. John's was a general model, but it derived from his frustration with the abuses that were typical on the international stage (Dunn 1995). What we now take for granted is what was once quite novel and heretical, that large groups, even including nations, behave like traumatized individuals. There is a consistency to conflict across levels of analysis. So when analyzing the conflictual behaviors of an abused Polish girl in early twentieth-century Chicago, the insidious terrorist plotting of a Saudi scion of a prominent figure in public works, or a young nation's rise to global power after the fall of Germany and Japan, the same set of right distinctions from Table 7.1 must be taken seriously.

Conflicts for Burton were rooted in human needs (the tricky idea), and once an individual's core needs were violated the person would act to satisfy them no matter how much power was exerted to insure that he could not. In contrast to strict lines of power, social conflicts follow the contours of the kinds of civil forces that unite social movements in society, those narrative interpretations of political issues that circulate in the public sphere and concentrate attention through agenda setting and taste formation. While a person in a dispute wants to settle it by attaining concrete results, people in conflicts are confronted with the need to repair breaches in the moral order. When moral orders are breached, this is the result of some kind of abuse of power, and this gives rise to emotional damage and deeper commitment to causes that become consecrated in the struggle. When such damage has been done by supposed abusive powers, there is no hope of negotiation, but only of reconciliation, and reconciliation in any escalated conflict is difficult because the discursive environment is suffused with codes that mean different things to people who feel them in different ways. No content comes cleanly uncoded and it is therefore the job of the analyst to decode the conflict in supportive ways that allow all parties to save face, to imagine the repair of the civil fabric and to reconfigure the boundaries of solidarity so that interdependent parties can project themselves in a new moral space. All of this is implied in the Burtonian model of conflict resolution, and many of us have expanded on his ideas so that this kind of binary model makes sense to a variety of scholars who see their work very much opposed to what John was up to.

The key piece of Burton's puzzle was to flesh out his axial concept of basic human needs, and it is a shame that as this concept has fallen on tough times so too has the larger Burtonian project. Voltaire famously mocked the Holy Roman Empire for being neither holy nor Roman, nor an empire. For students after the cultural turn, basic human needs often appear to be neither basic nor human, nor needs. We can all readily think of cases where absolute deprivation has been suffered in silence for generations. We need not be Machiavellian to recognize that strategic interests often drive confrontations even where the language of grievance is deeply involved. Basic human needs is also a confusing idea because it brings to mind things like food, clothing and shelter, and therefore draws on a misleading materialism at the same time that the theory enjoins us to embrace a numbing utopian attitude that conflates mere wants with something less negotiable.

Taking this or a similar line of critique is a temptation but a mistake. It is a mistake because John was on to the core of what makes this field worth studying. The temptation arises because John himself made a crucial mistake in his theoretical specification that subsequent theorists like John Paul Lederach have since corrected. John's needs theory was a psychosocial theory where it should have been a socio-cultural theory; his critics, foremost among them Kevin Avruch, buried the theory in this very ground. A post-Burtonian theory will have to exhume the remains and animate them by conceding the effectiveness of weapons that laid the body low.

Human needs are human in the sense that they arise in the processes of political culture, but they are not features of individual experience. The proper ancestor of Burtonian needs is not Abraham Maslow, rather it is W.I. Thomas. No one has yet recognized this or worked through the implications of the insight, but once we recognize it, the entire project is clarified in a new light. Needs are, in today's parlance, socially constructed, but they are also essential properties of socio-cultural systems. They provide us with "the definition of the situation" through which we can channel our deeper frustrations and consecrated aspirations. The contents of needs, being products of cultural competition, are as variable as the political cultures that produce them. As Avruch and Black (1987) clearly recognized, there is no use in speculating about some abstract and innate universal human nature which plays out in all conflicts everywhere in the same way. The project is doomed to failure when conceived of in this way.[2] We cannot read off moral systems directly from their psychological micro-foundations. This means that we cannot identify one set of moral ideas as an attempt to make an individual feel secure, another as one intended to insure he feels recognized and still another that provides him with a sense of identity. Instead we have to assume that the common richness of human sensibility is worked into every driving creed that we encounter in the political talk of ongoing conflicts. The creeds satisfy different individual needs, even while they play on a common stock of cultural themes. To rectify the deep and distracting error of Burton's foundational fallacy, we will have to turn to culture as his critics demanded that we do, but to turn to culture with an aim to reduce complexity and abet parsimonious analysis much as John had hoped to do. This has implications for practice as well; our task becomes less one of satisfying individuals in problem-solving workshops and more one of decoding and redirecting destructive political talk in public discourse. In such a view, peace work requires the addition of what I call "communicative practice." We have to learn to engage in strategic ways in the public sphere to direct the moral imagination where we would like it to go.

A neo-Weberian needs theory: security, freedom, equality and tolerance

In a devastating review of Burton's *Conflict: Resolution and Prevention* (Burton 1990), the sociologist Lewis Coser attacked basic Human Needs theory at its weakest point (Coser 1991). He wondered how many needs there really were and why this list that John had settled on was any more convincing than some other random assortment. Why not have one need? Why not have 57? Coser was ultimately unconvinced by what he interpreted as a utopian project that would amount to little. Many of us have followed Coser's lead even if we have not read his review. We wonder why this basic set of needs is the right one and why one might not legitimately select a different set of needs – ontological features of human nature – that would play out much like John's did, but with different implications. This number-of-needs problem has always been the Achilles Heel of Basic Human Needs theory. Ironically, I think we can rediscover the power of Burton's vision by bolstering his project at this weakest spot.

I propose that we can specify a small set of distinctive needs and we can anchor them in something real that is susceptible to empirical verification. Instead of locating the font and origin of needs in the individual human psyche, we should instead locate them in the varieties of the uses of power and therefore in the distinctive ways that people always and everywhere have narrated its abuses. I claim that the needs that will be satisfied and cannot be negotiated away are the seeds of the civil forces that have mobilized around particular stories about the abuse of power and the fragmentation of moral order – the "good reasons" that people offer to justify their actions. In this view, human needs are categories of the moral imagination which correspond to the institutional varieties of forms of power and therefore of abusive behavior. So how many needs are there? Four.

Because institutions are as variable as the rhythms of history, the cultural content of aggregated representations will vary accordingly, while the basic arguments will fall into a distinctive set of categories with four divisions. Following Weber and a reformulation of Weber's analysis of power develop by Michael Mann (1986), I suggest that abusive powers can be sorted into the categories of what Weber described as "class, status and party," with one additional category recognized for military organization that represents Weber's core conception of the state as the institution that upholds the claim to the monopoly of the legitimate use of physical force in the enforcement of its order (Weber 1978). Put simply, the categories of the moral imagination (to be used for good or ill) correspond to Weber's categories of state, party, class and status. This scheme can then be translated to a set of positive values: security, freedom, equality and tolerance. When a person, group or mass of people uses any of these four sources of institutional means to victimize others, they risk being cast in a popular story as enemies of the common good, villains against whom all decent people must rebel.

This is the yeast that leavens the bread of conflicts wherever we might find them. Post-Burtonian needs theory is therefore a theory of the uses of the moral imagination both by peacebuilders and selfish strategic interests. Only through a process of what Jeffrey Alexander called "civil repair" can we hope to bring about the lasting transformations that will constrain future abuses of social power (Alexander 2008). Only through a process of public deliberation can we isolate and civilize what Richard Rubenstein has artfully labeled "Reasons to Kill" (Rubenstein 2010). That is the task of conflict resolution theory and should become a major focus of resolution practice.

I propose that we can locate the energy and vital force of an argument in its capacity to serve as a mass communicative vehicle for the narration of civil disorders located in four distinctive types of abuse of power. These sources of abusive power are state, party, class and status, and I claim that the major divisive genres of the reasons to kill provided by partisans in societies always and everywhere can be sorted into the categories defined by these four mechanisms and the value domains associated with them: security, freedom, equality and tolerance (see Table 7.2). The major conflicts in the world from the Mongol invasions to the French revolution to the Marxist rebellions to the post-colonial impulse can be rendered sensible in terms of the performance of the kind of social dramas that channel human need to collective purpose against an abusive form of institutionalized power.

My suggestion is that for theoretical purposes, we need only four basic human needs and that, contrary to the name, they should be imagined as complex constructed contingencies as much as they are foundational features of simple originality. In discovering needs, we have not escaped

Table 7.2 Four abuses of power

Need	Uncivil adversary	Abusive power	Rights focus	Anti-value
Security	Barbarians (Anti-criminal)	Faction (The Enemy)	Sovereignty (Reaction)	Chaos
Freedom	Bureaucrats (Anti-tyrannical)	Party (The One)	Individual (Revolution)	Tyranny
Equality	Bigwigs (Anti-corporate)	Class (The Few)	Social (Redistribution)	Exploitation
Tolerance	Bigots (Anti-supremacist)	Status (The Many)	Cultural (Recognition)	Bigotry

culture; far from it. As one of the first great Human Needs theorists Erich Fromm put it:

> Although there are certain needs, such as hunger, thirst, sex, which are common to man, those drives which make for the differences in men's characters, like love and hatred, the lust for power and the yearning for submission, the enjoyment of sensuous pleasure and the fear of it, are all products of the social process. The most beautiful as well as the most ugly inclinations of man are not part of a fixed and biologically given human nature, but result from the social process which creates man. In other words, society has not only a suppressing function – although it has that too – but it has also a creative function.
>
> (Fromm 1994)

Nevertheless, the simplifying work done by reducing the variety of cultural and discursive phenomena to a manageable set of considerations is immense. I argue that we can find in the patterns of political talk features of each of the four semantic systems, often overlaid on top of the other in intricate temporal patterns like a palimpsest. Each draws its moral force from its opposition to an uncivil adversary, has a distinctive if fluid conception of what kind of abusive power has been at work, focuses attention on the entitlements that the victims of such abuse have a right to expect and allows parties to position their adversaries in a space defined by a holy value and a polluted anti-value. In short, each aspect of human need touches on the ways in which moral order has been destroyed and how human dignity might be restored.

The major normative political philosophers have provided us with virtuoso performances which can be variously classified in these categories: Hobbes and Machiavelli with security, Locke and von Hayek with individual freedom, Marx and Sorokin with equality and J.S. Mill and Franz Fanon with tolerance. Some of these masters of the moral imagination have been gentle in the uses of their craft while others have embraced the darker side, but all of them worked within the Hilbert space of axiological distinctions that comprise the semantic facts recognized by John Burton as basic human needs. Taken as a field of distinctions and semantic codes as Alexander has described them, we can think of needs less as innate psychological drives and more as rhetorical traditions. They become the categories of evaluation that define the space in which we position social issues and objects of political discussion (Harré and Lagenhove 1999; Rothbart and Bartlett 2008). One way to describe them is as rhetorics – ways of speaking, feeling and thinking about novel social facts and of painting them in the moral colors that allow us to give them the hues of meaning that we require all relevant things to have (Simmons 2012).

It is important to recognize the expansive spirit in which John proposed his theory of Basic Human Needs. It was meant to capture the complexity of all the extant political philosophies and popular slogans that have been employed in settings as diverse as the plains of ancient Ilium and the coasts of the today's Gulf of Aden. John's project was roughly equivalent to what John Paul Lederach describes in this passage from his *Moral Imagination* (2010: 5).

> Transcending violence is forged by the capacity to generate, mobilize, and build the moral imagination ... we must understand and feel the landscape of protracted violence and why it poses such deep-rooted challenges to constructive change. In other words, we must set our feet deeply into the geographies and realities of what destructive relationships produce, what legacies they leave, and what breaking their violent patterns will require.

The semantic categories of human need and the sets of axiological distinctions that each presents as premises of moral order are the geographies and realities produced by destructive relationships; setting our feet in them demands that we translate political interpretations into intelligible categories of moral evaluation. Burton's theory was almost absurdly ambitious; a discursive translation of his ideas will be confronted with no lesser task. In order to capture some of the complexity embedded in such a framework, I have introduced a few conceptual distinctions that advert to the features of each.

Un-clashing civilizations: the peril and promise of needs theory

The real test of a theory lies either in what it can do for guiding novel research or what it can do for guiding practice. I think this post-Burtonian needs theory has much to offer various research traditions, but I will hold this for a discussion in another place. The most promising use of a re-imagined Basic Human Needs theory can be found just where John Burton imagined it would be, in the practice of resolving deep-rooted conflicts. This utility emerges just as newer techniques like narrative practice have begun to demonstrate their promise. Developed in the right way, a post-Burtonian needs theory describes the constraints on and conditions under which compelling conflict narratives can be developed. If it is true, as I claim, that needs are more useful as descriptors of the categories of the moral imagination than they are of the primary sources of human motivation, then they can be used as elemental templates for decoding political talk. The task of conflict resolution becomes one of looking for the way that practical issues have been portrayed in contrast to distinctive kinds of abuses of power. By working backwards from the vivid images surrounding the details of political debate to the consecrating principles that animate and propel them, we can see how deep-rooted conflicts are typically framed as clashes of civil principles. By decoding these consecrated causes and subjecting them to close analysis, we can either help riled parties through the Rashomon-like process of recognizing contradictory positioning of identical events or assist deserving groups to better frame their arguments for greater success in an unfriendly environment. The point is to discover how meaning has been worked into social issues (people, problems and positions) and how they have been granted an almost sacred power in the history of their prior performance in the public sphere. Post-Burtonian needs theory therefore undergirds a new approach to practice that we might describe as communicative.

To take a specific example, consider Samuel Huntington's famous and notorious clash of civilizations thesis. In an ominous and then celebrated passage, he predicted the coming confrontation of whole cultural groups that would rise above the existing divisions based on ideology and traditional national rivalries:

> It is my hypothesis that the fundamental source of conflict in this new world will not be primarily ideological or primarily economic. The great divisions among humankind and the dominating source of conflict will be cultural. Nation states will remain the most powerful actors in world affairs, but the principal conflicts of global politics will occur between nations and groups of different civilizations.
>
> (Huntington 1993: 22)

First published in the summer of 1993, once this thesis had been tested and amplified by the events of 9/11 and the coming War on Terror, they appeared either incendiary and provocative or prescient and transformative. Within the field of conflict resolution it has become a commonplace to attack the clash hypothesis for its overgeneralization and simplification. For example, Rubenstein and Crocker (1994: 119) challenged the theses for its failure to recognize the complexity of and uses of culture:

> Huntington's civilizations, it seems clear, are ideological constructs as "recent and modern" as nations, and equally rooted in "structures of inequality." The cultural materials available to define a politicized "civilization" are so rich, varied, and contradictory that any political definition reflects choices made by modern leaders in response to modern problems.

As with all powerful arguments, it is tempting to either embrace the thesis as politically incorrect but true nonetheless or to comfortably dismiss it as simple-minded, non-starter nativism. But from the vantage of a post-Burtonian needs theory, we might approach the hypothesis in a different way.

In escalated conflicts, modern leaders tend to use the cultural materials available to them in exactly the way that Huntington did in his Clash of Civilizations thesis (and by extension what Rubenstein and Crocker did in their critique of it). What leaders do, specifically opinion leaders, is to use the categories of the moral imagination to change what Johan Galtung, invoking the imagery of a traffic light, called the "moral color of an act," shifting it either from green to yellow and then red, or from red to green (Galtung 1990). What Human Needs adds to this discussion is the claim that the "moral color" that leaders imbue in political acts and social issues derive from a small set of universally applicable themes. There are only so many ways to condemn an action as violent and repugnant and these correspond to the distinctive ways that people can abuse power. In this view, leaders encode political objects as supportive of security, freedom, equality and tolerance or as productive of abuses in the form of chaos, tyranny, exploitation or bigotry. What makes this a needs theory is that once these distinctive civil forces have been put in motion in living contexts, they move people from their depths; they must be satisfied in some way.

In this case, Huntington painted much of the developing world in the thrall of backward ideology and ancient hatreds that were patently incompatible with the traditions of stability and freedom that were the basis of western civilization. Huntington's argument triggered solidaristic energies on many sides of his construct. In his home country, the portrait suggested that trends toward multiculturalism and cosmopolitan attitudes in the West were a path toward Spenglerian decline. On the other side, Rubenstein and Crocker positioned Huntington's argument itself as a social issue in its own right, suggesting that the proliferation of this worldview was productive of exploitation and a circle-the-wagons, top-dog bigotry.

Which side is right is beside the point; what matters is how each mobilized cultural resources to consecrate their moves in the battle of ideas. When important issues of this kind flare up, they tend to be most brilliantly fueled when they can be portrayed in the service of contrasting civil principles: principles that are defined by their opposition to abusive power. In the Huntington debate, it is the clash of liberty and security against equality and tolerance. In another round, the same authors, gifted as they were, might well present their cases in the inverse, with Huntington drawing on the equality and tolerance portion of his palette and Rubenstein and Crocker framing their arguments in terms of liberty and security. What would not change is the power and persuasiveness of the elemental axiological distinctions. The authors tap needs as the depths of our connections to others. Their goal is the construction of new solidarities, what the Arab scholar Ibn Khaldun called "asabiyah" (Cherkaoui 2012).

Similar positioning dynamics are in play in any other conflict worth its salt. Things heat up when civil traditions can be played off one another. In the United States, the tropes of liberty have increasingly animated so-called conservatives while tropes of tolerance have animated the so-called liberals. Political labels have lost their meaning and factional lines have been crossed and re-crossed. Left out of this debate is a powerful constituency that could mobilize the language of equality in support of practical programs. If a Democrat would pollute an opponent's plan, the best bet is to frame it as incompatible with the norms of tolerance. If a Republican would pollute her opponent's plan, it would be within the dramatic repertoire of freedom. In this, we can explain the rising appeal of both multiculturalism and the Tea Party. These movements tap into the dominant civil forces by performing principle and making meaning out of the detritus of daily life. These traditions correspond to elemental patterns of the political imagination. Their power derives from their conception of humanity. They will find expression unless satisfied. These aroused civil forces are manifest basic human needs. All effective leaders "manufacture consent" by triggering the urge to dignity. Their vehicle is the moral imagination and they can use it for good or ill.

All of this points to a way out of (and indeed into) escalated confrontations. As the sociologist Phillip Smith has argued, we can explain the rise of conflict by the genre of arguments that obtain in the narrative environment, escalating from the descriptive to the romantic to the apocalyptic (Smith 2005). It is as if the point is to ascertain how much moral color has been imbued in the issues of the day. To put pressure on the system, invoke the codes typical of one's folk creed and get your people hopping mad about the unholy racism of the other side or their monstrous tendencies to hate our freedoms. Perhaps the color comes from the need to rise above the bigotry of the western Great Satan or the devious exploitation of blood sucking capitalist pigs. All of these symbolic triggers invoke the four civil traditions and provide partisans with a clear sense of how political action is necessary (hence need) to preserve their civilization (however locally defined it may be).

The converse is also true. To walk a conflict down from the mountaintop, you have to wash out the moral color and shift the genre to "low-mimetic," descriptive forms with few heroes and no villains. Axiological distinctions become implicit rather than explicit and partisans must act as if they share some common civil conception. For example, rather than pitting liberty against diversity as competing value domains, all parties might strive to find a common folk idiom that demonstrates how everyone demands security, values freedom, embraces equality and condemns bigotry. Great leaders do just this and petty ones do their best spoil the emerging folk syntheses.

The path back across what has been described as the "tail of Cerberus" (Pruitt and Kim 2003) toward peace is coeval with the emergence of a genre that Phillip Smith pays less attention to: comedy. De-escalation requires that once this colorless state of discursive practice has been invoked, that the story of how history had become encoded in these folk idioms and narrative fragments must be explored by cooler heads, and to channel conviction, color must return in less explosive form. Non-virtuosos have to be allowed to make discursive mistakes and risk offense. These mistakes and minor offenses should be rendered as silly and absurd rather than evil. Consequences for a slip of "right speech" must be accommodated. Because offense is the norm in reconciliation processes, the cool heads have to become anthropologists of the politically incorrect and translators of apostasy to their own partisans, teaching all sides to laugh at themselves, even where they are not yet comfortable with the other laughing at them. When wit is used as a weapon (Speier 1998) it indicates nothing but desolation, but when people on both sides of a normative breach can housebreak salient atrocities with mirth without provoking outrage and offense, parties are on the path to peace. What emerges with the entrance of the comedic genre is a new solidarity that transcends identity. It then becomes clear that identity is just a word for stale solidarity. What the future demands is that old identities are shed to make room for the solidarity that is bursting the old skin. Human needs will be satisfied, the point is to be deliberate in managing how.

Is there a future for Basic Human Needs theory in the development of this new, humanistic science of peace? I think there is if we break with the conventions that have led to confusions in the recent history of the field. The central problem with Basic Human Needs theory emerges in the connotations of the term itself. Basic human needs are basic in that they are categories of moral evaluation shared by all people, always and everywhere; human in that they work on the plane of universal humanity and the dramatic mobilizing capacity of abusive atrocities; and needs in that once the fiery stories of dignity degraded have been lit in the hearts of the people, they will be satisfied in ways either positive or perverse. Needs-based practice is therefore cultural, historical and deeply implicated in narrative traditions from myth, to folk wisdom to political discourse and media representations. Whatever else one might argue, needs theory deserves to survive under that name if only for its uncompromising focus on those aspects of the human condition that cannot be negotiated, traded or bargained away.

Notes

1 We should immediately recognize that various Human Needs theories have come and gone over the last century. Compelling examples in this vein include, the sociology of W.I. Thomas (Thomas 1924), the Marxist psychoanalysis of Erich Fromm (Fromm 1947), the humanistic psychology of Abraham Maslow (Maslow 1954), the communitarian sociology of Amitai Etzioni (Etzioni 1968) and the conflict theory of John Burton (a list which excludes more overtly materialist variants). The explanations for the rise and fall of each needs theory are broadly similar; in one story, a scholar-practitioner recognizes the striking psycho-social commonalities in human experience for people always and everywhere, and

documents them in relation to some practical task. Then, sharp-minded theorists recognize the limitations of the specification of the universals that the scholar-practitioner has proposed. Common questions emerge that recurrently seem to stagger the enterprise: How many needs are there? Don't considerations about the situation and the social context matter more than those about the person? Is it really possible to separate the need from the satisfier? And aren't needs satisfied differently in Papua New Guinea and Germany?

2 In passing, we should note that the most compelling current work in moral psychology, that on the paradigm of Jonathan Haidt is falling into the same trap that John did. The moral, foundations approach is exactly right in the identification of the mechanisms of moral consciousness, but by building up a moral philosophy from distinctive innate properties of the psyche it re-commits the foundational fallacy that John's work fell into.

References

Alexander, Jeffrey C. (2008) *The Civil Sphere.* New York: Oxford University Press.

Avruch, K. (1998) *Culture and Conflict Resolution.* Washington, D.C.: United States Institute of Peace Press.

Avruch, K. and Black, P.W. (1987) "A Generic Theory of Conflict resolution: A Critique." *Negotiation Journal,* 3(1): 87–96, 99–100.

Avruch, K. and Black, P.W. (1990) "Ideas of Human Nature in Contemporary Conflict Resolution Theory." *Negotiation Journal,* 6(3): 221–228.

Burton, J.W. (1979) *Deviance, Terrorism and War: The Process of Solving Unsolved Social and Political Problems.* New York: St. Martin's.

Burton, J.W. (1990) *Conflict: Resolution and Prevention.* New York: St. Martin's.

Burton, J.W. (1991) "Conflict Resolution as a Political Philosophy." *Global Change, Peace and Security,* 3(1): 62–72.

Burton, J.W. (1993) "Conflict Resolution: Towards Problem Solving." *International Journal for Peace Studies.* Online www.gmu.edu/programs/icar/pcs/burton.html.

Cherkaoui, M. (2012) *Why Groups Split.* Unpublished dissertation.

Coser, L. (1991) "Review. 'Conflict: Resolution and Prevention'." *Political Science Quarterly,* 106(3).

Dunn, D.J. (1995) "Articulating an Alternative: The Contribution of John Burton." *Review of International Studies,* 21(02): 197–208.

Etzioni, A. (1968) "Basic Human Needs, Alienation and Inauthenticity." *American Sociological Review,* 33(6): 870–885.

Fromm, E. (1947) *Man for Himself: An Inquiry into the Psychology of Ethics.* New York: Rinehart.

Fromm, E. (1994) *Escape from Freedom.* New York: Macmillan.

Galtung, J. (1990) "Cultural Violence." *Journal of Peace Research,* 27(3): 291–305.

Gurr, T.R. (1971) *Why Men Rebel.* Princeton, NJ: Princeton University Press.

Harré, R. and Lagenhove, L.V. (1999) *Positioning Theory: Moral Contexts of Intentional Action.* Wiley-Blackwell.

Huntington, S. (1993) "The Clash of Civilizations?" *Foreign Affairs,* Summer 72 (3): 22–49.

Lederach, J.P. (2010) *The Moral Imagination: The Art and Soul of Building Peace.* Reprint. New York: Oxford University Press.

Lukes, S. (2005) "Power and the Battle for Hearts and Minds." *Millennium – Journal of International Studies,* 33(3) (June 1): 477–493.

Mann, M. (1986) *The Sources of Social Power: A History of Power from the Beginning to A.D. 1760.* Cambridge: Cambridge University Press.

Maslow, A.H. (1954) *Motivation and Personality.* New York: Harper.

Merton, R.K. (1968) *Social Theory and Social Structure.* New York: The Free Press.

Mill, J.S. (1993) *On Liberty and Utilitarianism.* Bantam Classics.

Pruitt, D. and Kim, S.H. (2003) *Social Conflict: Escalation, Stalemate, and Settlement.* 3rd edn. McGraw-Hill Humanities/Social Sciences/Languages.

Rothbart, D. and Bartlett, T. (2008) "Rwandan Radio Broadcasts and Hutu/Tutsi Positioning," in F.M. Moghaddam, R. Harré and N. Lee (eds) *Global Conflict Resolution through Positioning Analysis.* Berlin: Springer, pp. 227–246.

Rubenstein, R.E. (2010) *Reasons to Kill: Why Americans Choose War.* London: Bloomsbury Press.

Rubenstein, R.E. and Crocker, J. (1994) "Challenging Huntington." *Foreign Policy,* 96 (October 1): 113–128.

Schumpeter, J. (1950) *Capitalism, Socialism and Democracy.* New York: Harper Torchbooks.

Simmons, S.J. (2012) "Civil Identity and Communicative Practice: The Rhetoric of Liberty in the United States," in K.V. Korostelina (ed.) *Forming a Culture of Peace: Reframing Narratives of Intergroup Relations, Equity, and Justice.* New York: Palgrave Macmillan, pp. 165–194.

Smith, P. (2005) *Why War? The Cultural Logic of Iraq, the Gulf War, and Suez.* 1st edn. University of Chicago Press.

Speier, H. (1998) "Wit and Politics: An Essay on Power and Laughter." *American Journal of Sociology,* 103(5) (March 1): 1352–1401.

Thomas, W.I. (1924) *The Unadjusted Girl: With Cases and Standpoint for Behavior Analysis.* Boston: Little, Brown.

Waltz, K.N. (1979) *Theory of International Politics.* New York: McGraw-Hill.

Waltz, K.N. (2000) "Structural Realism after the Cold War." *International Security,* 25(1): 5–41.

Weber, M. (1978) *Economy and Society.* Vol. 2. Ed. Claus Wittich. Berkeley: University of California Press.

Part II

Basic Human Needs in practice

Chapters 8–12 are all written by scholars who have had extensive experience in the practice of conflict resolution and peacebuilding. Chapters 8–11 describe work in the form of practice pioneered by Burton (interactive problem solving in the context of the analytical problem-solving workshop), while in Chapter 12 Dukes describes a much less formal sort of intervention in a community-environmental conflict. All the authors, nevertheless, pay attention to how the notion of BHN figures in their work. Mitchell begins this section by considering the list of "rules" Burton set out in 1987 for how these workshops should be run and, reflecting on his own decades-long experience, describes how these rules have been altered over the years. Abu-Nimer places the concept of BHN at the center of his practice, while warning that invoking it naively may result in negative as well as positive outcomes. Fisher takes us inside two different workshop settings (Cyprus and Darfur) to show how the idea must always be fitted to context and the exigencies of each conflict situation. Nan and Greiff, meanwhile, focus on the Georgian–South Ossetian conflict and use the notion of BHN as "lens" with which to view specific (and often rather concrete) issues. Abu-Nimer, Fisher and Nan and Greiff, in fact, all point to the importance of understanding the place of BHN in the context of the conflict, as well as the structure (or stage) of the particular workshop. Finally, as noted, Dukes takes us beyond the formal setting of the workshop while, like Nan and Greiff, using the idea of BHN as a lens through which to view and understand the more affective (emotional) aspects of deep-rooted conflict.

8 Beyond the "classical model" of problem-solving workshops

25 years of experience, experiment and adaptation

Christopher Mitchell

Introduction

The early experiments in applying ideas from group dynamics, industrial relations theory, social work and T-Group theory to complex, and often violent, social conflicts were very much a matter of trial and error. True, they were informed by theories developed in social psychology, sociology and political science, backed up by knowledge about practical peacemaking techniques familiar from what were then called "simpler societies" by ethnographers and anthropologists. However, these ideas tended to be used in an ad hoc manner and it was only gradually that systematic attempts to develop an empirically based theory of problem solving developed – attempts that continue today as the number of cases where problem-solving workshops have been used increases and systematic – if not statistical – comparison becomes possible.

It was only in the mid-1980s that the Australian scholar-practitioner, John Burton, wrote out the draft of his "handbook" for resolving deep-rooted conflict (Burton 1987). At the time, Burton was attempting to integrate sets of ideas about "basic human needs," drawn from the work of Paul Sites (1973), E.O. Wilson (1975) and, more distantly, Abraham Maslow (1954) into his practical intervention work using problem-solving workshops. The ideas would, ultimately, offer a theoretical basis – via the concept of alternative "satisfiers" – for the resolution in principle of even the most intractable of social conflicts. However, the resultant handbook was, in essence, a collection of empirically developed guidelines for what might be termed the original, "classical" model of problem-solving workshops which Burton himself, Richard Walton, Herbert Kelman, Leonard Doob and others had tentatively pioneered in the 1960s and 1970s (Burton 1969, 1987). Up to that point, save for a small number of articles – the most distinguished of which were those authored by Herbert Kelman (1972, 1982) and later by Ronald Fisher (1972, 1983) – the practice of problem solving had been very much a "hands on" process. Practitioners felt their way tentatively into the details of protracted conflict and used theories in a somewhat opportunistic manner. Burton's brief volume represented an early attempt to delineate what a classical problem-solving workshop should – ideally – look like, and what theories, often used implicitly, contributed to a workshop's likely success.

The circumstances that led to Burton setting himself this task were unusual, in that the need seemed to have arisen from the third of a series of workshops held during the period 1983–1985 at the University of Maryland in College Park. The series focused on relations between Britain and Argentina following the short, but intense, war in the South Atlantic over the Falklands/Malvinas Islands, during which over 1,000 young men had lost their lives. The three workshops, which had taken place at intervals of approximately nine months, had been an attempt to restore the previously good relations that had existed between the two countries. The organizers also hoped to help to start up some meaningful "Track One" negotiations as a means of constructing a durable solution to what was, at base, a conflict mixing disputes about territorial ownership with elements of identity, decolonization and self determination (Little and Mitchell 1989).

The third of the workshop series had not gone well. For the first time a representative of the British community living on the Falkland Islands had been persuaded to attend the workshop so that the other participants from London and Buenos Aires had been faced with some of the realities of a people whose homes and livelihoods were directly involved in the conflict. There had been a number of temporary "visitors" to the week-long discussions, while members of the facilitating panel had moved "in and out" of the meetings. Both factors made for much distraction in the participants' ability to focus on possible moves towards confidence building. Nonetheless, after much effort, texts consisting of suggestions for some conciliatory gestures and possible principles for a settlement had been agreed at the last minute, and an agreement reached to carry this confidential document back to the relevant decision-makers in the Argentine Canceleria and the Foreign and Commonwealth Office in London for their perusal. The participants departed College Park with a sense of accomplishment, only to find the details of the meeting and the agreements headlined in the London Sunday newspaper for which one of the British participants – a journalist who was also a Conservative Party Member of Parliament – worked and wrote.

Needless to say, the workshop sponsors and facilitators were not pleased by this, and a great deal of repair work had to be carried out subsequently, particularly with representatives from Buenos Aires. The workshop series never resumed.

A classical model: the structure of "the rules"

Burton's reaction to all this was to look back on the many things that had, in his view, gone wrong with the third of the "Maryland workshops" and to try to devise some guidelines to ensure that at least some basic errors were avoided in future work. The book that emerged from his reflections was short and divided into two main sections. The first was an introduction to the underlying philosophy of the "problem-solving" approach and the second a list of 56 "Rules" for conducting a successful problem-solving exercise, mainly with the assumption that these would apply particularly to the first of a series – although Rule 2 states firmly that a sponsoring organization should always be sure that "it is possible to stay with the situation until the services offered are no longer required" (Burton 1987: 34).

The list of "Rules" then followed sequentially through the various stages of a "classical" problem-solving workshop, starting from the basic assumptions that the participants in the group process would not be officials from any of the involved parties, that the group involved would be small and that the sponsoring organization would be neutral, in the sense of not having any direct stake in the outcome of the conflict.[1] The typical sequence of stages would involve analysis of the conflict and the definition of (often underlying) issues through a discussion of options; changes needed; likely obstacles, negotiations that would be needed to overcome these; and steps that could be taken by participants, both jointly and separately, at the conclusion of the workshop. The "Rules" ended with the admonition that the facilitators should "always have in mind the earliest possible termination of the seminar series" (1987: 70).

Since 1985, many, many problem-solving series, interactive dialogues and interactive conflict resolution initiatives, collaborative and analytical problem-solving exercises have taken place as part of the huge growth of "Track Two" initiatives carried out by unofficial sponsors and facilitators from a variety of backgrounds – national, professional, academic, ad hoc. Some have used various versions of "the classical model" outlined in Burton's writings. Others have adapted basic ideas, changed settings and sequencing, and used their own approaches, methods and objectives. Still others have developed their own techniques in complete and often fruitful ignorance of the origins of the problem-solving approach.[2]

Twenty-five years on, and following much varied experience of various models of Track Two activity, it seems appropriate to re-examine the "classical model" – at least through reviewing some of Burton's core rules – to see how they have been used or adapted – and broken – and with what effects. What follows is a retrospective look at some of Burton's most firmly stated guidelines in the light of a number of subsequent workshop series, among them one that took place in the early 1990s focused on a conflict in the former Soviet Union and under the sponsorship of a loose partnership of some of Burton's colleagues and followers (Camplisson and Hall 1996; Hall, with Camplisson 2002).

Relevant parties and crucial entrance points

One of the first and most crucial decisions for any sponsoring organization in considering an intervention into a deep-rooted conflict is the issue of who the actual participants should be, so that the workshop or series should have the most effective impact on *the* conflict. This is actually two questions, the first and perhaps the most important concerning the "level" of a complex conflict, at which intervention is to be aimed. The issue actually came up in the Maryland series when there was much debate about whether some representatives from the Falkland Island community should be key participants in the discussions, particularly given the fact that the Islanders thoroughly mistrusted elements of the British Government (especially the Foreign and Commonwealth Office) whom they regarded as only a slightly lesser danger than the Government in Buenos Aires.

Burton's Rule 4 starts with the assertion that "the starting point in any analysis and resolution of any conflict is where the closest relationships have broken down" (1987: 35).

This idea that those most directly affected by the conflict should be the key part of any resolutionary process seems a good guiding principle until one considers the issues of asymmetry and the fact that many contemporary protracted conflicts involve governments and intra-state dissidents. In many cases, answering the question about who are the parties to this conflict turns out to be far from simple. If one starts a workshop series with local Georgians and Ossetians, or Georgians and Abkaz, should one, at some stage, also involve representatives – "voices" in the problem-solving jargon – of Russia as a genuine "party" which clearly would have the ability to veto any locally derived resolution? It is clear that Israelis and Palestinians are key parties to their conflict, but what should be the role of the United States as Israel's chief patron? The Unionists and Nationalists were clearly those who had their relationship thoroughly broken in Northern Ireland, and a logical starting point of many problem-solving and relationship repairing initiatives, but where in this complex process were the British and the Irish Governments?

The question of participation arises in another form when one or other of the adversaries is split into competing – sometimes viciously warring – factions, especially in the light of the theory which states interveners have a better chance of securing a durable solution when the adversaries are *not* riven by rivalries and intra-party antagonisms – a situation that makes the undermining charge of "treachery" or "selling out" all too easy to level – successfully – by potential spoilers. Burton's answer is contained in Rule 9: "The participation of all factions within a party should be sought."

However, practically speaking, this seems easier said than done. It might be possible to include voices from Hamas, the PLO and Palestinian civil society in an Israeli-Palestinian workshop series. However, the question of who might best "represent" the numerous (at times almost a dozen) and constantly changing factions among the armed Darfurian resistance movements in the post-2003 civil strife in Darfur Province in the Sudan has frustrated sponsors and conveners alike, at both official and unofficial levels. One answer, which Burton practiced but did not write about, is to aim to enter a conflict system at the level of what might be called "intra-party" conflict to try to resolve issues at that level in preparation for moving the process "up" a level to the inter-party conflict. In such a situation, however, one has to ask how a sponsor's value as a potential third party might have diminished in the eyes of a party now confronted with a more coherent, organized and united adversary, undoubtedly capable of negotiating a durable peace, but equally capable of waging a more effective struggle through negotiation or through coercion.

One final aspect of this "dilemma of representation" is the perennial question of excluding "extremists" from a workshop series in order to make it easier to achieve some kind of consensus – about analysis or action. The assumption underlying efforts to exclude certain factions, organizations or movements is that agreement can be reached more easily between reasonable "doves" or "owls," but including "hawks" reduces the chances of any successful outcome. Thus, even in an unofficial workshop series on Northern Ireland held in the very early 1990s, it was possible to meet with participants representing the Unionist community (both from the Official Unionists and the Democratic Unionist parties) and the Nationalist community (the Social Democratic and Labour Party) but it proved impossible – even in the later stages of the series – to include representatives of Sinn Fein, the political wing of the IRA.[3]

In the Northern Ireland case, however, it should be noted that almost no progress towards a durable resolution was made via any "Track" until the extremists of both sides (Sinn Fein/IRA and organizations like the Unionist UVF) had been brought, directly or indirectly, into preliminary talks about talks and eventually into negotiations; and that though the discussions proved very difficult, nonetheless they resulted finally in a workable agreement. It often seems to be the case that "extremists" turn out to be the most innovative in their thinking and – ultimately – most flexible in devising and considering options, having the least to lose and the most to gain through change.

Participants and representative "voices"

One of the issues that had plagued the Argentine/British workshop series that eventually gave rise to John Burton's decision to lay down some firm rules for the future of classical workshops was the whole question of who should sit around the table in such workshops, and hence how they should be invited. Who would be ideal participants in a "classical" problem-solving exercise and how would it be best to arrange that they were actually there?

In the case of the Maryland series, there was a clear problem of imbalance, in that the Argentine group involved a number of persons, admittedly there in an individual capacity, but with excellent access to decision-making circles in Buenos Aires. They included a former Foreign Minister and a political advisor to recently elected President Raoul Alfonsin, together with notable academics and lawyers. Facing them was a group consisting of out-of-favor Conservative Members of Parliament, members of the Labour Party parliamentary opposition and academics from chronically under-resourced Latin American Studies departments in British universities. As I have noted elsewhere (Mitchell 2002), the ease of access to decision-making circles of the Argentine representatives was matched by almost complete absence of access – not to mention the levels of official mistrust and hostility – enjoyed by the British.

Burton's response to this frustrating imbalance was to follow up on his colleague Herb Kelman's hypothesis that the closer workshop participants were to official decision-making circles, the less flexible they would prove to be in discussion, analysis, reframing issues and creating options – a hypothesis borne out by the willingness of the British group to countenance non-traditional ideas and approaches countered by the Argentine participants' consciousness of legal and political limitations on what could be discussed as serious alternatives:

> Rule 8. Parties should be invited to send participants who are not official representatives but who have easy access to decision makers.

This is an interesting starting point to open a discussion about the whole issue of what subsequently became known as "Track One and Half" and the role of discussions held at an unofficial level which nonetheless involves individuals with official positions within adversaries.[4] What effects might ensue from involving officials attempting to act in an unofficial capacity in informal processes like problem-solving workshops with no official standing – and, almost equally contentious – who gets to decide who can come to such exercises?

One extreme example of this mixing of Track One participants with Track Two processes is provided by the series of four "Canterbury Workshops" which took place in the mid-1990s and which focused on the conflict between the largely Rumanian community and government of the newly independent state of Moldova (formerly part of the Soviet Union) and the mainly Russian minority and their (unrecognized) government in the breakaway eastern region of Transdniestria (Camplisson and Hall 1996; Williams 1999). After a number of preliminary visits and with the credibility gained from organizing helpful community development projects in the region, the sponsors for this initiative (who were organized under the umbrella of MICOM – the "Moldovan Initiative Committee of Management") obtained the support of the rival Moldovan and Transdniestrian Presidents, who not only agreed to permit a series of problem-solving workshops to take place but actually appointed which participants from each side would be permitted to attend week-long meetings in Canterbury in England.

In the event, the two rival groups of participants turned out to be the official negotiating teams (the "Experts Groups") who were even then involved in a limping negotiation process over future political, social and economic relationships between the two entities. The two sides proceeded to treat the meetings in Canterbury as a continuation of this official process, often in spite of the best efforts of the panel of facilitators to get participants to stop acting as members of hierarchically organized negotiating teams, to investigate values underlying the official negotiating positions, to brainstorm options and to abandon legal frameworks and historical precedents as a basis for discussion. Workshop processes often became bargaining sessions with both "teams" comparing negotiating positions on various contentious issues in side-by-side negotiating texts, which could be modified in preparation for subsequent meetings away from Canterbury and back in official OSCE meetings. The culmination of this "Track One and One Eighth" process was the involvement of some of the official OSCE mediation team as "observers" of the workshop process, which in actuality meant their eventual full participation in the exchange and an abandonment of any pretence that this was, in any way, separate and different from official level bargaining.

Such a workshop series throws into sharp relief the Burtonian assumption that Tracks One and Two should really be kept physically separate from one another and that cross over in participations should be avoided:

> Rule 20. Sponsors should give special consideration to the transition stage between the unofficial discussions ... and the official negotiations, and to take whatever steps are required to prepare for this even before viable options have emerged in the seminars.

However, what happens when, in a long drawn-out series of meetings, previous "un-officials" take up official positions, something that can happen quite often when workshops involve members of a political opposition or when new ruling coalitions are formed from previously rival factions? This seems a far more likely scenario than the one outlined above, and it actually occurred during one Israeli-Palestinian workshop series in the mid-1990s, when a new Israeli Government came to power and several out-of-power members of the workshop series suddenly found themselves in very official positions (Kelman 2002). This seems to contrast markedly with the experience of the Canterbury workshops, in which official negotiators were asked to don different hats and miraculously become "individual voices" willing to brainstorm and discuss underlying values and creative options – as opposed to being staunch defenders of official bargaining positions and seekers after every possible advantage for their side. Such roles seem contradictory – and probably beyond most people.

Facilitation: nature and composition

One set of issues that had seriously disturbed John Burton during the Maryland series had been the structure and performance of the facilitating panel, and this was especially so during the third workshop of the series. Ideally, Burton had wanted a stable and continuing panel throughout the whole series but this had not proved possible to arrange. Moreover, during the last workshop, panel members had been invited in an uncoordinated manner, many turned out to have been invited for purely public relations reasons, and there had been constant absences during the week-long discussions, with panel members appearing and disappearing from one session to the next as they tried to fit attendance at the workshop into their own timetables.

Probably it was with these concerns in mind that the rules included a number of very firm requirements for a classical facilitating panel:

> Rule 13. Panel members should be drawn from several key disciplines and they should be widely informed about different approaches in their own field, have an adequate knowledge of conflict theories and be experienced in the facilitation process.

> Rule 14. It is necessary to have balanced viewpoints and perspectives represented on the panel including gender and ... ethnic and class perspectives.

Clearly Burton was trying to ensure that the panel should be well briefed, prepared and organized to avoid the ad-hoc-ery that seemed to him to have marred some of the conduct of the Maryland process:

> Rule 17. Panel members must prepare before and during the seminar, even adjourning discussions for this purpose, so that they are always acting together and with mutual understanding.

In a number of workshop series that have taken place after Burton wrote up his summary "Rules" other crucial questions have arisen about the role of the facilitation panel and the qualification of the facilitators. One of these involves the issue of whether panel members could or should be drawn from a particular ethnic, religious or national entity that is a party to the conflict under analysis (and thus will also be represented round the table as members of the group of (rival) participants); or even whether panel members should be drawn from a country or group seen as a patron or constant supporter of one side or the other.[5]

Could Greek or Turkish Cypriot facilitators successfully conduct a workshop on the Cyprus conflict? Could scholars from Northern Ireland – or from Britain – be part of a panel analyzing interactions in a workshop on that province during "the Troubles"? This whole question is part of a broader issue about the nature of the interveners raised initially by Paul Wehr and John Paul Lederach (1991). The two writers contrasted their experiences with the work of "insider partials" with the classical idea of "outsider neutrals" and discussed the advantages enjoyed by intermediaries who shared the values and cultures of the rival participants in a peace process, who understood and empathized with the aspirations of those involved in the conflict relationship and who could thus inspire *confianza* in the minds of the adversaries and their representatives. In subsequent works (Lederach 1995, 1997), Lederach argued that the whole idea of an outsider coming into a complex set of relationships embodied in a very different culture was fraught with dangers involving ignorance of local norms, being oblivious to subtle nuances and the likely imposition of foreign values and alien processes onto the search for solutions. These might well end up being crafted to satisfy outsiders' norms and values, rather than those held by local communities.

In reality, Lederach's thesis involved a broad criticism of the whole concept of outsiders conducting alien procedures – including problem-solving workshops – in cultures where local, elicitive techniques were more appropriate. Framed slightly differently, the issue could be seen as a question of how intermediaries established trust and credibility among representatives of rival parties, and whether this could best be achieved through empathy, identification or expertise – and what this last was based upon. For those advocating the use of insider partials, the answer involved empathy, existing, balanced relationships and familiarity with the local culture. For those following a classical problem-solving approach, key factors were impartiality, balance and perceived fairness (at the very least while interacting with adversaries as participants), transparency about what they were doing and why, plus theoretical knowledge of conflict processes.

As far as the practicalities of conducting problem-solving exercises were concerned, the problem to be faced in the 1990s and 2000s increasingly came to involve the likely construction of mixed panels of insiders and outsiders, as opposed to a classical outsiders panel advocated by Burton, who even argued that

> Rule 15: The panel should not include persons who have made an exclusive speciality of the particular dispute being analysed or of the region in which the dispute takes place.

This becomes a serious and increasingly likely potential problem when sponsors from outside a conflict arena partner with institutions (NGOs, universities, research centers, foundations) from that region. On the one hand, local expertise on a panel can be helpful in providing detailed insight into the nuances of position shifts, changes in analytical frames used in conversation by participants, options floated as possibilities, retreats undertaken from previous (non-negotiable) positions, or recognitions offered of others' claims, concessions or conciliatory moves. Moreover, local members of an involved community sitting on the facilitation panel as perceived "experts" would also – for good or ill – enable some participants to feel comfortable in that their side was represented as part of the third party. Thus, there were one or more facilitators with whom they could identify and who might more easily identify with their side's problems and perspectives.

On the other hand, the effects of having a panelist who might well be perceived as being a representative – even if only through perceived ethnic, national or religious affiliation – of one of the involved adversaries, could be to fatally undermine any possibility of that panel being seen as minimally credible by other participants – and this effect might only be partially avoided by having facilitators from both (or all) adversaries balanced on the panel. Even when this form of balance is actually achieved, it has sometimes proved difficult for the facilitators involved to maintain a clear distinction between their roles as professional facilitator and representative of this or that involved community group or faction.

Facilitation tasks

In the early, experimental days of problem-solving workshops, the precise tasks and functions – and even the size and composition – of the facilitating panel were worked out pragmatically, almost on a case-by-case basis. A facilitator's basic task was – as the name suggests – to ease the difficult exchanging of positions, aspirations, interests, values and perceptions of people who inevitably would distrust and discount everything "the others" might say. It was to soften and interpret exchanges that would inevitably, and frequently, become accusatory, challenging, contestable and – at times – downright insulting. It was to make it easier for adversaries to listen to one another in order to understand rather than rebut, to be analytical rather than confrontational. Burton summarized this basic task initially in a somewhat negative fashion:

> Rule 12. The Role of the panel in conflict resolution is not to seek compromise. It is initially to facilitate analysis so that goals and tactics, interests, values and needs can be clarified and later to help deduce possible outcomes.

From the beginning, most sponsors, organizers and practitioners shared a firm belief in the practical advantages of having a workshop conducted by a mediating panel rather than a single mediator supported by a back-up staff. Early experience seemed to confirm the benefits of using a group of facilitators that was almost equal in numbers to the participants present. The panel could work to model a group culture of openness, informality, respect for others and a willingness to entertain and examine others' ideas and aspirations. Intra-group success thus involved what De Reuck (personal communication) once described as the creation of an informal "island," safe for all participants to be open, analytical and creative. Others talked about the – perhaps temporary – transformation of rival participants into "honorary academics" willing at least to entertain new ideas and options.

Whatever the results of the underlying workshop dynamics, a crucial determining factor was the facilitators' ability to work as a team, and this remained a part of Burton's classical model in the mid-1980s:

> Rule 18. Panelists must be selected not only for their professionalism in facilitation but also for their talents and abilities to work within a team and, even then, only if they can be available if and when required.

> Rule 35. The panel acts as a *unit* [emphasis added] in conducting the seminar, with one member acting as the host/hostess and formal chairperson.

As general principles, the unity of the facilitating panel seems simple common sense (although some facilitators have also argued that part of the process of modeling a productive process has, on occasions, involved panel members disagreeing publicly among themselves, thus demonstrating that it is acceptable to disagree, at the same time as demonstrating the nature of "productive" disagreement). However, what was implied by that guideline? Clearly, under ideal circumstances, there was a set of interlocking roles, but even by the mid-1980s the only one clearly delineated was that of a chair or a lead facilitator who conducted the various sessions. Early on, however, it was recognized that this lead role was a demanding one and it was best for individual facilitators to hold it on a rotating basis. Rule 35 argues that one person should act in the role of "host" and "formal chairperson" and much later experience has shown that a single figure has to be the ultimate arbiter for the panel, who orchestrates the whole process and chooses among courses of action when disagreements arise among panel members. Nevertheless, for the hour-by-hour conduct of the workshop, passing the "lead facilitator" role among the panel members has proved to be good practice.

Apart from the rotating role as lead facilitator, what other roles have been identified within well functioning panels? Quite early on in many problem-solving workshops it became obvious that the role of lead facilitator was better shared by at least two people, with a back up "chair" ready to intervene if necessary:

1   When the lead facilitator was temporarily at a loss or "in trouble" and needed a few seconds to recover;
2   When possible openings into a productive line of discussion had been missed;

3   When something had been said that needed highlighting, repeating or emphasizing;
4   When the discussion required re-focusing back to an original or an incomplete theme or it needed to be emphasized that a new theme or line of discussion had been broached without having achieved satisfactory closure on a previous line of thought;
5   When tensions had grown and some form of tension relieving move was needed.

Of course, any member of a facilitating team could fulfill these functions and act effectively in these and many other circumstances to maintain a productive flow of discussion and analysis. However, some prior agreement about roles and functions obviously would prevent confusion and contradictions among panelists.[6] On an effective panel, at least one member has often been assigned the task of simply listening and observing interactions – body language, revealing silences etc., – and making sure that important ideas or statements do not get lost or inadvertently dropped from the agenda. Other facilitators can take up roles of:

CLARIFIER: "I don't quite understand why…"
TRANSLATOR: "Would it be just as accurate to say…?"
HIGHLIGHTER: "If I have understood you correctly, this is very important because…"
DRAWER OF PARALLELS: "In another situation I have studied…"
THEORIST: "This is not entirely unique, as recent work on escalatory spirals emphasizes…"
ELDER STATESMAN: "In my experience…"[7]

Much subsequent experience with PSWs has shown that these roles can easily be passed from one facilitator to another as the workshop process unfolds – apart perhaps for the role of elder statesman, for which grey hair is something of a necessity. Played appropriately, the combination of roles can emphasize that one of the tactical aims of a problem-solving workshop is to get all present – participants and facilitators – involved in a search rather than a debate or a contest, and that a major initial task for the facilitation team is the analysis of the conflict processes at work within the case under study – "How and why might you all have arrived here?"

   This does start to answer the question posed above as to the functions of an effective facilitation team – apart from the basic task of making easier the exchange of accurate information between adversaries. Inputs from the facilitation team at appropriate stages in the workshop process are initially aimed at helping with analysis and understanding of why adversaries have arrived "here" – at violence, profound mistrust, hostility verging on hatred, a sense of victimhood, and an unwillingness to assign any but the most malign motives to anything the other side does or suggests. At this stage, as Burton and others have emphasized elsewhere (1969), an input of abstract theories regarding conflict dynamics can be helpful in avoiding competitive blaming. At later stages in the process, inputs about parallel situations or solutions employed in other conflicts can help creativity and get participants "thinking outside the box."

One final task for a facilitation panel has revealed itself in many recent workshop series and this has often occurred at the stage of a workshop in which participants are facing the question of what might be done in order to move their sides' relationship towards a durable peace. Here the panel's role is to become what many have characterized as an "agent of reality" by pointing out the constraints that still exist on both sides in any effort to abandon current strategies of coercion and to move towards a conciliatory pattern of interaction. It has often proved difficult for a panel of facilitators to act as a brake on enthusiasm, but it is a role that often needs to be played.

When considering the way in which the classical workshop model – as exemplified in Burton's 1987 handbook – came into being, one should recall the very experimental and tentative way in which the process had been developed. Whatever the subsequent image that this form of "outsider-neutral" intervention actually developed, in its classical form it was highly non-directive, with its format and procedures extremely open to influence by the participants. The latter set the program of what could be discussed and what might be off limits, which ideas from panel members were accepted and which rejected outright, what outputs from the discussions were useful to carry back to leaders, and what steps might cautiously be taken at the end of the exercise. Most practitioners hoped that participants would be able to get away from the simple reiteration of public bargaining positions and be able to dig more deeply into the under-lying sources of the conflict and thence to possible remedies, but were realistic enough to recognize the difficulties of doing this:

> Rule 40. When the panel asks the participants to make their opening statements they should ask them to focus on the values and goals at stake in the conflict situation.

By the mid-1980s the few practitioners of problem solving had merely arrived at a point where they had a general idea of the stages through which a typical workshop could be expected to pass. However, even after devising a clear rule based on this template, Burton insisted on a high level of flexibility in its practical application:

> Rule 36. The step by step progression from initial perceptions, through analysis of the situation, to evaluation of these perceptions and to finding an agreed definition to exploration of options that meet the needs of all should be maintained. However, there should be no fixed agenda....

Practitioners knew that the basic tasks of the facilitating panel included: (1) devising and providing a non-provocative language for participants to use in describing their situation – should they wish to do so; (2) providing through their own behavior a role model for productive interaction within the workshop setting, which included the idea that disagreements were acceptable but demanded further analysis of why they existed; and (3) acting as a lightning rod for participants' anger, animosity and resentment of one another but also (4) providing something – an idea, a model, a scheme, a narrative – that could focus attention other than on the "crimes and cruelties" of the other side. One key aspect of this last task, therefore, involved attempting to repeat back to the participants what seemed to panel members to be the underlying causes and dynamics of the conflict. Successfully executed, this would help the participants dig below the surface bargaining positions of their adversaries – usually fully familiar to one another – to provide insights that might allow them to reframe the situation in which they found themselves and suggest some possible ways out of current dilemmas.

> Rule 42. The panel should prepare [overnight probably] a statement of what appear to be shared and unshared values for submission to the participants.

Underlying all of these interlocking practical tasks was the principle that the facilitators should control – to the best of their ability – the process but the participants would obviously control the content and the outcome of the workshop or the workshop series. Burton admittedly did want to control the process as closely as possible, and wanted all the interaction between the participants to take place within the physical confines of the workshop itself:

> Rule 26. Parties should be met separately and housed separately if possible.[8]

Not for nothing were his first writings on the subjects given the title of "controlled" communication (1969), although he did initially also use the label "case work" to describe the approach (1967). Subsequent practitioners, in contrast, have stressed the importance of relationship building among participants and the opportunities afforded by informal as well as formal contacts within the overall workshop environment. In many subsequent workshops, much fruitful work has been carried out in conversations outside formal meeting rooms and through contacts away from the eyes of facilitating teams, entirely "uncontrolled" by such "outsiders."

However, the classical model also acknowledged the fundamental dilemma inherent in wishing, on the one hand, to give the participants free rein to take the discussion where they wished, yet on the other wishing to keep the nature of the discussion largely analytical rather than accusatory or confrontational:

> Rule 43. The panel should allow discussions which help to clarify values to proceed freely while intervening constantly to ensure that the dialogue remains analytical and does not regress to point scoring debating exchanges.

Subsequent experience has indicated that, while such a rule may be necessary – even essential – in the earlier, tension ridden meetings envisioned by the classical workshop model, it may be necessary for panelists to withdraw – perhaps even physically – and let participants take over the workshop process, remaining on the sidelines ready to assist when asked with ideas, information or suggestions about resources. This often occurs when cooperative work on a detailed set of outputs from that workshop becomes the focus of activity.

This last leads us to the point of asking what sort of an outcome was envisaged in the classical workshop model and how this has changed subsequently as the basic formula of a PSW was applied to different kinds and different levels of conflict and with different ends in view.

Outputs and outcomes

Early practitioners of problem-solving processes as a remedy for protracted, social conflicts were not without ambition for the technique, arguing that the outcome from its use would – at least ultimately – be the resolution of the conflict under analysis, or at least would contribute to the achievement of a resolution. The expansion of the use of problem-solving approaches to many different types of conflict, but above all the application of the technique to different levels of complex social conflict, produced a set of very different answers to the question: What do you hope will be the outcome of this workshop series?

In cases where conditions leading to the establishment of a classical process existed – an impasse at Track One level, a major breakdown in communication, participants with excellent access to elite decision-makers, profound degrees of mutual hostility and misunderstanding, a willingness for leaders to try an alternative Track Two approach (perhaps motivated by desperation) – maximalist hopes could be entertained, as they clearly were for the Moldovan-Transdniestrian workshops held at Canterbury in the mid-1990s. At the very least, sponsors and facilitators could hope to restart a stalled Track One process, based on some promising alternatives generated at the Track Two meetings. However, the practice of using problem-solving approaches began to spread to other levels of many complex conflicts as it began to be recognized that peacemaking at an elite level needed to be accompanied by peacebuilding at other levels, so that opinion leaders and grassroots constituents also needed to be involved in the overall process.[9]

This expansion of the number and the range of PSWs over the last two decades has led to an altered focus on what such initiatives might achieve along two dimensions – relationship building and tension reduction. This more modest approach to what problem-solving approaches could achieve had already become evident in the early 1980s and could be exemplified by some of the outputs from the problem-solving series on the Falklands/ Malvinas carried out at College Park, Maryland, the third of which had occasioned the production of Burton's "rules" for the classical model. Having built some positive and respectful relationships during the first and second of these one-week meetings, the work of the participants started to focus on the development of tension reduction processes that could involve both British and Argentine Governments and reduce the costs of the continued stance of wary suspicion that had characterized relations between the two governments since the 1982 war. One further result of this workshop series took the form of institution building, and resulted in the establishment in London of the South Atlantic Council, an organization of political, economic and academic opinion leaders dedicated to the task of finding a long-term, sustainable solution to the conflict.

In this respect, over the last 20 years, one common result of relationship building among participants in problem-solving initiatives has frequently taken the form of creating an organization to work on mutual problems or fulfill super-ordinate goals. Sometimes the institution has been for a specific project involving both sides of a protracted conflict, as when, in the early 1990s, a workshop series on the Cyprus problem agreed to organize an art exhibition of works by both Greek and Turkish Cypriots artists and to make arrangements for it to open at venues on both sides of the Green Line dividing the island. At others, a bilateral or multilateral institution has been set up on a permanent basis with support and funding from both sets of adversaries as well as from outside organizations. Following a workshop series on the civil war in Liberia in the mid-1990s, an informal institution was formed by participants involving members of many of the warring ethnicities – Mandingo, Kran, Americo-Liberian. The Liberian Initiative for Peacebuilding and Conflict Resolution (LIPCORE) was set up to maintain communication, exchange ideas and work towards a sustainable peace. Another process involves the establishment of linkages between outside sponsors and internal NGOs already working on humanitarian or development projects, who then take up the peacebuilding process and carry it forward. Such a process ensued between the Moldovan Initiative Committee of Management (MICOM), the Northern Ireland organizer of the Canterbury workshops and the Joint Committee for Democratisation and Conciliation (JCDC), a group initially engaged in community development work in both Moldova and Transdnestria, both groups subsequently working closely together to organize a series of cross community dialogues and workshops in the late 1990s.

On other occasions, workshop series have been initiated with the specific purpose of bringing together specialist participants from adversarial parties unable to meet to discuss mutual interests or shared goals. Workshops on Cyprus during the 1990s have involved teachers from both sides of the Green Line talking about history textbooks and material that could be presented in a less xenophobic way. Workshops and dialogues in the Middle East have brought together journalists from Israel and Palestine to talk about problems both experienced in carrying out their work.

These and many other initiatives may have little to do directly with resolving the conflict between the parties but all have to do with establishing more positive relationships across often profound divides, building bridges between mutually suspicious sectors of otherwise adversarial societies and ultimately preparing "followers" for new relationships with the other side's "followers."[10] These efforts may been seen as straying far from the original idea of the classical model of the problem-solving workshop, with its focus on influencing leaders and elites, but it can be argued that the process is, at base, the same, that participants usually go away from the initiative with an enhanced – and more nuanced – understanding of the conflict dynamics in which they are all caught up, and that the outputs from such meetings make an important – if not decisive – contribution to the process of overall peacebuilding.

Re-entry and follow-up

The last aspect of the "classical model" that needs reviewing is that which deals with the whole issue of "return" and some of the problems participants might face when stepping off the "island" and back into the reality of the ongoing conflict and the suspicions of the many who have not been through the workshop process. Again, this is not an aspect that has been totally neglected by those early practitioners who wrote about problem-solving approaches. For example, the final four "rules" in Burton's Handbook deal with issues of re-entry and follow up:

> Rule 52. Towards the end of the discussion ... the panel should make sure to include a preliminary discussion of transitional policies. It should also find out what special seminars may be required in the future.

Beyond this, however, Burton simply discusses steps to arrange for a next meeting and says little about "transitional policies" or helping the participants with problems likely to arise when they "go home." This may, of course, be because Burton's own use of the classical model involved elite individuals with contacts to and – presumably – tacit approval from leaders for their unofficial activities, but this may not necessarily be the case for grassroots or middle-ranking opinion leaders who have increasingly become involved in Track Two work over the last two decades.

Much practical experience has shown that participants in many workshops tend to become increasingly defensive as the end of the workshop nears and realization of the possible perils they face on returning begin to loom much more realistically. Reversion to more intransigent positions and statements sometimes occurs and participants can begin to look harder and less favorably at options discussed and tacitly accepted. In many problem-solving processes, sponsors and facilitators have found it useful to build in at least a penultimate session to consider how participants might jointly deal with problems likely to arise for individuals when they return home – for example, generally unfavorable publicity about "consorting with the enemy" or even breaking laws about not having contacts with that enemy. (In spite of efforts to maintain a low profile and exhortations from sponsors about confidentiality and the need to keep at least the contents of the discussion secret, experience has shown how difficult it is in the era of instant news and transparent communications to keep any kind of Track Two contacts confidential.) In fact, one indicator of how successful the discussions have been can be provided by the recognition of participants about the problems the other side may face on their return home, and the willingness of all concerned to regard this as a joint problem and something that has to be worked on jointly.

Even if this re-entry stage of the problem-solving process can be circumnavigated successfully, there remains the whole issue of follow up and trying to ensure that whatever comes out of the workshop of any value is not lost in the aftermath of business as usual. Contacts have to be maintained and encouraged, communication with relevant decision-makers followed up, new cross-party institutions supported and maintained, desires for future meetings encouraged and arrangements put in hand.

It has to be admitted that the classical model has offered few guidelines as to how this can be achieved and practical experience shows that this is the model's weakest link. In many cases, the process has deteriorated in this aftermath, perhaps because sponsoring organizations and facilitation panels have exhausted themselves and their resources in planning and conducting the actual workshop and have little time and energy for the follow up. The Liberian institution mentioned above fell apart after just over a year owing to the difficulties of maintaining contacts in the midst of renewed fighting, the absence of outside resources to keep the network in being, and pressure on local members to become more closely and officially linked with one faction or the other in the renewed civil war. A more recent post-workshop process focused on the Sudan also fell apart because of sponsors' neglect and failure to keep communications networks alive in a crucial period for three months after the ending of the first, initially highly successful workshop, partly owing to a lack of resources to keep open expensive cell-phone linkages.

Such examples, while idiosyncratic in themselves, indicate that there might be a general problem in ensuring adequate follow up after successful problem-solving encounters and that breaches of confidence among participants, as in the Falklands/Malvinas debacle, are just one of the problems that sponsors, facilitators and participants will face in the period after a workshop. If one were to add to Burton's "rules," then obvious additions would need to be made to those offering guidelines for how to keep the process from foundering in the gaps between one meeting and the next:

> Planning for a workshop needs to focus on likely continuing action that will be needed in the aftermath of a successful workshop, so that resources of funds, time, energy and attention need to be reserved for this stage of the overall process.

Conclusion

All of the discussion above clearly indicates that the use of problem-solving workshops and dialogues over the last two decades has involved numerous adaptations, modifications and revisions of the original model developed by the pioneering practitioners from the 1960s and 1970s – and that, to their credit, some of these pioneering practitioners themselves have played major roles in introducing these adaptations. Some of the basics remain of what I have termed the "classical problem-solving model" – informality, absence of a set agenda as opposed to a flexibly arranged set of tasks to be undertaken by unofficial participants aided by a facilitating panel, an analytical as opposed to a judgmental mind-set, a search for understanding rather than accusation, and efforts to find mutually beneficial options for the future rather than a win for one side that makes up for damage suffered in the past. However, what we seem to have now is a whole family of problem-solving approaches that have been adapted to suit various purposes and varied situations.

Amid all this welter of difference, the one thing that seems clear is that this adaptation and innovation is going to continue as sponsors and practitioners seek to modify basic principles that have worked in the past to new challenges. The aim remains the same – to help produce solutions that are non-violent and durable and produce benefits for all the involved parties. The classical model may have turned out to be applicable to a limited range of situations and circumstances, but the adaptations demonstrate that the model was flexible enough to allow its modifications to be applied, with some level of success, to non-classical circumstances that do not involve unified adversaries, sovereign states or influential participants.

The one curious omission from Burton's handbook is the complete absence of any mention of the other set of ideas he was working on at the time – Basic Human Needs as the theoretical underpinnings of the reason for believing that problem-solving workshops could bring about a fundamental resolution as opposed to a possibly temporary settlement. The work is essentially about technique. As such, it is always open to challenge and revision as new applications provide alternative lessons. However, this would not have worried John Burton, who was always much more flexible than his reputation would have some of us believe.

Notes

1 Some of the "Rules" now seem obvious – see especially Chapter XII – while others remain remarkably hopeful in the light of subsequent experience, for example Rule 22. "Before approaches are made, there should be adequate funds for a first meeting so there are no unnecessary anxieties or economies"; or Rule 24: "Reserve funding is necessary so that no opportunities are missed."

2 To the collective astonishment of key ICAR faculty, the Norwegian facilitators of the Oslo Process once strenuously denied even being aware of Burton's work in their process that involved (initially) unofficial and (subsequently) official representative voices from the Israeli and Palestinian sides of the conflict – as well as being unaware of Roger Fisher, Herb Kelman, Leonard Doob or, indeed, anyone at all connected to Track Two.

3 Another workshop series, organized at roughly the same time, sought to hold discussions between representatives of "moderate" and "extremist" political organizations in the Basque country of Spain; these had entrapped themselves though repeated public refusals even to converse until "extremists" had finally abandoned support for violence as a strategy.

4 The gradual process through which the Oslo meetings became more and more "official" provides one interesting model in which "official" participants gradually become more involved in what starts off as a wholly unofficial – and hence deniable – process, but gradually gets taken over by involving more and more officials at higher and higher levels until it becomes wholly a "Track One" enterprise.

5 Here it should be noted the initial Argentine resentment of members of the first Maryland panel who came from the United States, a country that was perceived in Buenos Aires as having perfidiously sided with Britain in the South Atlantic War.

6 Increasingly, further experience with PSWs showed that facilitators become comfortable and effective working with colleagues they trust and whose working styles have become familiar.

7 Workshops that have involved participants from traditional cultures indicate that, in many societies, respect and credibility are accorded axiomatically to elders in a way that is not the case with younger facilitators, no matter how skilled or knowledgeable they might be. Perhaps unfairly, youth has to earn trust and respect.

8 Burton wrote well before the era of instantaneous electronic communication offered by the internet, cell phones, skype etc. Nevertheless, while anticipating the effects of such innovations, he wrote that, "it may well be that continuing interaction of selected persons can be sustained, still *with the third party in full control of the dialogue*" (1987: 71, emphasis added).

9 The need for constituent support – or at least tolerance – for deals worked out at the elite level was increasingly recognized after the rejection of the Sunningdale Agreement by mass Unionist opinion in Northern Ireland in 1974 and, a decade later, by the rejection of the Oslo Accords by different "streets" in Palestine and Israel. The recognition was made official with UN Secretary General Boutros Boutros Ghali's call for multilateral-linked processes of peacekeeping, peacemaking and peacebuilding in his 1992 report, *An Agenda for Peace*.

10 For an account of the varied Track Two initiatives undertaken in South Asia during the decade following the publication of Burton's 1987 guidebook, see Behera (1997).

References

Behera, Navnita Chadha (1997) *Beyond Boundaries: A Report on the State of Non-Official Dialogues on Peace, Security and Cooperation in South Asia*, Toronto, University of Toronto–York University, Joint Centre for Asia-Pacific Studies.

Boutros Boutros Ghali (1992) *An Agenda for Peace*, New York, United Nations.

Burton, John W. (1967) "The Resolution of Conflict by Case Work," *Yearbook of World Affairs*, London: Stevens.

Burton, John W. (1969) *Conflict and Communication*, London: Macmillan.

Burton John W. (1987) *Resolving Deep Rooted Conflict: A Handbook*, Lanham, MD: University Press of America.

Camplisson, Joe and Hall, Michael (1996) *Hidden Frontiers: Addressing Deep-Rooted Violent Conflict in Northern Ireland and the Republic of Moldova*, Newtownabbey: Island Publications.

Doob, Leonard W. (ed.) (1970) *Resolving Conflict in Africa: The Fermeda Workshop*, New Haven: Yale University Press.

Fisher, Ronald J. (1972) "Third Party Consultation: A Method for the Study and Resolution of Conflict," *Journal of Conflict Resolution*, 16: 67–94.

Fisher, Ronald J. (1983) "Third Party Consultation as a Method for Inter-Group Conflict Resolution," *Journal of Conflict Resolution*, 27: 301–334.

Hall, Michael (in collaboration with Joe Camplisson) (2002) *From Conflict Containment to Resolution: The Experiences of Moldovan-Northern Ireland Self Help Initiative*, Newtownabbey: Island Publications.

Kelman, H.C. (1972) "The Problem Solving Workshop in Conflict Resolution," in R.L. Merritt (ed.) *Communication in International Politics*, Urbana: University of Illinois Press.

Kelman, H.C. (1982) "Creating the Conditions for Israeli-Palestinian Negotiations," *Journal of Conflict Resolution*, 26: 39–75.

Kelman, H.C. (2002) "Interactive Problem Solving: Informal Mediation by the Scholar-Practitioner," in J. Bercovitch (ed.) *Studies in International Mediation: Essays in Honor of Jeffrey Z. Rubin*, New York: Palgrave Macmillan.

Lederach, John Paul (1995) *Preparing for Peace: Conflict Transformation across Cultures*, Syracuse: Syracuse University Press.

Lederach, John Paul (1997) *Building Peace: Sustainable Reconciliation in Divided Societies*, Washington, D.C.: United States Institute of Peace Press.

Little, Walter and Mitchell, Christopher (eds) (1989) *In the Aftermath: Anglo-Argentine Relations since the War for the Falklands-Malvinas Islands*, College Park, MD: CIDCM.

Maslow, Abraham H. (1954) *Motivation and Personality*, New York: Harper & Row.

Mitchell, Christopher (1981) *Peacemaking and the Consultant's Role*, Farnborough, Hants.: Gower Press.

Mitchell, Christopher (2002) *Ripe for Contribution? The Falklands/Malvinas War and the Utility of Problem Solving Workshops*, Working Paper #15, Fairfax, VA: Institute for Conflict Analysis and Resolution.

Sites, Paul (1973) *Control: The Basis of Social Order*, New York: Dunellen.

Wehr, Paul and Lederach, John Paul (1991) "Mediating Conflict in Central America," *Journal of Peace Studies*, 28: 85–98.

Williams, Andrew J. (1999) "Conflict Resolution after the Cold War: The Case of Moldova," *Review of International Studies*, 25: 71–86.

Wilson, E.O. (1975) *Sociobiology: The New Synthesis*, Cambridge, MA: Harvard University Press.

9 Basic Human Needs

Bridging the gap between theory and practice

Mohammed Abu-Nimer

Basic principles of Human Needs theory

The field of conflict resolution has few theoretical frameworks. Basic Human Needs (BHN) theory is one of the few that aims to explain, understand and even predict the eruptions, dynamics and resolutions of all conflicts. The theory itself has its roots in psychology, political science and sociology. Articulated mainly and originally by psychologists like Erikson, Fromm and particularly Maslow (1976) (see Salkind *et al.* 2006), their lists of basic physiological and psychological human needs were not widely applied to interethnic or international conflicts, until John Burton pioneered the process of attempting to conceptualize these principles and theoretical propositions into a comprehensive conflict resolution theory. The principal assumption behind all these theoretical frameworks (from psychology, political science or conflict resolution) remained the same: a deprivation of physical and psychological needs leads to unhealthy psychological behaviors and may lead to behavioral problems and instability in relationships. Thus, when psychologists needed to address these developmental dysfunctionalities, they suggested certain methods such as psychoanalysis or behavioral therapies – or medication.

Scholars and practitioners of conflict resolution who used the idea of BHN followed the same principle and assumed that when societies experience conflicts, they are disrupted in their "linear developmental process" and need to be "cured" in order to remain on the correct path of human and social development. Bryant Wedge, for example, along with others who used medical metaphors speaking of social conflict, wrote of the "pathologies of conflict" (Wedge 1971). When BHNs are not fulfilled people face deprivation that may escalate into destructive dynamics of violence and war. The suppression of these needs by authorities leads to frustration, victimhood and a sense of alienation, which are the seeds for violence and the escalation of conflict and violence.

Thus, the basic "cure" for this social illness or disease is the satisfaction of the basic human needs. Until these needs are satisfied, BHN theory claims that conflicts will continue and may even escalate beyond social means of control to become destructive. The theory rests on several other basic assumptions (some ontological): First, all humans, regardless of their culture, religion or ethnicity have the same type, number and order of basic needs. Second, the *satisfiers* of these needs differ according to cultural values and norms. Third, needs are fulfilled in a linear manner and the process is generic and universal. All persons seek the fulfillment of their needs, regardless of the hierarchy and ranking of these needs. Fourth, there are inherent social, political and economic structures in a conflict context that generate tension and deprivation. Unless these structures are challenged and changed, conflicts will continue to arise and escalate.

Like the psychologists who originally devised the psychotherapeutic process, Burton developed analytical problem solving as the process through which a cure might be effected. This process relies heavily on rational cost-benefit calculations. It assumes that parties involved in a conflict can be rational; they will weigh the cost of their conflict behavior and are able to modify their actions accordingly. The process is described by Burton (1987) as highly analytical, and it aims to help parties identify their universal basic human needs by formulating a conflict analysis, including a "mapping" of parties, power bases, conflict history, while separating conceptually deep-rooted BHNs from more superficial analytical concepts such as positions, interests or values.

Despite several critiques that have been put forward by scholars such as Avruch *et al.* (1991), Mitchell (1990) or Laue (in Rubenstein, 1999), regarding the conceptual clarity of BHN theory, I maintain that there are points of strength that the theory possesses in understanding the root causes of conflicts in deeply divided societies when the conflict mainly concerns issues of acknowledgement, identity and recognition. In addition, BHN theory offers a way for practitioners, as third parties, to structure their process.

While acknowledging the theory's strengths, in this chapter I also reflect on some of its weaknesses, particularly for practice. I ask two questions. First, how can the third party in a conflict resolution process utilize or put into practice the various theoretical principles of BHN theory? Second, how can the shortcomings and limitations of the BHN theory affect its utilization in various conflict resolution processes? In attempting to answer these questions, and in that way to help bridge BHN theory and practice, I will capture some of the potential applications of BHN theory in various conflict resolution processes, particularly dialogue, problem-solving and skills-based training, and discuss the main limitations of the theory (around issues of culture, rational choice assumptions, emotions and asymmetric power relations), together with their implications for the field of practice.

Processes of practice and basic human needs

There are various processes and tools utilized by practitioners of peace-building, including training, facilitation of dialogues, mediation, arbitration and problem-solving workshops. The following section will focus mainly on the utilization of BHN in the practice of facilitation, training, dialogue and problem-solving workshop in a conflict within a divided society. The context of applying these processes is mainly in intractable conflicts in Sri Lanka, Palestine–Israel, Mindanao and Iraq, and in race relations in the USA.

Despite the limitations of the BHN applied model as presented by Burton, there are a number of theoretical principles that can be detected or reflected in the practice of various conflict resolution processes. We apply BHN theory in our practice through a variety of these principles.

Humanizing the enemy

As a result of the workshop encounter (or other form of third-party intervention, such as dialogue), conflict resolution practice aims to have the contesting parties come to realize their shared humanity, that is, "humanize the enemy." The new awareness or insight emerges or begins to take shape in the minds and hearts of the participants when they understand that the other side has similar needs, along with the realization that some – if perhaps not all – of these needs are valid and legitimate. However, at this stage of the intervention this does not necessarily mean that these needs can be satisfied or addressed according to their historical or current positions or demands.

Such realization has been reported by many scholars and practitioners as successful outcomes of their intervention in conflict situations. For example, Kelman (1997), Rouhana and Korper (1997) Abu-Nimer (1999), Halabi (2004), Maoz (2004) have all reported that after Israelis and Palestinians met in a problem-solving workshop, Israelis discovered that Palestinians have the need for self-determination and Palestinians have discovered that Israelis have the same need for self-determination. They also both realized as a result of the process that they need the "acknowledgment" of the other side, too. Mutual acknowledgment becomes a key for unlocking the stalemate and the deadlock in the relationship that characterized many of these meetings – and the Israeli–Palestinian encounter in general.

Similar dynamics take place at dialogue groups between Catholic and Muslim Filipinos in Mindanao in their "encounter meetings" for peace and dialogue. The Muslim participants are surprised to realize, as a result of the encounter, that the basic human needs of the Catholics (or "Settlers" as characterized by some Muslim participants) for security, identity and even recognition are similar to their own. Many Muslims in these settings did not expect the dominant Christian Catholics to demand or expect recognition from them as legitimate residents of the Island of Mindanao. The Muslim participants had planned or been determined to demand self-determination and to seek an acknowledgment from the dominant majority of their basic need for security, identity and development. However, they were surprised to discover that the other side was also seeking satisfaction of the same needs. Similarly, when Sri Lankan Muslims, Hindu Tamils and even the Sinhalese settlers in the North and North Eastern parts of Sri Lanka met in an encounter, participants from the three ethnic groups often discovered that they all sought the same basic human needs of development, identity and security.

When such a realization emerges "in the room" after certain peace-building processes, it becomes much easier for the participants and the third party to move on to the next level of interaction, an exploration of the obstacles that obstruct the fulfillment of these needs. At this point of the encounter, the realization of basic human needs commonality and connectedness between the participants serves as the glue that holds the participants from different groups together despite their deep political, historical and religious differences. After this realization of "we all seek the same things"[1] a new shared subculture inside the encounter is created within and among the group's members.

This is the core and seed for the formation of a new awareness and relationship between the group members from different ethnic or religious parties, if the workshop is to be successful. Based on this foundation or realization of shared and similar BHN, the participants build their new and shared identity as peacemakers, which counters the destructive conflict dynamics of polarization and win-lose assumptions. In addition, it forms the core of the peacemakers' profiles of "we are different from our own people," and "we do not fully belong in the camps in either side." Such statements often indicate the emergence of a new subculture among the dialoguers or problem solvers, a culture that is governed by a conflict resolution orientation or ethos.

Nevertheless, the process of BHN discovery is not as simple as it might appear from the above descriptions. For the participants to reach the realization that their needs are identical and universal as human beings, is indeed a painful process. It entails critically examining several conflict coping mechanisms that they have developed throughout their lives, both to survive the conflict and to form their national/ethnic/religious identity. Some of these coping mechanisms that block the realization of the universality of basic human needs as a path toward genuine acceptance of diversity include: total denial of the existence of different identities and needs; competition over victimhood; the illusion that shared needs implies "sameness"; and the passive acceptance of rights to differ while pursuing mutual satisfaction of BHNs. I examine each of these mechanisms in turn.

Denial of the identity needs of the other

Participants in conflict resolution processes make statements throughout the encounters or discussions that reflect a denial of the other's need for identity. In the context of the Israeli Palestinian conflict, Israeli Jewish or Jewish Americans have sometimes said: "Palestinians are not a separate national group; they are Arabs or Muslims. There is no such thing as a Palestinian people – this is a new invention in response to the creation of the state of Israel." Certain Palestinian or Arab participants in general have also stated: "Jews in Israel are not a nation. They belong to religious minorities from different countries." Similarly, in the encounter between Christians and Muslims in Mindanao, they mutually exchange denial statements: "Muslims in Mindanao are not one separate ethnic group, they are different tribal groups. Their tribal affiliation is the most important aspect of their identity and not their religion." The Muslim response to this discourse of denial is rooted in their own denial of the right of Christians to settle in their land in the southern Island of Mindanao and an insistence on labeling them as "settlers" or "land grabbers." These terms deny the majority Christians on the Island their identity as "residents of Mindanao" for at least 50 years. The same conflict game or dynamic is played out in Sri Lanka between the three ethnic groups from the Sinhalese majority and the Tamil and Muslim minorities. In his response to the question of why Muslims are not included in the peace process between the Sinhalese government and leaders of the Tamil LTTE, a Sinhalese participant responded: "Muslims in Sri Lanka are not one ethic group. They are separate groups, and they are not united under the same leaders. They are not Tamil. They are a religious minority and have no aspirations for self determination."[2]

All the above are illustrations of how certain members of the majority and minority groups in a conflict articulate their denial of the other side's quest for recognition. While refusing to recognize the other side's separate identity, participants strive to highlight their own national or ethnic identity as the only valid one, and they solidly define their own identity by subjective criteria. The denial of the other's identity is a base on which to establish their superior sense of moral, national, ethnic or religious identity over the other and, as a result, to claim a right to the land, statehood or other resources.

Throughout such exchanges, Israeli and Palestinian participants compete to prove that the other side does not have the same needs for identity, recognition or development. Similarly, Sinhalese Buddhist participants reject the "sameness" of Sri Lankan Tamils or Muslims in terms of their quest for a separate national or recognized cultural identity. The implications of such recognition in the minds of the dominant majority members are often related to territorial secession or delegitimizing the existence of the majority's right for a state or land, especially if the conflict is between new settlers and existing indigenous groups, as in Mindanao, the Philippines or Palestine/Israel. Such exchanges are also connected to dynamics of relative (asymmetric) power and "standing."

Competition over victimhood

Another obstacle to participants' realization of their common pursuit of BHN is related to the typical conflict dynamic of "self-victimization." Participants in dialogue groups or problem-solving processes also engage in a competition over who has been more victimized by the conflict. In this context, the need for recognition as a victim is essential for participants in order to establish the moral superiority of their side over the other. Each side's conflict identity and discourse have been formulated based on the assumption that "our people" are the only or the main victims of aggression. There is no doubt in the minds of the participants from each group that their side has suffered more than the other groups in the conflict. In the encounter, their description of the suffering and degree of loss and victimhood can be meticulously detailed and even visualized, for the sake of establishing the notion or belief that "we are the victims in this conflict." An Iraqi Sunni woman from Diyalla said, in a recent dialogue session to the Shia participants who competed in describing how much Saddam Hussein's regime has destroyed and had tortured Shia leaders and symbols:

> We are confined to our homes and surrounded by Hussainiya (a Shia worshipping site) everywhere. We no longer can sleep because of the religious chanting that lasts for 40 days. We are under attack from both al-Qaeda as well as the Mahdi army. So do not compare what Saddam did to us Iraqis (Sunni and Shia) with what we (Sunni) are facing since 2003.[3]

As a way of coping with the horrible reality of violence and war, such mechanisms or common conflict dynamics have helped socialize and shape the participants from each side to negate the suffering of the other, either as less important, less painful, less serious, or simply "less." This socialization is an outcome of the experience of conflict, and motivates the participants in the initial stages to compete over the status of being "the victim" of the conflict. In turn, this obstructs the realization that both sides are victims deprived of their basic human needs, and no matter how much each has suffered, they both have lost enough to think about other ways to handle their conflict. (Ironically, this is the reason why they agreed to participate in such peace programs in the first place.)

The universal basic human need of recognition is a powerful tool on which to build feelings of connectedness and awareness of commonalities, once the participants realize and acknowledge that they are all victims of the conflict. No matter how they measure or weigh their suffering, they all share the feelings of pain, sense of deep loss, anger and sorrow.

Throughout a dialogue intervention, third-party facilitators utilize certain tools that allow the participants to engage in a careful and slow-paced process of exploration and re-examination of their assumptions about their own identity and the identity of the other. One of these tools is *mirroring* the sense of victimhood expressed by one side to the other. For example, a facilitator insists that no-one interrupts the story telling of a painful memory associated with the conflict when narrated by one participant. Also, the facilitator asks someone from the other side to repeat the story and takes the time to ask clarifying questions in order to highlight the sense of victimhood expressed in the story. The facilitator completes the intervention with an open-ended question of: "What happens to our sense of identity when we recognize that people from our side have committed such actions and brought such unnecessary pain and victimhood on other innocent people?"

Another tool that can assist a third party in confronting participants with their denial of the other's victimhood (or identity) is a joint "visit" or "walk" through the history of the conflict from one side's perspective. Christian and Muslim participants in Mindanao agreed to walk together to visit the various historical sites that belong to the Muslims and indigenous communities, especially those commemorating both victimhood and cultural pride. The journey was carefully planned by minority participants who wanted to prove to majority members that they have been fighting for their needs of self determination and identity for centuries – and that their cultural practices were source of pride and dignity for them.

"We are all humans; we are all the same"

Realization of the same basic human needs among participants is neither a mechanical step nor simply a statement. It has deeper implications for the relationship between the conflicting parties via its capacity to shift power dynamics and to suggest new approaches to satisfy these common needs. Nevertheless, there is also some danger in the mutual recognition of shared BHNs. Thus, a third party ought to be careful when, on many occasions, certain participants in a dialogue process insist on adopting the language of *sameness*, in which dominant majority members and (perhaps some) minority participants agree that there are no differences among them at all or that their differences are so minor that they should not be in the center of their dialogical conversation.

In such a phase, members of the dominant majority group often acknowledge the existence of different cultural or religious values and beliefs. However, they still resist carving out a special place for such differences in the public space or within their hegemonic identity framework as the dominant majority. Thus, for the dominant, the way to "address" these differences is by adopting the language of: "We all have the same BHN and we all can fit under the umbrella of one unified identity." This call for unity by dominant majority participants typically means: "Let us all accept the ways in which the dominant majority has defined the identity of the state, the common public space and the satisfiers to fulfill that identity." The "satisfiers," in turn, are often based on the cultural, religious or ethnic identity of the majority. Here, in fact, the discourse of BHN connects to existing asymmetries of power and standing among the parties.

For example, turning to race in the USA: Certain White American participants in race relations dialogue sessions, once they no longer can deny or invidiously compare the cultural and ethnic differences between themselves and various American minorities, will adopt the discourse: "After all, we are all Americans – we are all humans and have the same basic needs." However, after a brief exploration of such a call for unity, one realizes that the terms to achieve this unified identity are based on the assumption of English language domination (unifying language), plus "Anglo-Saxon" cultural values and beliefs (especially liberalism and free-market capitalism). White participants who determine that being American should be the wider identity framework, do not feel comfortable with Hispanic, Native American or African Americans who claim different ways to fulfill their needs, or seek to demonstrate different manifestations of their identities, ones that contradict or challenge a definition of American unity – for example, by claiming rights to ancestral land or calling for a reshaping of the existing education system (or any other existing structure) to reflect a genuine respect for diversity and pluralism.

Another example: A Sri Lankan Sinhalese Buddhist insists that all participants are Sri Lankan and therefore there is no need to emphasize a unique Tamil Hindu or Muslim cultural or religious heritage. He emphasizes the unity of the Island; "We all live on the same Island and have no other place to go ... we are all suffering from a lack of security." This majority Sinhalese narrative already delegitimizes the quest for territorial secession which might be a tool for Hindu Tamils (or even Muslims) to secure their unique ethnic and religious identity within a larger Sri Lankan civic identity. Those Sinhalese participants who believe in keeping the Island as one territorial unit under one government, often also see this government as run or controlled by the dominant Sinhalese majority. Thus, this is not a genuine recognition of the BHN of Muslims or Tamils for a separate and unique set of cultural and religious symbols, but is an attempt to recognize only the aspects of this identity that are in line with the dominant Sinhalese Buddhist majority identity and ideology. Minimizing these identity differences and their actual manifestation is a more challenging task for the dialogue facilitator than the denial and defensive modes of interaction between these identities. The participants have partially recognized the commonalities and connectedness among the conflicting identities and see the need for recognition of citizenship rights (equality). However, such participants who belong to the dominant majority often reject the remaining aspects of the minority identity that do not fit within their definition of how the country – or state – should be defined.

On one hand, the basic human need for equality is recognized (especially on an individual level), but on the other hand the need to recognize the unique features of national, ethnic or religious identity (on a collective level) is not recognized. Ironically, this process becomes more challenging for the facilitator due to the positive self image that the participants have now developed when they recognized the sameness of basic human needs; "We are all humans, we are all the children of Abraham, we are all citizens of the state, we all want to live on the same island or land." Participants in this frame of mind see themselves as holding moderate and tolerant attitudes in comparison to those who deny the existence of the other or view them as lower or in derogatory terms. They tell participants from the minority groups: "I am not like the others of my people – those who do not want to live with you or look down on you, I want to live with you – in one state" – my state.

Addressing this sense of *false or partial recognition* is one of the harder tasks facing the third party in a dialogue process. In fact, when utilizing the BHN theory in such an applied context, this has been one of the critiques often voiced by members of minority groups who oppose the simplification of their conflict relationships and aspirations within a universal and generic Human Needs approach. Such opposition is partially explained by a lack of understanding or capacity to fully implement the principles of BHN theory at a later stage of the dialogue or interaction.

Palestinians in a dialogue room scream that:

> Yes – the Israelis are human and they have their needs, yet the asymmetric reality of the conflict, both currently and historically, indicates that we have paid a higher cost in terms of loss of property, and number of people killed and displaced, as well as lack of control over our basic human rights of mobility or self-governance.[4]

By accepting the BHN principles and approach and shifting the conversation so that both sides are equal in their rights for security, identity, recognition, control and development, Palestinians feel that the conflict resolution process has become biased towards the dominant Israeli majority. Such participants assume that the simple recognition of universal BHN is a step towards delegitimizing their historical claims for justice. It also assumes that the two sides enjoy the same power basis to influence their reality and the conflict.

Minority members reject such assumptions if the third party uses BHN principles at this stage of the process without making it clear that the process of BHN identification and fulfillment of the needs is based on *recognition that a differential treatment of their needs' satisfiers will be central to the success of the process.*

This means that the fulfillment of the Tamil need for security or identity or self determination will be different from the definition derived from a Buddhist's view of appropriate satisfiers. Therefore, when the latter offer "equal rights for all Sri Lankan citizens" as a formula to satisfy the needs of Tamils for identity, this does not necessarily satisfy these needs based on the Tamil's own definition of their identity and their satisfiers. Moreover, differential treatment of satisfiers would mean that certain arrangements might be required in order to change the structure of relationships between the minority and majority as this existed in the past – or the present.

Such assurances and further exploration of BHN principles are often confirmed by the minority members as assurances that the simple generic and universal existence of BHN will not mean continuing injustice for them.

Acceptance of the "right to differ" in pursuing BHNs

Recognizing the universal existence of BHNs is an essential first step for workshop or dialogue participants in adopting a level of awareness that leads to tolerance of differences. But after this a further step is required. The realization of universal BHN should not imply minimizing and trivializing differences which continue to exist among the parties. These differences are often about the means to satisfy BHNs. Thus the movement should be in the direction of accepting a *relativity of difference* in the face of universal and shared BHN. For example, when a Pakistani Sunni accepts the right of the Shia to practice their rituals and build their mosque in the neighborhood, this becomes a solid ground for coexistence, especially if the rule of law and state institutions are able to guarantee that the Shia will practice their religious rituals in a safe and free environment. Similarly, when an American white resident of Fairfax in Virginia accepts a Sunni Pakistani immigrant in his neighborhood and recognizes that they both are citizens of the state, have the same rights, and the same universal BHNs – yet that they are different in their cultural and religious practices.

As mentioned above, this sort of understanding of BHNs constitutes a core for the individual's acceptance of basic coexistence among minority and majority. It might also be a sufficient condition for preventing interethnic or interreligious violence, if the state institutions supporting this are strong and the rule of law is enforced. Under these circumstances, the person has already recognized the fact that all humans have the same BHN, yet the articulation of these needs is different based on their differing cultural and religious identities. Nevertheless, a person even in this state of awareness in a conflict often continues to believe that his own identity satisfiers (cultural and religious identity symbols or rituals) are more "superior, important, or correct" in comparison with the other side's identity satisfiers. Nevertheless, such a person might respect the identity of the other and coexist with him not because of deep understanding or appreciation of the differences, but because of certain structural obstacles (such as a legal system that prohibits discrimination and prejudice or strong social taboos) that prevent the privileging of one identity over the other. (See Merton's theory on Norms and Conformism in Hill (1980).)

According to BHN theory, this awareness might be sufficient to reach structural arrangements between the conflicting parties in order to resolve their conflict peacefully. Certainly, a cost-benefit approach can be effective in exploring different arrangements that the parties require to guarantee the fulfillment of their deprived basic human needs. However, as one knows from Northern Ireland, or from the South African post-Apartheid model, and even from post-civil rights laws in the USA, passive acceptance based on simple recognition that all people have needs that should be respected through laws is not enough to develop genuine understanding and appreciation of human connectedness among conflicting groups or even to create strong bonds against future conflicts. Such connectedness can only be a result of principles and tools that aim to transform the entire system of relationships, including inner values and belief systems. A basic BHN framework does not reach out or explore such tools in enough detail, either in theory or in practice. The theory, in particular, overemphasizes the parties' capacity for analytical and rational behavior and action.

Cultural differences in identifying BHN

John Burton's initial articulation or conceptualization of BHN theory did not take culture much into consideration and as a result it has been criticized by scholars and practitioners in the field (see Avruch 1998, Abu-Nimer 1999, Sandole 2009). In fact, when reviewing Burton's volumes on BHN theory (1990) or the analytical problem-solving manual (1987), it is clear that Burton assumed that the majority of diplomats and politicians belonged to the same cultural heritage or orientation. In addition, such differences as existed did not constitute a major obstacle in the engagement to identify their BHN and their satisfiers. Nevertheless, his claim of universal and generic applications of needs across cultures remains provocative and challenging to many conflict resolvers who emphasize the role of culture in conflict resolution processes and dynamics. In addition, the original BHN framework assumes that there is a hierarchical and linear relationship between the universal needs, the values that people use to pursue the satisfaction of these needs and the satisfiers themselves (see Figure 9.1). In the triangular framework of BHN, needs are in the lowest base, articulated through values that can only slowly – or with great difficulty – be changed. Thus, negotiation in analytical problem solving is

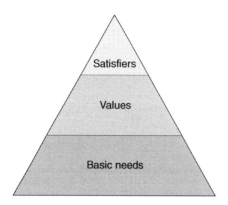

Figure 9.1 Needs, values and satisfiers.

mainly focused on the satisfiers (interests or positions) which can be exchanged, traded and modified.

In terms of application, to what extent do such arguments affect the practice of conflict resolution? How do cultural differences affect the parties' realization of common BHNs? Do they affect these at all?

For example, when Shia and Sunni from Iraq meet to dialogue over their current and historical grievances, or when an Israeli and a Palestinian meet on European ground to explore their current relationships and how to move forward, does culture play a major role in their realization of their BHN? How should practitioners who lead such meetings handle cultural aspects of the dynamics in order to facilitate the common realization of BHN? Obviously, these are complicated questions that require a great deal of analysis. Thus, the purpose of the following discussion is mainly to tease out the difficulty that practitioners face when applying BHN theory with little information about how it works in different cultural settings.

Cultural differences (including religious differences and differences in rituals and symbols) between participants in dialogues, problem-solving workshops, or skills-based training workshops, add to the complexity of relationship building. Lack of understanding of different cultural codes (verbal and non-verbal) adds another layer of difficulty to establishing proper communication and understanding between the conflicting parties. Thus, on both levels, cultural differences – as concrete norms and behaviors and as a "meaning system" through which the parties view their worlds – obstruct parties from realizing the common universal BHNs that they pursue. For example, when Israeli participants are seeking security and recognition through certain cultural practices, such as developing a discourse of being superior (through military capacity, technology or art), Palestinians – and Arabs, in general – view such actions or statements as a sign of arrogance and domination, and refuse to see it as a way to fulfill the Israelis' need for security. On the other hand, Palestinian participants are also seeking security and recognition through an emphasis on the need for statehood and independence. However, they express such need for security through cultural metaphors – and resultant methods – of sacrifice and martyrdom. For many Palestinians, suicide bombing and other forms of attack on Israelis (settlers, soldiers, or even citizens) are legitimate ways to seek recognition of their national identity. In addition, Palestinian Muslims insist on their own cultural symbols, as means to fulfill such needs. They utilize Islamic religious sources (Hadith and Quran) to explain the legitimacy of the argument as a normal – and even a typical – cultural strategy in any verbal exchange to persuade someone about one's point of view. Thus, when a Palestinian dialogue participant tries to explain their need for security and recognition to an Israeli participant in such terms, the Israeli participant, who rarely has an understanding of such a "meaning system," rejects it and cannot see beyond his/her Israeli cultural lenses. Ironically the two sides are arguing about and seeking the same needs of mutual recognition and security, yet both are unable to see such commonality, partially due to cultural differences.

The same cultural dynamics characterize the Sri Lankan Tamil (Hindu and Catholics), Sinhalese and Muslim participants in conflict resolution processes. All three groups are seeking recognition and security, yet the cultural and religious expressions of their basic human needs are manifested and pursued differently due to their cultural differences. For example, in 2008, an interfaith dialogue meeting took place to discuss the events in the town of Trincomali in the North Eastern Province, in which riots erupted following the erection of a statue of Buddha in the center of the city by the Sinhalese community members. Making claims to the central location of a shared public space in this equally mixed city (a third of each ethnic group) through this Sinhalese religious symbol, immediately triggered threats to the security and identity of the other three religious groups. During their exchange to explain their communities' reactions to this action and its destructive consequences, the religious leaders struggled to recognize the other groups' need for security and for religious and ethnic identity.

Eventually, through third-party facilitative intervention in the 2008 process, participants sorted out the assumptions that they had about each others' cultures (religious practices and values), and recognized each other's basic needs for a safe and secure space to express their religious identity. Some of these facilitative interventions included paraphrasing and reframing what each participant meant when they explained their ways of achieving security and a recognition of religious identity. The facilitators also emphasized the different intracultural meanings attached to various religious symbols and how they were perceived by the other religious groups. The realization that the four religious groups were seeking the same set of needs was not as shocking as the realization that they had enough space for each of the groups to practice its rituals and symbols without imposing limitations on the others.

It is clear that all parties in such conflicts are seeking the same basic universal human needs, but that their ignorance or lack of understanding of the cultural differences was obstructing such realization. However, even once the parties manage to gain such an insight as: "We all have the same needs,"[5] there remained two more major challenges to be overcome. First, there was the necessity to discover the culturally appropriate satisfiers of these needs and explore the world views and perceptions of each side. These things comprise the unique cultural ways to exercise, practice or fulfill their needs.

A basic BHN framework offers no guidelines on how to sort out or deal with these cultural differences, yet anthropology, cultural studies, and certain conflict resolution processes and framework have accumulated knowledge and experience in how to assist groups in advancing their competencies and skills in gaining cultural understanding and sensitivity when dealing with others. In advancing the BHN framework as an effective tool for conflict resolution, there is a pressing need to link the theory with these sources of knowledge about culture.

The second challenge, once the parties have acknowledged the universality and commonality of their human needs, is related to the complexity of sorting out a path to go beyond this simple realization. The challenge is to begin handling the power dynamics that influence the parties' relationships within their reality. In the cases of Sri Lankan dialoguers in the town of Trincomali, Israelis and Palestinians in Jerusalem, or Muslims and Christians in Mindanao, participants have to address the fact that the military commander and the army in each town or region mainly represent the dominant majority. They also have to find a way to convince those who hold a position of power in these dominant majorities to give up their privileges and enter a new BHN paradigm, in which power and domination are actually (as Burton maintains) irrelevant in resolving their conflict, as opposed simply to suppressing it.

Power dynamics and basic human needs

BHN theory, especially as utilized by Burton, assumes that power – asymmetric power dynamics and in fact the entire realist approach to power – becomes irrelevant once the parties adopt the new paradigm of seeking to satisfy their universal set of BHNs. However, while asserting this, the theory offers little or no answer to the question of how practitioners and policy-makers may achieve such a shift in interaction within existing intractable conflicts, despite the fact that parties themselves are often wholly immersed in a power paradigm that assumes certain inherent characteristics about individuals and collectivities. These assumptions include:

- Individuals and people are in general selfish or self-interested;
- Parties (individual and collective) will unilaterally compete to pursue their self interest;
- Competition is better than cooperation;
- Adversaries devalue the "soft bases of power" (morality and relationships) by measuring their strength in tangible economic and military terms;
- Rivals dismiss or de-emphasize the role of non-state actors.

In the context of conflict resolution processes such as dialogues, trainings or problem-solving workshops this realist "power paradigm" mentality manifests itself through various interactions between parties or participants of these meetings.

For example, when a group of Iraqi officials explored the history and current relationships in Iraq in an attempt to agree on an educational policy for teaching history and religion, the Shia ministry of education officer declared that "In post-Saddam reality, power relations have changed and this is *sunnat al hayat* ['the rules of life']. Today you are a majority, tomorrow you are a minority." Similar dynamics often emerge among Israeli and Palestinians when they debate their historical relationships. The Palestinians argue that they were majority and ruled the land prior to the arrival of Jewish settlers in Palestine from the early 1880s. The Israelis take the stance: "We are here and we are more powerful and can enforce our rules." A "power competition" occurs when participants in such interactions engage in a race to measure who is more powerful and who can force the other side to give up – or accept – the former's terms of how their needs will be satisfied (or not).

A BHN framework offers several tools to address or shift this dynamic. In addition to pointing out the commonalities in pursuing the same BHN, Burton suggests a cost-benefit calculation – or the "rational choice" approach – in persuading the parties to see the costs of their decision when engaging in destructive conflict relationships and power competition. However, in real-world practice, these tools are limited in their effect. Thus, the core challenge remains as why and how to convince the powerful party and its members and constituencies to give up their perceived position of superiority and domination and adopt a new attitude of shared power or win–win, and to venture into exploring a new set of arrangements for mutual satisfactions of BHN. Both in theory and practice, BHN theory comes up short in detailing how, practically, to respond to the question of power asymmetry, as this constitutes the "rules" by which the parties themselves play, or frame their conflict generally.

Approaching official negotiators to shift their calculations from a power paradigm to a joint exploration of BHN, mainly by utilizing a cost–benefit analysis, is certainly necessary and in theory possible, especially if one assumes that all parties and participants in such workshops are "acting out of purely rational thinking" without much emotion or without involving specific cultural values that (pre)determine what is "reasonable" (rational) and what is not.

However, it is clear to any practitioner and policy-maker that relying solely on a rational approach of cost-benefit analysis in conducting negotiations, dialogues, or problem-solving workshops is not sufficient to shift the positions and perceptions of the participants. Even if the third-party intervention manages to cause some perceptual changes, in general these are temporary and easily reversible once participants return to their home environment. The changes based on cost-benefit and pragmatic considerations are good to manage the crisis manifestation of a conflict temporarily or perhaps good for political negotiators who benefit from making short-term decisions. However, longer-term change can be less assured.

For this reason, to complement a cost-benefit rational approach, practitioners or third party have to invoke other aspects that affect the shaping and formation of the participants' conflict *identity* – for example, by engaging participants in a process to explore their religious and spiritual values involving peace, compromise or non-violence. In the first two days of a Mindanao Tri People (Muslim Christian and Lumads-indigenous) training and dialogue session, it was clear that participants had realized that they had the same universal BHN and that they were trapped in their conflict, which had heavy costs for each participant. However, participants from all groups were unable to move beyond their historical "power paradigm" relationships, in which the Christian majority controlled the governmental, economic and military institutions. In an attempt to secure its own national and religious identity the majority inflicted discriminatory policies against the two other groups. The other two groups, especially the Muslim minority, adopted militant means to resist and protect their threatened religious and cultural identities. Sadly and ironically, both groups – Muslims and Christians – had historically used the same means to marginalize and threaten the local indigenous tribes in their areas.

Having spent two days sorting out these relationships and evaluating the costs and benefits of current reality for each side through conflict analysis tools and a mapping exercise, a young Lumad leader who had combined art and spirituality in his work for peace, took command of the group and urged them to examine their peaceful spiritual and religious values and to bring *those* to the group. For the next three days, the group struggled to understand the similarities and differences between their cultural and religious traditions, during which time they sorted out the events and areas that had historically been perceived as threatening to each groups' basic human needs (identity, recognition, security, control and development). A series of breakthroughs occurred in the group that shifted the mode of discussion from the power paradigm into a joint exploration of satisfiers for their common needs. One of these breakthroughs was a shift in the Christian majority members' perceptions, led by a Catholic bishop and a civil rights activist. These two leaders urged and modeled for their constituencies how an apology and a call for forgiveness could open up a path to relationship transformation. Relying on the new deeper understanding of the Muslims and indigenous, the Catholic participants acknowledged their responsibility for certain historical injuries inflicted upon Muslims and indigenous tribes and admitted their collective responsibility in denigrating the cultural practices and values of Muslims and indigenous groups by holding to a superior ("we-are-more modern, they are backward") representation of their Christian identity.

When members of the majority who hold the power (and might thus naturally favor the status quo) move forward with an acknowledgement of some responsibility, they send a signal of their willingness to re-evaluate the existing power relations. Members of the minority groups often pick up on such signals and reciprocate by acknowledging their partial responsibility for historical injuries.

Such processes have taken place in many workshops among grassroot participants and even among middle-range leaders who leave these problem-solving and dialogue encounters with totally different views, plus a deeper understanding of the necessity to satisfy the basic human needs of all sides in an appropriate cultural context. As for practitioners in the field of conflict resolution in general, the challenge has been how to transfer such gains or changes beyond the workshop into the policy realm. How can one bring the decision-makers in such conflicts to adopt the process of joint exploration of BHN based on a new understanding of the identity (religious and cultural) of other parties? What are the incentives for a policy-maker to engage in such a risky process? Can a politician or diplomat survive his/her official position when abandoning the language of power paradigms and adopting a genuine BHN lenses?

Unfortunately, as a field of practice, we have very few examples or cases to illustrate that such a process has taken place. In fact, we have few opportunities to access these political elites leaders to experiment with, or implement, tools based on BHN framework.

Rational cost-benefit calculations and the problem of emotions

A BHN framework treated religion, cultural identity and political ideology as tools that parties used to manipulate political decisions and justify policies to suppress or deny human needs in a conflict setting. The theory assumes that, through a rational analytical problem-solving process, individuals will reach a rational conclusion that the costs of continuing in the conflict are too high for everyone, including their own side, and will act upon this realization.

However, in reality and practice, participants in conflict resolution process and parties to a conflict have emotional baggage associated with and accumulated from the experience of their conflict which obstructs their capacity to engage in any calm, rational calculation process. Injuries, victimhood, a sense of betrayal, distrust and many other emotions constitute an essential part of the participants' conflict identity. In practice, the Shia Iraqi trainees need to express these emotions and confront Sunni participants with this baggage. Similarly, Palestinians have to narrate their "tragedy of 1948" and what followed in their national history, and Israelis often have to describe in detail what happened to their children and to innocent people who are killed in suicide bombing – and even go back to the Holocaust and its horrible crimes as a source of their insecurity and fear of non-Jews.

Creating a space for the participants throughout a process to share these emotional burdens safely and to acknowledge their existence on all sides in a respectful manner is a crucial step for them to begin exploring and recognizing the universality of their human needs. Carrying out a basic analytical problem-solving process as outlined by the existing BHN framework can only get them to a limited realization. In fact, in many cases forcing such limited process on participants in these intractable conflicts, without proper handling of the emotional baggage of the conflict, will backfire on the third party and the workshop in general. There are many examples of Western trainers who conduct skills-based workshops in deep-rooted conflict areas and who manage to transfer knowledge of how to analyze and map a conflict comprehensively, yet who neglect the emotional and dialogical aspects of a conflict relationship. The result of such a project or workshop is often a well trained group of participants who know how to analyze their conflict cognitively and rationally. However, they remain fearful and distrustful of each other and mechanically train their communities in these alienating tools of conflict mapping or analysis.[6]

Conclusions

There is no doubt that a BHN framework offers a set of principles and concepts that can facilitate the process of conflict resolution in intractable deep-rooted conflicts. Its central assumption – that all humans have the same human needs and as long as these needs are deprived there is a potential for violence and conflict – is a foundational principle in the field. Furthermore, the success and effectiveness of all conflict resolution processes in such conflict arenas depends on the capacity of the third party and participants to engage in a process that leads to the realization that all people have the same basic human needs and they deserve to fulfill these needs equally. Without such a realization, there will be no effective conflict resolution arrangements.

Despite this foundational principle, conflict resolution scholars and practitioners have not yet seriously and systematically explored the specific tools that a comprehensive BHN theory can offer in leading participants beyond the basic realization that they have the same needs and that they can explore and agree upon structural arrangements to satisfy these needs. In addition, the field of practice is still struggling with conceptualizing practical tools and approaches to address the four core limitations of the existing BHN framework: cultural relevancy, asymmetric power relations, cost-benefit analysis based on rational thinking, and how to accommodate emotions. John Burton pioneered in setting up a powerful and comprehensive theoretical framework, which was further developed by many scholars and students. However, he himself and others paid little attention to how these theoretical principles could be implemented in real life situations through the various process of conflict resolution.

Finally, a preliminary examination of the BHN framework in the context of dialogues, problem-solving workshops and trainings shows that there are many opportunities to build upon the realization that we all have the same human needs regardless our culture, religion, race, gender or ethnicity. Nevertheless, from the practitioner's perspective, many questions remain unanswered, including:

- What are the interventions that a third party can utilize to lead an effective process in which participants from different conflicting groups can realize that their basic human needs are the same?
- How can practitioners utilize a BHN framework in the context of negotiation, reconciliation, trauma healing, dialogue and other processes of peacebuilding?
- What are the best practices to illustrate that a BHN framework and its tools can be applicable in a political elite context and not only at the middle and grass-roots level of actors?
- How can the utilization of a BHN framework bring more transformative changes than those produced by rational, analytical cost-benefit calculations?
- What tools need to be developed within a BHN framework in order to make asymmetric power relations less relevant in the pursuit of needs' satisfiers by the parties?

The idea of basic needs is a crucial and fundamental insight in conflict analysis and conflict resolution theory. But applying the notion unreservedly to productive and transformational practice continues to present us with unresolved problems.

Notes

1 Benjamin Broome's description of third culture also captures such realization (see Broome 1991).
2 Based on interethnic dynamics between the three ethnic groups in a Conflict Resolution Skills Training Workshop in Colombo, August, 2008.

3 Iraqi Shia–Sunni dialogue group, Turkey, April 14, 2011.
4 Typical statement made by Palestinian participants in Arab–Jewish encounter groups (Abu-Nimer 1999).
5 Interfaith Dialogue Workshop between clergy leaders in Sri Lanka (in Anuradhapura, 2008).
6 There are many conflict resolution programs (especially skills training oriented) in Iraq, Afghanistan and many other conflict areas. See reports on such trainings in USAID, Conflict Management and Mitigation (CMM), ARD, IRD, MSI etc.

References

Abu-Nimer, M. (1999) *Dialogue, Conflict Resolution and Change: Arab-Jewish Encounters in Israel.* New York: State University of New York Press.

Avruch, K. (1998) *Culture and Conflict Resolution.* Washington, D.C.: United States Institute of Peace Press.

Avruch, K., Black, P.W. and Scimecca, J.A. (eds) (1991) *Conflict Resolution: Cross-Cultural Perspectives.* New York: Greenwood Press.

Broome, B. (1991) "The role of empathy in interpersonal communication," in B.J. Broome (ed.) *Understanding Relationships: Selected Readings in Interpersonal Communication.* Dubuque, IA: Kendall-Hunt.

Burton, J.W. (1987) *Resolving Deep Rooted Conflict: A Handbook.* Lanham, MD: University Press of America.

Burton, J.W. (1990a) *Conflict Resolution and Provention.* New York: St. Martin's.

Burton, J.W. (1990b) *Conflict: Human Needs Theory.* New York: St. Martin's.

Furlong, G. (2005) *The Conflict Resolution Toolbox: Models and Maps for Analyzing, Diagnosing and Resolving Conflict.* Toronto: John Wiley and Sons.

Galtung, J. and Webel, C. (eds) (2007) *Handbook of Peace and Conflict Studies.* London and New York: Routledge.

Halabi, R. (2004) *Israeli and Palestinian Identities in Dialogue: The School for Peace Approach.* New Brunswick, NJ: Rutgers University Press.

Hill, B.R. (1980) *Merton's Role Types and Paradigm of Deviance.* New York: Arno Press.

Kelman, H.C. (1997) "Group processes in the resolution of international conflicts: experiences from the Israeli-Palestinian case," *American Psychologist,* 52: 212–220.

Maoz, I. (2004) "Coexistence is in the eye of the beholder: evaluating intergroup encounter interventions between Jews and Arab in Israel," *Journal of Social Issues,* 60(2): 403–418.

Maslow, A.H. (1976) *The Further Research of Human Nature.* New York: Penguin Books.

Mitchell, C.R. (1990) "Necessitous man and conflict resolution: more basic questions about basic human needs theory," in J.W. Burton (ed.) *Conflict: Human Needs Theory,* New York: St. Martin's Press.

Mitchell, C.R. and Banks, M. (eds) (1996) *Handbook of Conflict Resolution: The Analytical Problem Solving Approach.* New York: Pinter.

Rouhana, N. and Korper, S. (1997) "Power asymmetry and goals of unofficial third party interrelations in protracted intergroup conflict," *Peace and Conflict Journal of Psychology,* 3: 1–17.

Rubenstein, R.E. (1999) "Conflict resolution and distributive justice: reflections on the Burton-Laue debate," *Peace and Conflict Studies,* 6(1): 37–45.

Salkind, N.J., Margolis, L., Kimberly DeRuyck, K. and Rasmussen, K. (eds) (2006) *Encyclopedia of Human Development*. Thousand Oaks, CA: Sage Publications.

Sandole, D.J.D, Byrne, S., Sandole-Staroste, I. and Senehi, J. (eds) (2009) *Handbook of Conflict Analysis and Resolution*. London and New York: Routledge.

Wedge, Bryant (1971) "A psychiatric model of intercession in intergroup conflict," *Journal of Applied Behavioral Science*, 6(7): 733–767

10 Acknowledging Basic Human Needs and adjusting the focus of the problem-solving workshop[1]

Ronald J. Fisher

Introduction

The linkage between the Basic Human Needs (BHN) analysis of protracted ethnopolitical conflict and the central conflict resolution method of the problem-solving workshop (PSW) developed over an extended period of time in something of an ad hoc fashion. The primary creator of the PSW, John Burton, initially saw the subjective elements of escalated conflict as the primary focus of change using the problem-solving method (Burton 1969). Thus, his initial work identified misperceptions, inaccurate cost-benefit analyses and distorted communication along with destructive interaction as the cognitions and behaviors to be changed if the parties through his method of "controlled communication" were to move in more constructive directions in their decision-making and treatment of each other. However, over some years of application of the PSW, Burton and other pioneering scholar-practitioners, such as Herbert Kelman, observed in workshop interactions that the parties were not only concerned with threats and dilemmas related to security, but also put considerable emphasis on their collective identities, including the need for its expression and recognition as well as the threat it was under from the other party. Thus, the search for a deeper and broader explanation of destructive intergroup and international conflict led Burton toward BHN theory, first in the disciplines of sociology and psychology and then in the field of international development (Avruch and Mitchell, Chapters 2 and 8 in this volume). In applying BHN to situations of escalated conflict, Burton believed that he had found an explanation for the intractable and non-negotiable nature of such conflict that distinguished it from mere disputes over tangible interests which did not threaten BHNs (Burton 1990). From a scholar-practitioner perspective, there is no doubt that the application of BHN theory offered a fresh analytical perspective and additional theoretical support for the appropriateness and utility of the PSW as a means of helping to bring about improved intergroup relations and societal change required to resolve ethnopolitical conflicts (Fisher 1990). Some of the ways that the principles of BHN theory can be linked to practice in interactive forums, such as PSWs, dialogues and conflict resolution trainings, are fruitfully discussed in Mohammed Abu-Nimer's Chapter 9 in this volume.

The classic method of the PSW as defined in the literature and applied in practice typically involves the participation of influential and well connected individuals from the two primary parties of the conflict, who are seen to be most concerned with the central issues. These two primary parties are usually identity groups in ethnic, racial, cultural or religious terms, one of whom may be in control of the state apparatus. In his theory of practice writings, for example in his *Handbook* of rules, Burton (1987) prescribed starting a series of PSWs where the closest relationships had broken down. However, in taking a systems approach to conflict analysis, he also advised that the focus could move inward to factions exhibiting important differences within one or both of the parties. Furthermore, he advised that subsequent series of workshops could shift the focus externally beyond the primary parties, until all important parties and their issues had been addressed.[2] Both of these optimistic projections have occurred rarely in PSW practice, likely due to the high level of resources required to implement them as well as the urgent priority of dealing with the central conflict and parties.

This chapter will provide examples of both of Burton's possible foci beyond the central one of the two primary parties locked in destructive, intractable conflict. The first application of the PSW method to the recent violent and tragic conflict in the Darfur region of Sudan will illustrate the utility of beginning the focus on competing factions within one of the primary parties, before then expanding it to other stakeholders. The second case will look at the longstanding conflict on the Mediterranean island of Cyprus, and will illustrate the utility of expanding the PSW focus from the primary parties to the two "motherlands" of Greece and Turkey. In both cases, after initial engagement, the focus also shifts to a particularly salient issue identified in the initial analyses which is central to the current state of the conflict in question. For both cases, some description of the background and current state of the conflict will be provided, followed by the nature, purpose and outcomes of the PSW interventions.

PSWs on the Darfur/Sudan conflict

Conflict background and current expression

Darfur is the western region of the Sudan, about the size of France, and consisting of a mixed Arab and African population of about six million people, out of a total population of 30 million (before the separation of North and South Sudan in 2011). The predominantly Muslim population is compromised of both nomadic and settled Arabs alongside the mainly settled Africans from three main tribes along with numerous smaller ones.

Historically, Darfur has recorded more centuries as an independent entity than as a part of Sudan, which measures a scant 113 years (O'Fahey 2006). Conquered by Egypt in the late 1800s, Sudan and Darfur soon came under British rule, and gained independence in 1956 as one of the poorest countries in Africa. The central reality of the new country has been the extended period of recurring warfare between the North and the South, supposedly ending with a peace agreement in 2005, which resulted in the independence of South Sudan in July 2011. However, during the first decade of this century, violent conflict between armed rebels in Darfur and the Government of Sudan (GoS) along with their allied Arab militias has played out as a horror story that has competed with the North–South schism for international attention.

The primary themes of Darfur's recent existence are underdevelopment and a lack of political representation and power, which have been complemented in the current violent phase by high degrees of insecurity on all dimensions (Brosche and Rothbart 2012; de Waal 2007). Thus, a BHN analysis stressing the importance of the needs for security, identity, recognition, participation, freedom and distributive justice fits the Darfur/Sudan conflict like a glove, given that the people of the region have experienced severe frustration and denial of these fundamental rights of human existence. The causes of the current phase of the conflict can partly be found internal to Darfur, particularly in competition for the scarce resources of land and water, and partly in the long-running schism between the center of government in Khartoum and the periphery in Sudan, of which Darfur forms a large and neglected part. Traditionally, the competition for land between largely Arab herders from north Darfur and largely African farmers in south Darfur was managed through agreements that allowed herding in the farming areas during the dry season with the nomads heading back to the north during the rainy season. Unfortunately, the droughts and desertification of recent decades has exacerbated the situation with herders grazing their cattle further south and outside of the established time windows. This environmental squeeze has resulted in violent confrontations and the arming of tribal and village militias, which then provided armed combatants for both the Arab Janjaweed aligned with the GoS and the largely African rebel movements. The resource competition has taken place within an already underresourced region, due to the neglect of both the British rulers of the colonial period and successive GoS regimes. The economic imbalance has the capital region experiencing a degree of development, while the peripheries, including Darfur, suffer exploitation resulting in absolute poverty. This inequality expresses itself in the political, cultural and social domains, with all of the major institutions of the society based in Khartoum. Politically, the affairs and fate of Sudan have been controlled by the elite from a handful of small tribes based in the northern region, while the vast majority of Sudanese, particularly the Africans, gain few benefits from the state.

As the apparatus of the Sudan state developed, local tribal leaders were replaced with government appointees who were less effective in dealing with land disputes between herders and farmers, thus fueling the sense of insecurity. At the same time, the Islamist political parties, which were Arab dominated, tended to limit the engagement and advancement of Africans in their ranks. Even though almost all Sudanese are Muslim, the Arabs tend to see themselves as superior to the Africans, thus bringing an element of identity into the overall conflict. The alignment of the GoS with Arab militias and the subsequent ethnic cleansing of African villages in Darfur demonstrate the significance of tribal and ethnic differences. The combination and culmination of these processes of economic and political disenfranchisement of the African population of Darfur resulted in such a strong sense of marginalization that political and social protest transformed into armed rebellion, thus ushering in a highly violent period in Darfur's existence.

The formation of two main rebel groups, the Sudan Liberation Army (SLA) and the Justice and Equality Movement (JEM), representing leftist and Islamist sentiments respectively, took place in the early 2000s, and in early 2003 civil war was precipitated when the rebels began attacking GoS installations and personnel. The response of the government was harsh and insidious, forming alliances with Arab militias (the Janjaweed, literally "devils on horseback") to eradicate African villages in a wave of ethnic cleansing which many observers, including the then US Secretary of State, came to label as genocide. Over a five-year period, the estimates of displaced people and refugees reach between two and three million, with approximately 300,000 people killed. The internationally brokered Darfur Peace Agreement (DPA) negotiated in 2006 was signed by only one SLA faction (SLA–Minawi), with the majority of rebel groups continuing hostilities against the GoS and the Janjaweed. With continuing resistance from the GoS, an African Union peacekeeping force was employed and eventually merged into a combined AU/UN operation which, although it is one of the largest peacekeeping forces in history, has difficulty in providing security throughout the region. Alongside the attempts at peacemaking and peacekeeping, Darfur has experienced one of the worst humanitarian tragedies of the modern era, with hundreds of thousands of displaced people barely surviving in refugee camps in Darfur and the neighboring country of Chad. In 2009, the International Criminal Court issued an arrest warrant for the GoS President, as it has also done for a number of other GoS officials and Janjaweed commanders. On the political side, the Darfur rebel movements continued to experience fragmentation and reformation, but eventually an umbrella group, the Liberty and Justice Movement (LJM), largely a SLA combination with some Arab representation, was able to negotiate a peace agreement with the GoS in 2011 through an AU/UN mediation effort sponsored by the government of Qatar. The Doha Document for Peace in Darfur (DDPD) is a very comprehensive

settlement building on the DPA of 2006. However, significant rebel movements are not included in the deal, particularly JEM and the Wahid and
Minawi factions of the SLA. Thus, the violence in Darfur continues on a
sporadic basis with little attention to the denial of BHNs that precipitated
the conflict and with a significant humanitarian effort by international
and non-governmental organizations to address the human tragedy that
continues to affect millions of people.

A PSW response: the Sudan Task Group

The compelling tragedy in Darfur with its multi-faceted and egregious
human rights abuses and humanitarian emergencies seized the attention
of the international community and the conflict resolution field beginning in 2003 and continuing to the present day. In the fall of 2008, this
attention was crystallized at the Institute (now School) for Conflict Analysis and Resolution (S-CAR) at George Mason University at the Arlington,
Virginia campus. A mid-career doctoral student, who was from Darfur and
highly involved in the conflict, both as the principal of a humanitarian
NGO, and as a behind-the-scenes peace broker, approached his faculty
supervisor with a request to mount a conflict resolution intervention focusing on the conflict. This initial contact led to a query to other S-CAR
faculty members and to the International Peace and Conflict Resolution
(IPCR) Program at American University in Washington, D.C. about
scholar-practitioners in the field who might be interested in mounting a
program of intervention. An initial meeting in September 2008 led to the
formation of the Sudan Task Group (STG), consisting in the first instance
of three S-CAR faculty, one IPCR faculty and the Sudanese doctoral
student. Subsequently, graduate student assistants from both S-CAR and
IPCR were invited to join the team, and this number has varied from two
to four at any given time, with only one of the original graduate students
remaining a member at this time. Of the original three S-CAR faculty, two
remain on the STG and have been joined by a third adjunct faculty
member; the original IPCR faculty member remains, while the Sudanese
doctoral student departed in September 2009, but remains as a valuable
consultant to the team. In addition to the core members, the STG formed
a "second circle" of consultants, consisting of faculty members from American University who have expertise in Darfur/Sudan and/or conflict resolution practice. The STG consults regularly with both official and
unofficial actors in the Washington, D.C. area, as well as internationally
with other institutes, offices and programs concerned with the ongoing
analysis of the conflict and the peace process.

The primary objective of the STG was to create an unofficial conflict
analysis and resolution process that could be offered to the various factions and parties in complementarity and support of the official peace
process, consisting of an international mediation effort between the rebel

movements and the GoS. Given the expertise of the STG members and the need for an ongoing forum for conflict analysis and resolution efforts, the PSW was chosen as the primary method of intervention. While other conflict resolution interventions in dialogue, issue analysis, training and consultation have taken place over the past few years, there have been no interventions on Darfur/Sudan following the theory of practice of the PSW. The STG thus believed that it could make a unique and valuable contribution to the peace process by organizing a series of PSWs. Unfortunately, the challenge of acquiring continuous funding, combined with some initial resistance from relevant US State Department officials who were concerned about creating a dynamic of "forum shopping" among the movements, has resulted in a less frequent offering of workshops than initially intended. Workshops have been held in July 2009 and February 2011, and a third currently being planned pending the acquisition of further funding. Initial and some ongoing funding has been provided by the Point of View Fund at S-CAR, but the primary source of funding has been provided by the STG's Italian partners, the University of Siena and the Italian Foreign Ministry. Minor contributions have come from other sources in the USA. In addition to workshop planning and implementation, the STG has worked consistently to maintain its contacts with both official and unofficial actors concerned with Darfur, including hosting a consultation visit by a former senior Darfur statesman in Washington, D.C. in April 2010 and sending a subgroup to meet with various contacts in Khartoum in August 2011.

The workshops

During the period that the STG was planning its first workshop, there was general agreement in the international community that reducing the fractionation and discord among the rebel movements was necessary in order to move the peace process forward. Thus, the STG began organizing a PSW focusing solely on the different and contending factions of armed rebel movements, united in their agenda to overthrow the GoS. The workshop was initially to be held at the S-CAR retreat center at Point of View, whose budget was providing the primary funding. However, relevant officials in the US State Department indicated that they would not approve the issuing of visas to a number of the intended participants, not because they were on the official US list of terrorists, but because they were espousing policies that were not in accord with US thinking. Thus, the STG through other contacts, primarily the Director of S-CAR, was able to make an arrangement to hold the workshop at the University of Siena, with partners who were also able to secure additional funding. Thus, senior and mid-level representatives of most of the major armed movements were brought together in July 2009 to jointly analyze the nature of their grievances and the overall conflict, to foster coordination and cooperation among the movements in relation to the peace process, and to seek unity of purpose in their negotiations with the GoS. The workshop was also directed toward improving intergroup relationships among the movements and renewing channels of communication that had broken down during the fractionation process. The 17 attendees represented the main factions of the SLA (Wahid, Shafi, Unity), the United Resistance Front (a JEM break-away group), the United Revolutionary Forces Front (representing certain Arab interests) and the non-military movement of the Sudan Federal Democratic Alliance. JEM and SLA-Khamis were also invited, but were unable to come at the last minute, due apparently to resistance from their Libyan sponsors. The formal plenary sessions were facilitated by the STG scholar-practitioners, while small group, informal sessions were moderated by local leaders from Darfur who were familiar with the dynamics of the conflict and the relations among the movements. Outcomes generated in the small group sessions were brought back to the plenary sessions for discussion and approval. Using this process, the participants drafted a joint statement of accord and a proposal for ongoing coordination and cooperation, which following the workshop were taken back to their respective leaderships for comment and endorsement. This process encountered some initial success, but was curtailed by a failure on the part of the third-party team to facilitate ongoing communication and coordination due to personnel changes, as the Sudanese doctoral student left the team to work more directly with the official peace process. Following the workshop, official actors continued their efforts to coordinate and combine the rebel movements into an effective negotiating party, and the US State Department was successful in bringing most of the Siena workshop factions into the so-called "Roadmap Group," which eventually developed into the LJM. Ultimately, the LJM was able to reach agreement with the GoS at Doha, but JEM and important SLA factions (Wahid, Minawi) did not sign on to the accord. In any event, the process and outcomes of the first workshop appeared to assist in the later efforts of coordination and cooperation of the rebel movements who endorsed the DDPD in 2011.

The second workshop was held in February 2011 at the University of Siena in partnership with the Department of Comparative History and with continuing support from the Italian Foreign Ministry. This session brought together again some of the senior representatives of several opposition movements, including JEM this time, along with influentials from civil society (non-governmental organizations, academia) to address the current situation, to assess commonalities in grievances and purpose and to develop strategies and a vision for Darfur within Sudan in political, economic and socio-cultural terms. Although armed hostilities in Darfur had declined from previous levels, the humanitarian crisis continued almost unabated, with little physical security in the region and millions of displaced people and refugees living in substandard conditions in camps

in Darfur and neighboring Chad. It was intended that bringing together
the movements and civil society would help identify commonalities and
build support for the ongoing peace process. Thus, the STG designed a
two-stage PSW, meeting initially with mid-level leaders from a combination
of rebel movements to analyze the current state of the conflict and their
ongoing relations, followed by inclusion of the civil society influentials to
facilitate a wider dialogue among the different constituencies. It was
acknowledged that relations between these two broad sectors were
strained, with civil society concerned about a lack of consultation with the
movements that had left them out of the peace process, while the movements had a sense of distrust for some members of civil society who were
seen as GoS collaborators. Nonetheless, the deliberations of the workshop
demonstrated a high degree of commonality in both analysis of issues, and
preferred outcomes, in the form of a shared vision for Darfur in political,
economic and socio-cultural terms. The participants also identified strategies by which they could disseminate the vision statements among their
existing social networks and media outlets. It was clear that there were
more commonalities than differences among those who had taken up
arms against the GoS and those who were engaged in quiet and constructive work to bring about change in Darfur.

Following the signing of the DDPD, members of LJM have taken up
positions in the Darfur Regional Authority (DRA) in cooperation with
the GoS, while rebel fighters from JEM, SLA–Wahid, SLA–Minawi and
smaller factions continue to engage in armed hostilities with the Sudanese Armed Forces (SFA). Within this context, the question of land
tenure and access remains high on the agenda of achieving a peaceful
Darfur, because land issues have been central in the causation, escalation and maintenance of the conflict, and will therefore be central to its
resolution. Thus, the STG plans a third PSW to focus on an initial analysis of land issues with stakeholders from various constituencies. In the
first two PSWs, the centrality of the land resource, both as an initial
causative factor in the conflict and as a continuing and evolving
concern, was highly apparent. In combination with environmental
changes resulting in a depleting resource, the erosion of traditional
dispute resolution mechanisms and the increased use of violence to
alter historical patterns of sharing, have rendered the land issue into a
volatile and complex problem of immense proportion. As the conflict
unfolded, the forced migration of people off their land, now coupled
with their potential return through the mechanisms of the DDPD, will
exacerbate the ongoing challenge of dealing with issues of land access,
management and ownership. In terms of the need for security, the
underlying conflict between largely Arab herders and mainly African
farmers is seen as a struggle for survival by both groups. In addition,
land is tied to the basic need for identity in both cases, thus adding an
element of non-negotiability to the mix. The manipulation of group

loyalties, the eradication of villages and the forced migration of peoples as part of the conflict, has left a legacy of hostility and revenge that will not easily dissipate.

Thus, there is a clear need for a multi-level unofficial track of inter-action on the land issue that provides the major players in Darfur and Sudan with a quiet, exploratory forum in which to engage in genuine dia-logue, mutual analysis and creative problem solving away from the con-straints and pressures of negotiation, policy-making and day-to-day administration. The primary workshop objective centers on developing a shared analysis and finding common ground among the major stakehold-ers of the Darfur conflict with regard to land usage. Only by engaging voices associated with the center of power, the peripheries of power and from various levels, will it be possible to forge a workable consensus on the future, which can then be communicated to official actors and intermedi-aries. Suggested workshop topics include the following: methods for res-olution over land-related disputes; the question of different cultural traditions of "ownership" and "stewardship"; the use of development resources (both from within and outside the society) in a manner that does not aggravate hostility; and the whole problem of methods of manag-ing economic resources in a sustainable fashion so that Darfur society does not experience a future "tragedy of the commons." Participants are to be invited from the major resistance movements and coalitions, including LJM, SLA, JEM and others that have a political character as well as or in place of a military character. In addition, influential individuals from groups and constituencies that share interests with the GoS and represent-atives from civil society in Darfur will also be invited. Included in the invitees will be specialists in land usage and management who have direct experience in dealing with the types of issues and problems facing Darfur. Consistent with the model of the PSW, the number of participants will be less than 20, with a small team of facilitators in attendance to organize and manage the agenda. Participants will be carefully chosen in consultation with our local advisors, other Darfur experts and official actors to represent essential constituencies in a manner that garners respect both within and beyond those constituencies.

PSWs on the Cyprus conflict

Conflict background and current expression

The longstanding schism on the Mediterranean island of Cyprus is a pro-totypical ethnopolitical conflict in which significant differences in group identity are crossed with contrasting political ambitions, thus creating the conditions for conflict escalation, including the use of violence, and for conflict continuance over an extended period of time.[3] Positioned in the Eastern Mediterranean and at the crossroads of three continents, Cyprus has been subject to conquest by every major empire over recorded history, the most significant for the current conflict being the imposition of Ottoman rule for approximately 300 years until the British took over administration of the island in 1878, with formal colony status occurring in 1923. The infusion of Ottoman soldiers and citizens from Turkey and other parts of the empire created a minority ethnic and religious group of Muslim Turkish Cypriots alongside the majority Greek Cypriots, who had inhabited the island since ancient times. Under British rule, the relations between the two communities were generally harmonious in functional areas, such as business and administration, with segregation in housing, education and of course religion given the presence of the Christian Orthodox Church. In the 1950s, the Greek Cypriots began to agitate for independence, but with the intent to join the Greek motherland, which alienated the Turkish Cypriots given the history of violence between Greeks and Turks in other parts of the Mediterranean. The use of guerilla and terrorist tactics was strongly suppressed by the British, who nonetheless were looking for a way out that protected the security and identity of both communities. In 1960 an imposed constitution and other treaties provided for a power-sharing arrangement to protect Turkish Cypriot interests in ways that the Greek Cypriots saw as excessive. Three years of political maneuvering broke down with intercommunal violence in 1963–1964 and a United Nations peacekeeping force was installed and remains on the island today. In 1974, ten years of suppression and harassment of Turkish Cypriots ended when a Greek-inspired coup d'etat led to civil violence between Greek Cypriot ideological factions, and then between the two communities. Turkey intervened militarily to protect the minority community and this action ultimately divided the island into two homogeneous ethnic zones. A large number of Greek Cypriots fled the north of the island and became refugees in their own country, while a later UN-brokered transfer of populations saw the vast majority of Turkish Cypriots move to the Turkish occupied zone. Round after round of UN mediated negotiations over the past three decades have attempted to forge a political agreement to reconstitute Cyprus as a bicommunal, bizonal federal republic, but to no avail. The latest package deal, dubbed the Annan Plan, after the then UN Secretary General, failed to gain approval in a 2004 dual referendum in the Greek Cypriot community as most political parties recommended voting No in search of a better deal. The latest round of negotiations began in 2008 and struggled to forge a comprehensive agreement on the major issues of territory, governance, the status of Turkish "settlers," the return of or compensation for vacated property and so on. These talks, in which the UN took a limited third-party role, reached an impasse in early 2012, but did provide the context and the impetus for a PSW intervention with the intent of supporting the peace process.

The Cyprus PSW initiative

There is a long history of PSWs focusing on Cyprus, dating back to one of the first workshops organized by John Burton and his colleagues in 1966 (Fisher 2001). However, there have been very few sustained and consistent efforts operationalized through a series of workshops. The impetus for the current intervention grew out of a two-day symposium at the University of Denver in 2007 on the state of peacebuilding in the conflict that brought together a combination of Cypriot peacebuilders engaged in bicommunal work, along with a number of conflict resolution practitioners who had been engaged with the conflict over the past 20 or so years. The participants analyzed the current situation on the island and thought about ways to help move the peace process forward. It was agreed that the climate among the peace constituencies on the island was largely negative, with a degree of disarray and demoralization since the failure of the Annan Plan, and with the subsequent manipulation of the European Union accession as another means of prosecuting the conflict. Nonetheless, a small group of US-based peacebuilders continued their discussions after the symposium and agreed to develop a proposal for bicommunal work focusing largely on rapprochement without prejudice to the form of an eventual settlement.

The Cyprus team which formed out of the Denver symposium consisted of several scholar-practitioners, with extensive collective experience in the Cyprus conflict and based at a number of university centers for work in conflict resolution. These included two scholar-practitioners from the Peace Initiatives Project (PIP) at Portland State University, two from S-CAR at George Mason University, and one each from IPCR at American University, Tufts University and Arizona State University. The organizational tasks required for workshop implementation fell primarily to PIP and S-CAR, with minor contributions from IPCR, while all of the scholar-practitioners have contributed to the design, facilitation and evaluation roles required for workshop execution. Graduate student assistants from PIP, S-CAR and IPCR have also played an instrumental and essential role in carrying out the workshop project. The primary financial support for the workshops has been provided by a private donor through PIP, with S-CAR and IPCR also making contributions to the effort.

The workshops

In light of the analysis extending from the Denver Symposium, the first workshop in December of 2009 was designed to assist Cypriot peacebuilders in strengthening civil society involvement and support for the renewed peace process and for eventual rapprochement, without prejudice to the nature of an eventual settlement. A four-day workshop was held at S-CAR's retreat and conference facility in Mason Neck, VA, about 20 miles south of

Washington, DC, aptly named "Point of View." The sessions brought together Greek and Turkish Cypriot peacebuilders, many of them previous participants and then trainers in the bicommunal conflict resolution movement of the 1990s, who were heavily engaged in promoting the peace process and its potential benefits to their two communities. The participants and facilitators (as Cyprus experts) shared their perspectives of the current situation, including an analysis of the level of public support for the negotiations geared toward reunification in a federal state. With the assistance of the facilitators, the participants developed a force field analysis of the factors and dynamics supporting the peace process, as well as the resistances and barriers to it. Following the analysis, the discussions focused on identifying the opportunities and strategies for civil society actors to influence public opinion and to increase support for the peace process. In addition, the participants identified supportive strategies for external stakeholders (the "motherlands" and other members of the international community) to enact if the negotiations resulted in a proposed settlement. A number of conclusions were articulated by the participants. It was agreed that civil society organizations (including those represented in the workshop) should use all available electronic means (including social media) to disseminate the potential benefits of a federal solution, and to communicate the basic framework agreement that already existed (Cyprus as a federation with a single sovereignty consisting of two equal status states). It was agreed that the participants through their organizations should work to identify and articulate a common vision in order to mobilize the peace constituency alongside of the efforts by the political parties. It was also proposed that civil society needed to work at the intercommunal level (as well as within each community) to create an infrastructure for action in support of the peace process. Finally, it was asserted that Greece and Turkey should be encouraged to share their perspectives on negotiations and to make their support for a federal solution clearly known to the public in both communities. Following the workshop, a comprehensive report was prepared by the consortium in consultation with the participants and was made available for dissemination to interested parties. In addition, members of the consortium visited the island at points over the next year to discuss participants' reactions to the workshop and subsequent activities in support of the peace process.

A second workshop was held approximately one year after the first in January 2011, the timing being determined by a combination of available funding and a sense of what focus would be useful at what point in time for another unofficial intervention. In light of the continuing importance of the support of the two motherlands in the peace process (and its relative absence), the consortium in consultation with local associates decided to plan a two-phase workshop. The first two-day phase of the five-day workshop brought together some of the same Cypriot peacebuilders, who had attended the first session and could thus provide continuity, supplemented by advisors to the two leaders, who could provide a closer connection to the peace process. The second phase of three days engaged the Cypriots with influential participants from Greece and Turkey, two of whom were high-level policy advisors to the two Presidents, along with well known journalists from each country, who could influence public opinion. The goal of the workshop was to develop strategies for the Cypriots to continue to support the peace process and to discuss strategies for the two motherlands to influence negotiations in a positive direction. Both potential outcomes were of course predicated on progress in the negotiations, which has been mixed and has now moved into a period of impasse. In the first phase, the Cypriot participants developed their shared analysis of the current situation on the island with a focus on negotiations and public opinion. In the second phase, this analysis was provided to the Greek and Turkish participants, and their perceptions were then integrated into the analysis to produce a wider and more complex picture. In the problem-solving phase of the workshop, the participants developed options for potential confidence building measures that both the primary parties and others could implement. A number of strategies were identified that Greece and Turkey could take in order to directly support the negotiation process and also to influence public opinion toward greater understanding and approval. Finally, the group identified some of the incentives and disincentives for Greece and Turkey to become more engaged in the peace process. In its conclusions, the workshop noted that opportunities for moving the peace process forward existed, and indicated that an integrated package of confidence building measures was most likely to be successful as opposed to single efforts. It was proposed that at some point the negotiations needed to be broadened to four-party talks, particularly around issues such as security guarantees, in which the "motherlands" would join the two primary parties. Overall, the call was for Greece and Turkey to become more active and visible in the interest of a settlement, and also to work to promote a Cyprus settlement to their own citizens to reduce the resistance to an agreement that might be forthcoming. As with the first workshop, a comprehensive report was produced by the consortium and distributed to participants for use in their communication and interaction with their various constituencies.

Unfortunately, the impasse in the negotiations means that the various opportunities and activities envisaged to support the peace process have become inoperable in the current situation. At the time of writing, the UN and the various parties have indicated that the talks are stalemated and further that the holding of an international conference to address the conflict is not presently viable. At the same time, the discovery and development of hydrocarbon deposits (mainly natural gas) in the Eastern Mediterranean off the southeast coast of Cyprus has created a new and very contentious issue among the parties. The Greek Cypriots are intent on developing the hydrocarbon reserves in cooperation with Israel, and the

Turkish Cypriots and Turkey have raised vehement objections to this course of action. Drilling is proceeding in the Republic of Cyprus field, and in response Turkey is carrying out test drilling in north Cyprus. Thus, not only is the rhetoric heating up, but also the maneuvering, and the prospects of renewing the peace process are receding every day. It is clear that a situation which could be turned into a cooperative venture to build confidence will likely escalate to a contentious interaction with multiple negative consequences. Thus, the opportunity exists to bring influentials and experts from the various parties together for objective analysis and creative problem solving on the hydrocarbon issue. Plans are now underway to hold a third Cyprus workshop with participants from the two communities and the two "motherlands" in the spring of 2013.

Conclusion

A systems perspective on conflict, such as that taken by John Burton, alerts analysts that a wide range of actors and dynamics are involved in complex ethnopolitical conflicts which escalate to violence and continue over a period of time. Thus, there are multiple options for intervention by conflict resolution specialists in terms of participants and issues. It is therefore possible and desirable to adapt a PSW intervention to the salient characteristics and actors in a conflict at any point in time. The focus of the first Darfur workshop was chosen as the relations among the rebel factions as these were critical at that point in time to progress in the peace process. In contrast, the focus in the first Cyprus workshop was on the two primary parties and participants who were engaged in peacebuilding activities in order to carry out an assessment of how the struggling peace process could be better supported. Then in both cases, the focus was broadened to bring in more constituencies from Darfur and to bring in representatives of the "motherlands" of Cyprus respectively. Lastly, in both cases, a currently critical issue has been identified as the next substantive focus for a PSW – an issue on which shared analysis and the creation of positive alternatives will be central to the next phase of the conflict interaction. Parties, stakeholders and participants will be chosen in accord with their engagement in the central issue and the potential they hold for a constructive resolution of it. The adaptability of the PSW method in these two cases thus demonstrates a useful flexibility that is not apparent in the existing literature on practice. At the same time, interveners need to be careful in exercising this flexibility, as a shift in focus can have repercussions on the future viability of the intervention. For example, in focusing on the factions within the Darfur rebel movement, the possibility of alienating or producing a perception of partiality in supporters of the GoS might hamper the ability to refocus on the two primary parties in the conflict at a later date. In the Cyprus case, the shift of focus to the two primary external parties might cause a negative reaction among the Greek and Turkish Cypriots in that the principle of a "made in Cyprus" solution has been violated.

The validity of a BHN analysis for these two PSW interventions is very apparent, both in an initial understanding of the conflicts, as well as how such an analysis is represented in the concerns and aspirations of the conflicting parties, particularly the ones whose BHNs are under greater threat. The importance of the need for security goes without saying, especially in the Darfur conflict where approximately 300,000 have lost their lives, thousands more have been injured, and two to three million continue to live in deprived conditions in IDP camps. At the same time, the workshop discussions demonstrated the importance of identity among Darfurians in terms of their identification with Darfur, its culture and its aspirations for the future as a viable collective entity within a Sudanese federation. Recognition of Darfur identity goes hand in hand with the redress that is being sought for the multiple forms of marginalization experienced by the people of Darfur. In the Cyprus case, fear over security has been a driver in the conflict for both the Greek and the Turkish Cypriots, although this has been differentially magnified at different points in the conflict. Given the events of 1963 to 1974, the Turkish Cypriots need for security drives many of the demands they still bring to the negotiating table (e.g. the "Turkish guarantee"), while for the Greek Cypriots the invasion and exodus of 1974 reinforce their perception of being locked in an existential conflict. The differing identities of the two collectivities help to create prisms through which the conflict's history, current expression and potential resolution are crafted into very different and incompatible narratives that render negotiation a perplexing struggle. The conclusion is thus that in both of these very different cases, PSWs can serve a valuable pre- or para-negotiation function in the context of an overall peace process.

Notes

1 Portions of this chapter were revised from two papers presented at the Annual Convention of the International Studies Association, San Diego, CA, April 2012: R.J. Fisher, "Problem-Solving Workshops on Cyprus: Extending the Focus to Greece and Turkey," and C. Thomas and R.J. Fisher, "Using Problem-Solving Workshops to Elicit Commonalities and Encourage Coordination among Rebel Movements and Civil Society in Darfur, Sudan." The author would like to thank anonymously the organizers, facilitators and participants in the Darfur/Sudan and the Cyprus problem-solving workshops for their willingness to allow participant observation of the workshops in creating this documentation, which is also available in more detail in the workshop reports. For inquiries, please contact rfisher@american.edu.

2 These and other rules offered by Burton in his 1987 *Handbook* are discussed in detail in Christopher Mitchell's Chapter 8 in this volume.

3 Given that the Cyprus conflict is generally better known in the field of conflict resolution, only an abbreviated description will be given and no references will be provided for what is essentially common knowledge.

References

Brosche, J. and Rothbart, D. (2012) *The Continuing Crisis in Darfur.* London: Routledge.

Burton, J.W. (1969) *Conflict and Communication: The Use of Controlled Communication in International Relations.* London: MacMillan.

Burton, J.W. (1987) *Resolving Deep-rooted Conflict: A Handbook.* Lanham, MD: University Press of America.

Burton, J.W. (1990) *Conflict: Human Needs Theory.* New York: St. Martin's Press.

de Waal, A. (ed.) (2007) *War in Darfur: And the Search for Peace.* Cambridge, MA: Harvard University Global Equity Initiative and Justice Africa.

Fisher, R.J. (1990) "Needs theory, social identity and an eclectic model of conflict," in J.W. Burton (ed.) *Conflict: Human Needs Theory,* New York: St. Martin's.

Fisher, R.J. (2001) "Cyprus: the failure of mediation and the escalation of an identity-based conflict to an adversarial impasse," *Journal of Peace Research,* 38: 307–326.

O'Fahey, R.S. (2006) "Does Darfur have a future in Sudan?" *Fletcher Forum of World Affairs,* 30, Winter: 27–39.

11 Basic Human Needs in practice

The Georgian–South Ossetian Point of View process

Susan Allen Nan and Jacquie L. Greiff

When individuals in conflict explain to us all of the varying reasons why their particular conflict is unique, why the specific details and the personal nature of their conflict make it unlike any other, we tend to agree with them. However, while acting as a facilitator or convener of a conflict resolution process, we encourage parties to reach beyond this sense of uniqueness and to learn from other cases of conflict and conflict resolution processes. How have others forged more constructive relationships during the aftermath of war? What of those approaches might prove useful tools when dealing with the conflict at hand?

Across many conflicts, we have found that the Basic Human Needs approach resonates deeply. In post-war contexts, survivors find hope in acknowledging that the "enemy" is human, has needs, and that the parties may even share some basic human needs. Moreover, a focus on basic human needs can also offer a path forward when all other conversations are at a standstill.

This chapter presents an example of ways that an implicit Basic Human Needs approach offered Georgians and South Ossetians direction in the months and years immediately after the August 2008 Russian–Georgian–South Ossetian–Abkhaz war. Basic Human Needs has informed many approaches to conflict resolution practice that have been detailed in the Analytical Problem-solving Workshop model (Mitchell and Banks 1996) and other practices within the family of Interactive Conflict Resolution (Fisher 1997). And Basic Human Needs can be seen as a fundamental rationale for other processes that build on, adapt and innovate to address particular conflicts. Such is the case with the Georgian–South Ossetian Point of View process, an unofficial "Track Two" or "Track One and a Half" process (Nan *et al.* 2009) that began three months after the August 2008 war and continues as of this writing in summer 2012 as a complement to the official Geneva Talks process.

Before focusing on the Georgian–South Ossetian Point of View process (POV process), a brief review of the conflict context illustrates the divergent understandings of the conflict and surrounding conflicts as seen by the various parties, and also the broader structure of the peace process within which the POV process takes place. Next, the POV process is presented, followed by a discussion of the ways Basic Human Needs approaches informed the process. Finally, further research should consider questions raised by this case of Basic Human Needs in practice. What challenges remain to guide further innovation in the next generation of conflict resolution practice?

The conflict context: which conflict?

The Georgian–South Ossetian Point of View process focuses on one particular relationship within a web of conflictual and interrelated relationships in the South Caucasus. As described in more detail elsewhere (Nan 2011), there are diverse understandings of the conflicts, different names for the conflicts and, of course, divergent views of the best ways forward. First, it is necessary to arrive at some clarity regarding the various names of the various conflicts. Georgians tend to speak about a "Georgian–Russian" conflict, while Abkhaz, South Ossetians and Russians emphasize a "Georgian–Abkhaz" conflict and a "Georgian–South Ossetian conflict." These differing terms highlight the deeply politicized nature of the conflicts. Place names are equally controversial and politicized. Georgians may refer to the "Tskhinvali region," avoiding mention of the ethnic "Ossetian" title of the larger region, while South Ossetians refer to the "Republic of South Ossetia," implying internationally recognized sovereignty. Abkhaz refer to city names in Abkhazia without the "i" at the end of most Georgian cities, thus referring to the largest city as "Sukhum," while Georgians refer to that same city as "Sukhumi." For a scholar-practitioner of conflict resolution seeking to engage impartially in the area, it can be hard to say anything without inadvertently privileging one discourse over another. Here, the written word allows use of "(i)" at the end of city names to signify the city by two different names simultaneously, such as Tskhinval(i). In cases such as Akhalgori/Leningor, two entirely separate names are used by the opposing sides in referring to the same region and its capital city. The writing here seeks to present the competing narratives surrounding these areas, thus, whenever possible, we use wording here that does not privilege one of the narratives over others, and we seek to use the words embraced by each narrative respectively when presenting that particular narrative.

While experienced peacebuilders throughout the region have woven together many complex and detailed views of the interlocking conflicts, acknowledging elements of many perspectives, several clearly contrasting stories can be identified as the dominant competing narratives. A consideration of these competing perspectives will therefore be introduced here, in brief, in an effort to offer some context to the later discussions. The contrasting views considered here are stereotypical Georgian, Abkhaz, South Ossetian and Russian viewpoints. As such, it is recognized that clearly not all individuals in the ethnic groups described will or do see things with the respective stereotypical views described below. However, these views provide a sense of the extreme divergence of narratives, and are therefore useful in contextualizing the more nuanced, complex understandings of the conflict(s) at play.

Relationships between political units form the basis for many of the conflictual narratives and viewpoints between the parties. Georgians tend to operate within the collective memory of a history of oppression by Russia, often describing their relationship with the metaphor of Russia as a big bear to the north of much smaller Georgia, and seeing that bear as a hungry intruder in Georgia today. Georgian President Mikheil Saakashvili stated that Russia "is dreaming about how to abolish Georgia's sovereignty" (*Civil Georgia* 2011). Parallel to this, there is also an Abkhaz view of Georgian oppression of the less numerous Abkhaz people, reflected in the image of then President of Georgia Zviad Gamsakhurdia calling for "Georgia for the Georgians" in 1991 (Cohen 2001). Similarly, South Ossetians also speak of Georgian oppression of the less numerous South Ossetian people, along with a relatively fresh memory of betrayal, when Georgian President Mikheil Saasashvili reassured residents of South Ossetia that he had instructed Georgian military and police not to return fire on the evening of August 7, 2008, just before more intensive fighting began that very night (Saakashvili 2008). On the Russian side, there is an understanding of Russian intervention as a beneficial and necessary process towards protecting Abkhaz, South Ossetians and also Russian citizens from Georgian attack. This view resonates with South Ossetian Eduard Kokoity's praising Russian Prime Minister Vladimir Putin: "decisions you have taken saved a whole nation from extermination" (BBC 2009). Of course, this view contrasts entirely with the Georgian view, which sees Russia as first an invading and now an occupying force.

In addition to these leading political narratives, relationships between individuals from each of these conflicting groups also influence perceptions. Many Georgians speak readily and fondly of particular friends who are Abkhaz or South Ossetians, and will recall many years of high rates of intermarriage between Georgians and South Ossetians in particular. There is a Georgian sense that general inter-ethnic relations were quite good in the years before violence broke out. Revealing a slightly different attitude, although Abkhaz will recall individual Georgian neighbors with whom they were friendly prior to these individuals fleeing during the war, they will also recount a litany of offenses committed against them in the years prior to the war. South Ossetians will also speak of good personal relations between themselves and individual Georgians prior to the conflict. However, this shared appreciation for positive personal relationships across the ethnic divides becomes clouded by a difference in perceptions of those relationships. The Georgian view (not universal amongst Georgians) that South Ossetians are guests in Georgia contrasts with the South

Ossetian view that the South Ossetian territory is their homeland. The Georgian view of Abkhaz and Georgians having always lived together in Abkhazia contrasts with Abkhaz claims of a Georgianization of Abkhazia. When the Abkhaz archives were destroyed during fighting during the 1990s, that loss resonated with a broader Abkhaz fear of the destruction of their language and culture and a resulting domination by Georgian language and culture. As a reaction to the heavy Russian linguistic influence during the Soviet era, Georgian school children are more likely to study English than Russian, as Georgians have very quickly expressed an interest in western European languages.

Along with these different views of the dynamics of friendship amongst individual people, equally disparate views exist in explanation for the cause of the problems between the ethnic groups. Georgian viewpoints tend to center on Russian interference, describing a Russian attempt to control Georgia by dividing and conquering it, with particular suspicion falling on Russian Prime Minister Vladimir Putin. On the other side, Abkhaz and South Ossetians tend to point to a series of actions by Georgian leaders that they see as inflammatory or at least as missed opportunities to engage constructively, with particular concern currently on Georgian President Mikheil Saakashvili's perceived willingness to use force to restore Georgian territorial integrity. The Georgian government's continual reassurance of its 2011 unilateral declaration on non-use-of-force is given little credibility amongst Abkhaz, South Ossetians or Russians. Russian views instead highlight a need for Russian intervention in an effort to protect the non-Georgian populations of Abkhazia and South Ossetia. While Georgians describe a Russian attempt to control Georgia, Russians see US military training shared with Georgia as unconstructive and threatening to Abkhaz and South Ossetians.

The views of where agency lies in these conflict settings also differ between the groups. Russians wonder why the USA cannot control Georgia's actions, frowning upon what they see as the USA having embraced Georgia as though it were a client state. Meanwhile, Georgians explain there is little reason to expect serious negotiations with Leonid Tibilov, whom the remaining population of South Ossetia regards as their recently elected president, because Georgians perceive Tibilov as certainly a "puppet" of Russia, and also perhaps continuing what Georgians see as a culture of rampant corruption within South Ossetia.

As can naturally be assumed, such divergent conflict narratives lead to incredibly different views of what would be appropriate and acceptable responses to the conflicts. From the stereotypical Georgian perspective, the necessity lies in reconciliation, in rebuilding ties, developing increased western support, and engaging with Abkhaz and South Ossetian people within the Georgian understanding of leadership structures and without acknowledging the leadership structures currently operating on those territories. South Ossetians on the other hand, particularly in the months just after August 2008, have expressed an interest in creating a "Berlin wall" separating the Georgian military forces from South Ossetia. Generally, this group appreciates Russian security guarantees, is in favor of minimal contact across the conflict divide and emphasizes that contact, when it is necessary, should be directed to the authorities. While Abkhaz did not have the "Berlin wall" reaction of South Ossetians, in part because of their different experiences of August 2008, and remain more critical of some of the Russian influence in Abkhazia today, they also approach limited contact with Georgians cautiously.

These differing goals do lend themselves to the discovery of at least two potentially common visions: the humanitarian vision and the related non-use-of-force or force-as-a-last-resort vision. The humanitarian vision in essence sees that concrete human interests, such as having a home, access to water, being healthy, connecting with friends and family and being gainfully employed, are interests that are appropriate and reasonable for people in all the involved ethnic groups. This provides some area for coop-eration across the conflict divides in efforts to open these opportunities to people who suffered from the wars and continue to suffer the after-effects of the wars. Cooperation to care for an urgently ill child or to repair a broken dam can provide an impetus for working across the conflict divide towards non-political humanitarian goals.

Finally, a resonance also exists across many sectors with the Georgian, Abkhaz, South Ossetian and Russian narratives, which call for a discussion of differences and possible ways of bridging these as preferable to return-ing to war. The Georgian non-use-of-force voices seek ways to settle what seem to be ongoing conflicts (primarily with Russia, but also with Abkhaz and South Ossetians) through such discussions and meetings. The Abkhaz and South Ossetian non-use-of-force voices, however, view the conflicts as already settled, and therefore see no reason for their side to attack. In this vein, they are vocal about their hopes that their neighbor Georgia will respect this same view, and not use force. As is probably clear by now, even committing not to start a war is a political problem because of the com-peting narratives described above. With this difficulty at the forefront of considerations, Russians insist that Georgia should, in cooperation with the Abkhaz and South Ossetians, sign commitments not to use force. Georgians see the need for a Georgian–Russian set of mutual commit-ments, and wish to avoid any signatures that could seem to imply recogni-tion of the Abkhaz and South Ossetian authorities operating on those territories today.

Overall peace process

The Georgian–South Ossetian Point of View process takes place as part of an interrelated web of many peace initiatives. During this writing in the fall of 2012, there are multiple initiatives aimed at bridging across the conflict divides, the first of which started as early as the fall of 2008. The goals of the Georgian–South Ossetian Point of View process were described by its participants initially as opening channels for communication and preventing a return to war (Nan *et al.* 2008). Early initiatives in the Fall of 2008 and early 2009 demonstrated to participants that constructive contact was possible and, as participants gained confidence in their ability to interact with one another without the fear of accusations or blame of being traitors, these efforts expanded in number.

On the official side of negotiations, the Geneva Talks have served as a forum for those in leadership positions in the various conflict areas to meet every few months. Several successes have emerged out of these talks, including the convening of the Incident Prevention and Response Mechanisms (IPRMs). One IPRM bridges across the Georgian–Abkhaz divide, while the other one bridges across the Georgian–South Ossetian divide. These working-level discussions address concrete incidents of concern, which may vary from missing or arrested persons to wayward cows that somehow made their way across the dividing conflict lines. These official processes, both the Geneva Talks and the IPRM, are referred to as "Track One diplomacy."

In addition to these official talks, several parallel dialogues also exist, providing a space where those in positions of authority, together with non-governmental people and organizations, are able to meet in their personal capacities and assess opportunities for improving conflictual relationships and planning confidence building measures. These meetings allow for the consideration of many perspectives, ensuring that the resulting confidence building initiatives take into account the views of the members of each affected side and are thus able to have maximum constructive impact in all areas affected by the conflicts. Such meetings are referred to as "Track One and a Half diplomacy" and, although they may involve individuals in positions of authority, participants do not represent their place of work and the meetings are entirely unofficial.

Finally, a wide range of "Track Two diplomacy" initiatives are underway. Diamond and McDonald's (1996) concept of multi-track diplomacy highlights eight kinds of "diplomacy" initiatives beyond official governmental diplomacy: professional conflict resolution; business; private citizens; research, training and education; activism; religious; funding; and public opinion/communication. Each of these areas of work are engaged in peacemaking initiatives in the Caucasus region.

The Georgian–South Ossetian view of the process

The first of the Georgian–South Ossetian Point of View workshops (POV workshops) was convened in the fall of 2008 at George Mason's School for Conflict Analysis and Resolution retreat center, called Point of View, in Lorton, Virginia, and brought together 13 Georgian and South Ossetian civil society leaders. Since this time, meetings have occurred approximately every three months, "with a goal of further catalyzing constructive confidence building, sharing highly informed understandings of the conflict dynamics with advisors and decision-makers on both sides of the divide, and ultimately contributing to peace and security in the South Caucasus and beyond" (Center for Peacemaking Practice 2012). The majority of the meetings have taken place in Istanbul, though a few have occurred in Yerevan, one was held in Jerusalem, and two (including the first) occurred in the Washington, D.C. region. The process has become known for the place of its first meeting, Point of View.

In the absence of regular face-to-face meetings in unofficial formats along the ceasefire line or widespread freedom of movement across the ceasefire line, the Point of View workshops provide a format for direct discussions amongst individuals working with the Georgian and South Ossetian leadership structures and civil societies, and international community peacebuilders engaged in the region. People participate in the Point of View discussions in their personal capacity without status complications.

By providing an impartial and welcoming format for informal discussions that increase understanding and shared planning for confidence building, the Point of View process contributes long-term toward increased confidence and increased Georgian–South Ossetian abilities to work out their differences non-violently. More specifically, the Point of View discussions continue to contribute to decisions Georgians, South Ossetians and the international community will take that will shape the peace process. For example, POV workshop discussions have preceded suggested shifts by one or both of the parties that support increased economic ties across the ceasefire line, and increased cooperation in various non-political sectors, such as education, culture, health and water initiatives. Long-term, such progress will build the relationships and renewed trust that will pave the way for non-violent settlement of the political status issues.

The POV process has contributed to numerous positive outcomes in Georgian–South Ossetian relations, including: joint research and analysis reports; former neighbors dialogues; permission granted for visits across the ceasefire line; missing persons cooperation; release of teenage prisoners after a visit by Georgian Point of View participants to the South Ossetian side to request their release; resumption of the Incident Prevention and Response Mechanism local meetings in October 2010 just two weeks after a Point of View discussion of how to restart these meetings; the collaborative rebuilding of the Zonkari dam coordinated by the OSCE with informal technical discussions facilitated as an additional stream of the Point of View process; and increased coordination amongst the various initiatives focused on Georgian–South Ossetian reconciliation.

Each of the workshop agendas includes some consideration of how the activities of the Point of View series, and related initiatives developed by participants, can best complement the other initiatives under development by groups such as IKV Pax Christi, Berghof Foundation, Conciliation Resources, University of California-Irvine, Kvinn-za-Kvinn, Russian–Georgian dialogue, etc. Currently, very few unofficial contacts are happening across the South Ossetian–Georgian dividing line. One of these, the series of meetings of women IDPs and their former neighbors, is led by a Georgian and a South Ossetian participant in the Point of View process, who further develop their women's initiative in light of Point of View discussions. The participants and facilitators of the Point of View process also seek a variety of ways to contribute constructively to the potential of the official Geneva process. Participation by Geneva participants in the POV discussions has aided the flow of information between the official and unofficial processes.

Stages of the process

The structure and progression of the series of meetings has moved from initial explorations of how the group can talk and learn together (the main focus of initial meetings in 2008 and 2009), on to an exploration of locally focused confidence building measures (2009–2010), and further towards explorations of an impact both locally and globally (2011 and beyond). These stages are explained in more detail below.

Stage 1: Initial explorations

Initial meetings in the Point of View series encouraged Georgian and South Ossetian participants to explore whether it was possible for them to talk together, and if there was a point to such discussions. The resulting discovery was that, in fact, there were several things that it was necessary for these individuals to learn which they could only learn from each other. The strongest result of these initial meetings was an acknowledgement that neither side had adequate information on the humanitarian needs of civilians living around the ceasefire line. This information would be needed by both sides in order to adequately address these needs, and thus this became the first issue on which participants decided that they were able to come together and cooperate to address. By cooperating with CARE International, Point of View facilitators followed up on this shared Georgian and South Ossetian desire, which led to a survey and CARE International report on the needs of individuals living on the ceasefire line, the process and results of which are discussed in more detail in the following section.

Stage 2: Confidence building measures with a local focus

With an understanding on basic relief needs accomplished, POV participants began to question what further types of confidence-building measures they could explore towards the goal of restoring some normalcy to life, regardless of the political situation. Discussions formed around issues of drinking water, irrigation water, gas, health care, journalists' cooperation, and many other important issues effecting daily life. Through cooperation and trust built during the workshop process, many (but not all) of these issues were addressed in ways that synergized efforts across the conflict divide. The POV workshops came to be a forum where those interested in carrying out confidence building measures would come to test out their ideas, make sure they were not duplicating ongoing initiatives, and seek out willing partners for implementation. The workshop agendas included time to meet in small groups on specific developing initiatives. Individuals affiliated with international governmental organizations began to attend some of the Point of View meetings, allowing the international community approaches to the region to be considered at the workshops. One international who participated was an advisor to an international mediator, thus, the portion of the workshops focused on international approaches became known as "advice to the advisors." The presence of internationals proved useful in highlighting potential avenues for pursuing funding for promising new confidence building initiatives developed at the workshops, and also paved the way for developing more of a global-level impact from the Point of View workshops.

Stage 3: Linking local and global

As the work towards confidence building measures in local settings grew and flourished, POV workshops began to raise the idea of expanding this cooperation to a larger scale. At successive meetings, Point of View workshops focused on one or two potential areas of broader impact. For example, health care became a focus at one meeting. Journalists' cooperation for increased cross-conflict understanding became a focus at another meeting. Health care professionals, journalists, researchers and analysts from both sides were invited to come and discuss possibilities for preparing appropriate responses to, for example, a region-wide health epidemic, or a major regional natural catastrophe. Existing cooperation on specific local level areas lent a sense of possibility to these discussions.

Stage 4: Taking ownership

Currently, the POV process continues to convene three workshops per year, with a momentum towards building an eventual fourth stage in which outside conveners would no longer be necessary, and participants would be able to take ownership of the process entirely. Georgian and South Ossetian long-term participants have begun taking on more and more facilitation responsibility. The full transfer of convening responsibility to Georgians and South Ossetians may still be several years off, as, until such time as increased freedom of movement is available to connect

Georgians and South Ossetians locally, outside facilitators appear necessary for the coordination required to arrange and prepare international meetings, and to raise the funds for participants to travel to these. In addition, outside facilitators currently serve as impartial arbiters, and are occasionally called upon to make impartial decisions without bias between the Georgian and South Ossetian facilitators.

An implicit Basic Human Needs approach

As was mentioned earlier, the Point of View process began with an implicit Basic Human Needs approach. Beginning the first dialogue with an awareness of basic needs on each side of the ceasefire line allowed participants to relate to each other on a human level, and to move forward in cooperation, despite the fresh memories of war. The benefits of this were evident as early as the first meeting, in 2008, during which, as was noted above, participants identified humanitarian concerns as a relatable, non-political issue on which they were able to connect personally and emotionally. Discussions surrounding issues of missing persons were critical to this meeting, and participants agreed that they would be able to come together and help each other find mutually workable solutions to humanitarian concerns, outside of the tensions of the political sphere.

This demonstrates the power of universal human concerns to overpower political positions that tend to create immobile "sticking points." While the participants of these early dialogues did not agree with each other on many large political questions, or on historical or ideological understandings of the conflict, they were able to come together and recognize the shared human concerns of, for example, families unable to find their loved ones.

This initial breakthrough in understanding and agreement led to the decision described above, during the initial meeting in December 2008, that more information was needed concerning the situation and needs of those individuals living on and around the ceasefire line. A request was put forward for a survey of needs and CARE International partnered with Point of View facilitators Susan Allen Nan and Lara Olsen to organize and carry out this initiative. Local residents were hired to conduct surveys on both sides of the line and, in a March 2009 meeting in Yerevan, a joint analysis of results was carried out. Finally, in the June 2009 POV meeting, the results of both surveys were shared and for the first time an overall understanding of the needs of communities on both sides of the ceasefire line was compiled. The resulting report (CARE International 2009) presented a comprehensive assessment of the humanitarian needs of both parties. The existence of this report led directly to the discussion and implementation of confidence building measures designed specifically to address these needs, as well as others that arose out of later meetings.

To give an idea of some of these measures and the ways in which a Basic Human Needs framework has supported and encouraged productive discussions, a few projects discussed at POV meetings will be considered as examples below.

Reconstruction of the Zonkari Dam

During the March 2011 POV meeting, participants "discussed the critical state of the Zonkari resevoir" and "noted the necessity of preventing an accident at the dam" (George Mason University 2011). A spinoff process was developed out of this discussion through which a series of several small meetings with engineering experts from both sides focused on technical issues of the Zonkari Dam repair. After the first of these technical discussions, an OSCE-coordinated effort to repair the Zonkari Dam was strengthened by the relationships developed between South Ossetian and Georgian engineers during the unofficial Point of View technical discussions. The technical discussions allowed a range of experts to consider particular technical obstacles that were delaying repairs. Cooperation has continued, with visits by a Georgian engineer within the larger OSCE-led rehabilitation team. The US State Department Bureau of Population, Refugees, and Migration funded a series of small, technical meetings in Istanbul focused on additional challenges of dam repair. These meetings provided an apolitical environment that allowed technical experts to problem-solve together in a neutral setting. In addition, at many POV meetings, one or two technical experts from each side participated in the full discussion and also held additional side conversations during meals and along the margins of the meetings. For example, in a January 2012 meeting in Bethlehem, Georgian and South Ossetian engineers sat together and collaboratively developed a new approach for raising a stuck gate at the dam. Eight weeks later, that new approach proved successful, the gate was raised, and water began flowing through irrigation channels that had been dry for many years.

Health care

The topic of health care has been raised at several of the POV dialogues. During the March 2011 discussion, "the sides exchanged information about the state of health care in both societies and efforts to improve healthcare, as well as about possible mutual contacts with an aim of developing more effective and rapid treatment procedures" (George Mason University 2011). The process of developing relationships between health care professionals on each side of the ceasefire line serves as one way of preparing to address any future health catastrophe, for example, an epidemic that crosses lines or a major accident on either side. Establishing connections and cooperation on a smaller scale now increases the possibilities for greater large-scale cooperation of this sort should the need arise in the future.

Gas and irrigation

There are many complex issues surrounding the repair of irrigation channels that cross back and forth across ceasefire line, carrying water from the mountains on the South Ossetian side to villages on both sides. Some of these discussions have been linked to discussions of a gas pipeline that used to carry gas to the Leningor/Akhalgori region. The POV dialogues have allowed a space for a consideration of the technical implications and needs of such projects, and an acknowledgement that this is separate from the politics surrounding these situations. In the March 2011 meeting, "the participants came to an agreement that the rehabilitation of irrigation systems, as well as the restoration of gas supply to Leningor/Akhalgori region are not only technical and political issues, but also humanitarian, and need to be resolved without their politicization and with the help of international organizations" (George Mason University 2011).

Each of the issues highlighted briefly here have been politicized by one or more parties in the conflict. However, the ability of participants to discuss these issues within the framework of basic humanity, and those things that unite us, rather than divide us, has made an enormous difference in terms of the possibilities for collaboration and constructive dialogue.

This subsection was intentionally titled an *implicit* Basic Human Needs approach because although, as is clear through the above discussion and examples, this framework played an enormous role in the POV process, it was never a decision on the part of the facilitators or the participants to introduce this as an explicit framework. Perhaps, in essence, what the participants of the POV process have implicitly accessed is the fact that an attention to basic human needs reminds us of that which is common about us, rather than that which separates us. And it is this that opens up doorways for listening, cooperation and collaboration.

Such an understanding draws largely from an understanding of basic human needs such as that presented by Maslow (1943), in which physiological needs are seen as the most fundamental of human needs, and the basis upon which all else is built. Thus, the recognition by the POV participants that the first issue on which they needed to work together was the relief of the humanitarian needs of those living on the ceasefire line, serves as an example of an implicit recognition of shared physiological human needs, and how these were able to serve as a source of bonding and understanding.

However, it should also be noted that the very design of the POV workshops lends itself to an implicit satisfaction of several of Burton's most fundamental human needs: those of recognition and identity (Burton 1997). In many of his writings, Burton sees these psychological needs as holding the greatest human import, even over Maslow's physiological needs (1979, 1990, 1997). As Burton (1997: 26) explains, "if we are to deal with problems of societies we cannot afford to work within a construct that assumes certain institutional givens, but disregards human aspirations and ontological needs." In other words, societal problems will not be solved (and conversations between conflict parties will not occur) unless a basic recognition and satisfaction of the ontological human needs for identity, recognition and security is achieved.

The essential format of the POV meetings, from their very inception, has been to bring together Georgians and South Ossetians and to allow them to speak across the conflict divide. Even in the simple act of a South Ossetian sharing a statement that is heard by a Georgian, whether the two agree on the essence of the argument or not, provides an essential return of agency, of identity and of recognition. The initial phase of the POV process as described in the previous section, in which participants explored the simple question of whether they could speak to, and be heard by, the other side, can thus be seen as one of the most crucial steps when considered within the framework of Burton's arguments. Having some part of one's identity valued by the simple fact that one is invited into the room and listened to, may have served as the groundwork that, implicit as it was, led to the possibility of any further or greater collaboration.

Conclusion

Participants in the Point of View process have continuously engaged with issues through a Basic Human Needs lens. This lens has set a tone of mutual respect for the humanity of "the other," regardless of political differences, and has been the cornerstone that has led to constructive engagement throughout many dialogues. Recognizing the humanity of the other, and the commonalities of all humans, is a fundamental shift in a post-war context. The initial act of bringing Georgians and South Ossetians into one room and allowing both sides to speak and be heard can be seen as the first step towards a satisfaction of ontological needs for recognition and identity, and the resultant collaborations highlighted above may be seen to serve as one example of the power of such needs-satisfaction in a conflict resolution process. Although the individuals engaged in the POV process do have political differences, they have moved forward in cooperation by honoring each others humanity, which has allowed them to talk to each other in a civilized way.

Further research should consider questions raised by this case of Basic Human Needs in practice. How can other post-war dialogue series be structured to take on an implicit Basic Human Needs agenda? In what forms and contexts will such agendas be constructive? What further innovation can guide the next generation of conflict resolution practice? And, for the Point of View process, how can the parties move beyond confidence building measures that address some basic human needs, to eventually address the long-term security, identity, and development needs on both sides? How will the Georgians and South Ossetians conclude a mutually satisfactory political agreement that offers both ethnic groups long-term security, identity and development?

References

BBC (2009) "Russia Vows to Protect South Ossetia." Online. Available: http://news.bbc.co.uk/2/hi/8223443.stm [accessed November 18, 2011].

Burton, J.W. (1979) *Deviance Terrorism and War: The Process of Solving Unsolved Social and Political Problems.* Australian National University Press, Canberra.

Burton, J.W. (1990) *Conflict: Basic Human Needs.* St. Martins Press, New York.

Burton, J.W. (1997) *Violence Explained.* Manchester University Press, Manchester.

CARE International (2009) *Community Perceptions and Conflict Prevention Needs in the Georgian–South Ossetian Boundary Area and among IDPs in Georgia,* March 2009.

Center for Peacemaking Practice (2012) *The Georgian–South Ossetian Civic Point of View Process.* Online. Available: http://scar.gmu.edu/south-caucasus-project.

Civil Georgia (2011) "Saakashvili: Russia 'Dying Empire Dreaming of Occupying Georgia'," February 25. Online. Available: www.civil.ge/eng/article.php?id=23186 [accessed November 18, 2011].

Cohen, J. (ed.) (2001) "A Question of Sovereignty: The Georgia–Abkhazia Peace Process." *Accord,* 7: 88.

Diamond, L. and McDonald, J. (1996) *Multitrack Diplomacy: A Systems Approach to Peace.* Kumarian Press, West Hartford, CT.

Fisher, R. (1997) *Interactive Conflict Resolution.* Syracuse University Press, Syracuse.

George Mason University (2011) *Continuation of the Civic Dialogue Series "Point of View" for Georgian–South Ossetian Mutual Understanding and Trust.* Press release, March 22, 2011. Online. Available: http://scar.gmu.edu/press-releases/12093.

Maslow, A.H. (1943) "A Theory of Human Motivation." *Psychological Review,* 50(4): 370–396.

Mitchell, C. and Banks, M. (1996) *Handbook of Conflict Resolution: The Analytical Problem-Solving Approach.* Pinter, New York.

Nan, S. (2011) "Conflicts in the Caucasus and their Resolution: A Framing Essay." *Eurasian Geography and Economics,* 52(5): 679–685.

Nan, S., Druckman, D. and Horr, J.E. (2009) "Unofficial International Conflict Resolution: Is there a Track One and a Half? Are there Best Practices?" *Conflict Resolution Quarterly,* 27(1): 65–82.

Nan, S., Kozaeva, T. and Khutsishvili, G. (2008) "At Work in the Caucasus." *Common Ground News Service,* November 25.

Saakashvili, M. (2008) "Saakashvili's Televised Address on South Ossetia." *Civil Geogia,* August 7. Transcript available online. Available: www.civil.ge/eng/article.php?id=18934 [accessed November 18, 2011].

12 Human Needs and conflict resolution in practice

Environment and community

E. Franklin Dukes

This chapter focuses on the impact of Human Needs theory on my own practice of environmental and community conflict resolution.[1] I focus specifically on how theory informs my practice, using an analog of theories as lenses that allow me to understand and intervene in such conflicts. I emphasize the primary needs of *identity*, *security* and *recognition* as driving factors in environmental and community conflicts. I will furthermore demonstrate how satisfying the need for *relatedness* provides a framework for intervention that goes beyond the positions vs. interests conceptual framework, first articulated by Mary Parker Follett (1924) and popularized by Fisher and Ury (1981), that is so influential among practicing mediators.

I write briefly about why those four needs are particularly important, using a case that I experienced that shows the continuing evolution of my thinking and practice as a third-party mediator and consensus builder. I do that not to show how conflict intervention should be done, but rather to demonstrate how much my own practice owes to this framework of needs.

I will also present ways of how needs theory helps us understand how people construct meaning out of their encounters with one another in conflict, and how that meaning may be guided to change during a conflict transformation intervention.

The origins of theory to practice: an eclectic approach to human needs

I owe the origins of the theoretical foundations of my work to an eclectic and, surprisingly, largely unrelated group of psychologists and political scientists who formulated the idea that human needs are drivers of human behavior and, hence, human conflict. These theorists, or rather my interpretations of their work, have helped me navigate my way through the conflicts that I encounter in my role as director of the Institute for Environmental Negotiation at the University of Virginia.

John Burton (1990) was first responsible for introducing me to a starting point for this foundation, but Burton by no means invented needs theory. In fact he was not a major contributor to the explication of that theory, at least when compared to more influential theorists such as Abraham Maslow (1954) and Eric Fromm (1955). My own work draws more upon those theorists and, by way of Burton, Paul Sites (1973), than on Burton's own writings about needs.

Maslow is best known for his argument that there is a hierarchy of human needs, and that the more fundamental physical and psychological needs must be satisfied before higher order needs may be fulfilled. The prominence of his thinking helped legitimize the concept of human needs, and brought awareness of needs theory to my attention, but his specific description of those needs had little influence on my own thinking and work.

Fromm, on the other hand, inspired me with his dialectic of healthy and unhealthy means of needs satisfaction. He studied the fulfillment of human needs within the framework of the social environment, under social, political, industrial, philosophical and other influences. The consequences of the frustration of these needs are neuroses and psychoses; there is a direct consequence for the inadequate satisfaction of each of the needs. There can be both unfulfillment *and* dysfunctional fulfillment. The proper basis for judging any social group is the fulfillment of these needs. The two most powerful (in the sense of explanatory power) needs articulated by Fromm, and those that make up the first half of the core needs in my own conceptual framework, are *identity* and *relatedness.*

Sites, a less original thinker than Maslow or Fromm, nonetheless added *security* and *recognition* to the core listing of absolute human needs. As will be demonstrated later, these two make up the other half of the core needs that I find with the greatest explanatory power in environmental and community conflict.

Burton's accomplishment, then, was not the identification of needs per se but in articulating how needs theory could apply to understanding the sources and dynamics of conflict and how such understanding could then be applied during an appropriate conflict intervention process. His major thesis wasn't just that needs drove conflict; it also was that efforts of authorities to control behavior without taking into account those fundamental needs were doomed to failure.

Beyond that, Burton insisted that practice must derive from theory. That theory must be explicit; that is, the practitioner must have sufficient understanding of the theory to be able to articulate it clearly. In addition, it must not be limited to a single arena of practice; rather, it must be general enough to have explanatory power whether working on a family conflict or a conflict between nations. Finally, it must be powerful enough not only to explain conflictual behavior but also to provide the grounds for an appropriate intervention.

This insistence occurred at a time when conflict resolution and especially mediation was growing in popularity. Mediation and what came to be called ADR (alternative dispute resolution) was beginning to proliferate not only within the international arena but within the judicial system, in schools, through community mediation centers and in commercial systems. A number of popular and, it must be said, often effective atheoretical "how-to" books such as *Getting to Yes* were being adopted by those such as myself who had little knowledge of theories of human behavior and conflict resolution. Burton's insistence on articulating the theory behind practice – indeed, on developing the theory and practice concurrently with one another – forced his readers and his students to take theory seriously.

This is evident to me in my practice; practitioners may well be able to accomplish much without being able to articulate any specific theory, but attentiveness to theory will offer new avenues and tactics when they encounter unfamiliar situations or they get stuck. Being aware of one's theoretical framework(s) also allows a practitioner to test hypotheses and to learn to be more effective over time.

The uses of theory in conflict and conflict resolution

Theory may be understood as an explanation of some phenomenon that interests us; in our case, that is human behavior, and in particular conflict behavior. The better the theory, the more likely we can use it to describe and understand the origins and dynamics of conflict and, what is particularly useful, to predict what might influence conflict behavior to change as well. For a practitioner such as myself, the more powerful the theory, the more I can understand and even anticipate behavior and thus intervene appropriately.

My work draws on a number of theories and analytical frameworks in addition to human needs; to appropriate common language that others use, I call them my theory "lenses." I use the language of lenses to describe how different theories may help me understand different dimensions of a conflict. Like a micro-biologist who must rotate the lenses of a microscope to be able to focus on the appropriate scale, I must draw on different theories, or lenses, to understand different dimensions of a conflict. I incorporate into my work these lenses – theories – involving race, class, sexual orientation, gender, religion and nationality. I have other lenses based on learning theory, organizational theory, theories of the person and theories of group behavior. No single lens is ever sufficient to understand any situation I encounter; their power varies by context and, often within that context, by circumstance.

For instance, I have a "latent conflict" lens that allows me to be aware of hidden, underlying dynamics in relationships that become overt conflict when aroused by a trigger of some sorts (see, for example, Kriesberg 1982 for a seminal article that identifies theories of conflict origins, triggers, emergence and dynamics). For example, living near Shenandoah National

Park in Virginia, where many families were displaced in the 1930s, I know that conflict that attended that displacement may re-emerge with any new issue that might arise, as I will demonstrate later.

On the other hand, not all lenses are useful in each scenario. For instance, in the region that formed Shenandoah National Park and in the area that surrounds the Park today there are few African Americans. The racial lens is of little use. Similarly, sexual orientation and nationality appear largely irrelevant to this conflict. But applying a lens of class means that I can appreciate how power and privilege helped shape the formation of the Park and the potential roles that class may play in the differences between a largely urban and higher educated group that uses the Park and the rural communities that continue to surround the Park.

I used to feel somewhat inadequate for this way of understanding the world, rather than having a single general theory of conflict and its resolution; this may be partly my sense of a lingering debt to Burton, for I certainly felt as though he wanted us to have that general theory and for that theory to be based on human needs alone. But Birkhoff (2002) relieved me of this burden with her assessment of professional practice, an assessment that draws on a variety of disciplines. She recognizes the following, which is worth quoting at length:

> whichever way individuals or groups know and learn it is always an approximation, a partial picture or pictures of reality. Human perceptions are bounded and limited. Since there are many valid ways of knowing and learning, our challenge is to learn how to synthesize learning from different ways of knowing to enrich our practice and improve the conflict resolution field.
>
> (Birkhoff 2002: 50)

Mediators working with parties on the ground have to rely on an accumulation of knowledge from many sources. In addition, "Mediators know in action. Their knowing is tacit and is contextual.... Mediators' combination of tacit knowledge, abstract knowledge, and action is no different from other professionals" (Birkhoff 2002: 51). Physicians, attorneys and social workers cannot be thinking about and focusing on which particular theoretical foundations of their work apply as they practice; they incorporate those theories within their practice. Her argument does not imply that such work is a-theoretical, although it may be. It means that effective practice, even when well grounded in theory, incorporates ways of knowing that are not always conscious.

Ultimately, with the assistance of many critics of needs theory, some of whom are contributors to this volume, I found a number of problems with needs theory: can we distinguish needs from acquired values and desires? Who determines what is a need as opposed to a strong desire? Is human nature such that our individual needs and our social needs will always be in conflict? And, of course, how can one separate cultural manifestations of needs from needs that may transcend culture?

But I also found an accommodation that sidesteps the ontological debate of universal Human Needs theory. My accommodation is this: basically, I have gained empirical evidence that identity, recognition and security, as well as relatedness (to person and place), are enormous drivers of human behavior. Furthermore, while needs are found in individuals, they find expression as well in communal channels. That is, by my definition of theory these are powerful predictors of behavior and therefore useful intervener lenses.

The environment, conflict and needs

Before turning to the case of Shenandoah National Park I will explore the nature of environmental conflicts. Why is it that these conflicts that may appear primarily to involve technical, scientific and economic issues are also, and perhaps more fundamentally so, expressions of competing visions of individual and community identity (Hirsch and Dukes, in press)?

Everyone is familiar with environmental conflicts; they are in fact "ubiquitous, inevitable, complex, and enduring" (Hirsch and Dukes, in press). Whether one lives in a first-world or a so-called third-world country one's experience of everyday social, political and economic conditions is shaped by decisions about the control, use, protection or preservation of the natural and built environments. How one determines who does or does not acquire, keep, or transform land, air and water, minerals, forest, or farm, are conflicts fought every day in virtually every community. These conflicts can be costly in financial and social terms; they can denote the difference between a community that is healthy and one that is not.

Because these environmental issues impact such key dimensions of human society as economics and health, even life and death, differences will naturally provoke intense fighting. But as salient as those differences are, the passion that many environmental conflicts evoke derives as much, and sometimes even more, from competing visions of, and claims to, individual and community identity that accompany those more visible elements of the conflict.

Most of my work as a third-party mediator and facilitator features the environment in some way as the presenting issue. This may involve sharply competing visions of whether and how land should be protected or used, different emphasis placed upon the value of water quality or the need for less expensive food, or fights over the impacts of natural resource extraction. These differences are substantial, they are real, and they impact people's health, their pursuit of well-being and their pocketbook.

The parties involved in these conflicts often explain them in dramatic, value-laden terms of right and wrong. For a community member who fears that nearby uranium mining may release harmful radiation, bring unwanted (and unsafe) traffic of trucks and other large equipment, and forever alter a treasured landscape, the proponents of such mining may be greedy, uncaring and devious. Such a community member may well believe that these proponents are driven by their economic interests to ignore science and public will, or, even worse, to promote pseudoscience and to buy off public officials.

Proponents of such mining, on the other hand, may believe that the opposition to their plans is equally misguided or venal. For mining advocates, opponents may be short-sighted, easily manipulated by a few zealots, and selfish. They may be driven by their parochial interests to ignore science and the larger public good, or worse, to promote pseudoscience and to exert influence over public officials far greater than their actual numbers or their cause merits.

I recognize that there may be, and often are, real bases for those arguments even when they may be wrong in particular circumstances. Sometimes public officials are corrupt. Sometimes businesses are unscrupulous. Sometimes citizens are short-sighted, or care only for their own piece of property or their own well-being.

At the same time, within all of these conflicts there are drivers – factors influencing behavior in conflict – that have little to do with those factors that parties themselves most often ascribe to one another. These are the fundamental human needs. In fact, most of the conflicts that I find myself working with revolve primarily around individual and community *identity*, *security* and *recognition*. These three needs – identity, security and recognition – are the trinity that drive conflict behavior in the types of environmental and community conflicts in which I work. The need for identity, in particular, is always a significant causal factor.

The fourth primary need that I noted earlier, the need for *relatedness*, is less often a source of conflict. But it may be equally important as the other needs in providing a vehicle for conflict resolution and transformation in these situations of community environmental conflict.

Shenandoah National Park: issues of identity, recognition and security

The Shenandoah National Park consists of about 196,000 acres in the rolling hills of the Blue Ridge in Virginia. Shenandoah National Park was authorized by Congress in 1926, although it wasn't established until 1935. In 1926, Congress reluctantly approved legislation that designated 521,000 acres as acceptable for the boundaries of the Park, with the provision that no federal funds would be used for purchase of the land. The reluctance derived from the (accurate) perception that, unlike other national Parks that sought to protect wilderness areas with spectacular natural features, the driver for Shenandoah National Park was the desire of some to have a summer vacation spot for the elite of Washington, D.C. and to make money (by providing lodging) while doing so.

While the boundary was drawn encompassing the 521,000 acres, only about 176,000 acres were acquired by the time the Park was established. Indeed Congress had to keep lowering the required minimum acreage a number of times before the Park could be officially accepted into the national Park system. That land was taken from a patchwork of over 3,000 individual tracts of land, purchased or condemned by the Commonwealth of Virginia and presented to the Federal Government. At least 500 families were displaced in the process, with all but a handful of their homes destroyed and replaced by imported vegetation. Although residents at the time as well as today believe otherwise, the Park does not have condemnation authority; the only way that it can grow is through gifts of land from private owners or land conservation organizations. Donations and some small land swaps between the National Park Service and private owners account for a modest increase in size since its establishment, such that the Park now totals nearly 200,000 acres.

In 1992, Park personnel, recognizing the impact of lands adjacent to the Park on the Park itself, stated publicly that they would like to work with adjacent counties to develop ways of protecting Park resources affected by actions on those adjacent lands. In addition, the Park Superintendent indicated that he would like to have criteria established about the suitability of accepting donations of lands that are offered to the Park from time to time. The Superintendent contracted with a professor of landscape architecture at the University of Virginia to conduct an inventory of the lands within the authorized boundaries of the Park, with the intention of using that inventory to decide which lands might be appropriate for addition to the Park. Because of funding constraints, initial studies were to be conducted in only two of the six counties that bound the Park. The hope was that the other counties would see value in the knowledge of natural and cultural resources that the study could provide, and that they would contribute funding to conduct the study within their own jurisdiction.

This was the concept that the Park Service hoped to realize. However, a number of residents of counties adjacent to the Park challenged the motivations for the inventory. Some of them were relatives of former inhabitants of the Park who were, they feel, unfairly kicked off their own land, inadequately compensated for the loss of their property, and insulted and abused as supposedly being backwards, ignorant, criminal, lazy and uncivilized in the process. For these residents, this study was not a research study at all – they viewed it as a way to justify taking more land and displacing more people.

My own introduction to this opposition occurred at a public meeting in which Madison County was to consider their participation in this study. I had no role in the meeting but was interested in the subject because of the level of conflict that had emerged.

As I approached the County building where the meeting was to be held, I saw a phalanx of opponents surrounding the building. They could be identified by their hats that contained a label representing the Park and a big slash through the label. One large and angry man asked me "Are you with them?" and pointed to uniformed representatives of the Park. I was relieved to be able to answer "no" and enter without any trouble.

Although the Park Service representatives were allowed to speak to the Madison County Board of Supervisors, there was no contest. The Board had no interest in putting itself into the fight and refused to participate in the study.

Later, and likely because of the vehemence of this opposition, the Institute for Environmental Negotiation (IEN) at the University of Virginia, mediators and facilitators of environmental disputes, and my relatively new employer of less than one year at the time, contracted with the funders of the study to develop a process for engaging the public during the study. Advocates for the study had managed to convince two different counties, Rockingham County and Albemarle County, to participate. IEN's role was to work with the research team from the University of Virginia, the National Park Service, and local planning officials to engage the citizenry in the study. What this meant in practice was conducting public meetings in which the purpose of the study would be described and residents asked to contribute their knowledge about the unique natural, historical and cultural resources in the lands adjacent to the Park.

Thus began a stormy battle over whether and how the study would be completed at all. At the initial, and, as it turned out, only public meeting held in Rockingham County, a school auditorium was filled to overflowing with some 300 angry residents shouting down anyone who dared argue in favor of learning more about these lands. Plans to hold small group sessions as part of this meeting were altered when a majority of people refused to leave the main room, and a local staff member from Rockingham County refused to facilitate one of the planned groups out of fear of what might happen.

A public meeting in Albemarle County went only somewhat better. With many more advocates for environmental protection and for effective land-use planning in Albemarle than in any of the other six counties adjacent to the Park, some advocates for the Park and for the study were willing to speak out despite the vocal opposition. But the response from the public was conflicted.

This case brought me a welcome opportunity to test my own working application of needs theory. My Institute's director at the time was convinced that a realpolitik analysis of this conflict provided the best explanation for its course. From his perspective, this was simply another manifestation of the "wise use" movement (Jacobs 1995). Proponents of this movement advocated for the elimination of centralized land-use planning and for the ability of landowners to do whatever they wanted with their land. While there were grassroots supporters in the wise use movement, our director believed that this movement was largely directed and funded by moneyed property interests, particularly real estate development, who shaped the terms of the debate in the public sphere as well as behind the scenes, depending upon circumstances.

For me, his assessment was largely incorrect. I believed that the roots of this conflict could be found entirely in local history and conditions. I hypothesized that the opponents of the Park and this proposed study may well have found the language of wise use attractive as a means of articulating their opposition and of gathering additional supporters, by framing the Park's proposed study of adjacent lands as an attack on private property. But the depth and extent of emotion and opposition to what was, after all, only a study, and for a Park that had no authority to use condemnation powers to take land from an unwilling seller, could not be explained by a love for private property rights. Rather, in my view, this conflict involved core needs of individual and collective identity, recognition and security.

How might I test this theory and these specific hypotheses about identity, recognition and security and the role that relatedness might play in conflict intervention? I decided to borrow an invention of John Burton and his colleagues (Burton 1969) and invite opponents of the Park to class to deconstruct their conflict with the Park Service. Would they identify with my analysis of this conflict in terms of human needs, including in particular needs for identity, security and recognition? If successful, I reasoned, this not only would test my theory of the origins of the conflict, it might demonstrate to these opponents my willingness to understand and empathize with their views, if not their actions. By so doing, I could better fulfill our role as facilitators of public involvement if building trust with them meant that they would be willing to participate in the process that we were providing.

I decided that this test would work best if I could bring the strongest opponents of the Park and the study to class. My class, titled "Negotiating Public Policy," met for nearly three hours at a time and would provide sufficient opportunity to engage the Park and study opponents. I called one of the leaders of the opposition who had been particularly outspoken in a small-group session that I had facilitated, and explained my intent. Despite his antagonism towards me and anyone else having anything to do with the Park and the Related Lands Study, and his strong suspicions about my motives, he agreed to attend as long as he could bring with him one of the other opponents. This companion was co-author of a lengthy, self-published, anti-Park Service screed titled "US vs. NPS," a play on words meaning both United States versus the Shenandoah National Park as well as "us," that is, everyone else, against the Park.

I readily agreed to having both visitors come to class. When the visitors entered the classroom, I began by inviting them to offer their reasons for their opposition to the Park and the Related Lands Study. I then asked if they would be willing to evaluate my own theory of the conflict. I offered them, and the class, an outline of the conflict similar to the following, based upon my assessment that the conflict fundamentally was concerned with the denial of basic human needs.

Identity: The mountain identity shared by inhabitants of this region of the Appalachians had been systematically abused as Shenandoah National Park was being conceived. This had been done deliberately by supporters of the proposed Park as a way of convincing elected officials and the general population that the forced removal of the inhabitants was actually good for those inhabitants. The people living where the Park was to be formed were called backwards, illiterate, shiftless, promiscuous and more. One particularly egregious claim had been made that they were "devolving"; that is, becoming not just socially but genetically less "civilized" (Perdue and Martin-Perdue 1979–1980).

As preposterous as this might sound today, the 1920s in Virginia saw the passage of Virginia's Eugenical Sterilization Act and the infamous approval by the United States Supreme Court of that law, along with the comment by Chief Justice Oliver Wendell Holmes that "Three generations of imbeciles are enough." Indeed, shortly after his visit to my class I called one of the visitors on a related matter and he had initially been unexpectedly rude; he then apologized and revealed that he had just learned that morning that one of his aunts had been one of the women sterilized under this legislation.

So the sources of the conflict between the Park and its neighbors originated not only because many hundreds of residents were displaced; their entire culture and identity was attacked in print. In addition, activities important to that mountain culture such as hunting, fishing and gathering of plants became illegal as well. This created substantial conflict that continues today with poachers still battling Park Service personnel over deer and black bears.

Recognition: In 1992, Shenandoah National Park had a number of interpretive areas for natural and cultural history. Yet none of the cultural interpretations mentioned the circumstances of the displacement in any but a cursory manner. None acknowledged any harm done to the community by this displacement. Furthermore, residents resented the Park Service for their failure to hire local community members to offer a local perspective of history. Instead, the Park Service relied on college students from other areas who would be hired on a summer basis and who would simply repeat what they were told to say.

Thus, the original conflict was exacerbated by the sense among opponents of the Park that their contributions to Virginia and the region were not recognized, and that their loss had never been properly acknowledged.

Security: The circumstance in which the original authorized boundary of the Park is far larger than the current boundary is unique to Shenandoah.

And because of this, residents and local elected officials (for whom donations of property to the Park would reduce tax rolls) were susceptible to
anything that might hint of an enlargement of the Park. Furthermore,
when the Related Lands study was announced and the public meetings
held, some residents learned to their surprise and dismay that their property was contained within the Park's authorized boundary. Given the
antagonism towards the Park, it is no surprise that what was formally called
the Related Lands Study was called by opponents the Take the Land
Study.

The response to this analysis was gratifying. They entered the classroom
with the perspective that the conflict was caused by the continuing bad
faith of National Park Service personnel and those who supported public
lands. While they remained suspicious of Park Service actions, my class visitors' views on the sources of the conflict expanded with this analysis. They
particularly appreciated what they viewed as a sympathetic interpretation
of their conflict. By acknowledging the community's legitimate needs for
recognition, identity and security, and acknowledging how the Park violated those needs in the past, we created an opportunity for honest
encounter. After my assessment, one of the visitors told the story of an
elderly relative, forced to move out of the mountain home where he and
generations had been born and raised. Near the end of his life, this relative had constructed in his backyard a replica of his former homestead.
My guest described how this relative pined for his lost home, implying that
this loss had led to an early death. It was an unexpected, personal, moving
sharing of what was most important to this visitor.

This story would not have been told during one of our normal meetings. The vulnerability that it revealed, the intimacy of a family member's
grief, the need for respectful listening and questioning; none of those
could be found in a more public setting of advocacy and action.

And although this visit to my class did not soften their opposition to the
Park's potential expansion, it did create a relationship between myself and
them that allowed me to engage them on much better terms throughout
the rest of the project. In public, afterward, their opposition was offered in
civil, even humorous terms, and they acknowledged the value in our work.

Relatedness and conflict transformation

My brief description of how identity, recognition and security offered
explanatory power as the sources of conflict in the case of Shenandoah
National Park gives no hint of how that understanding might be used for
conflict transformation. Following the completion of our work on the
project – and the eventual abandonment by the Park Service of any hope
of expanding the study to other counties, due to lack of funding – I wrote
a memo detailing why the history of the Park would continue to create a
basis for conflict unless change were to occur. That change needed to be

based upon meeting the needs for identity, recognition and security that were, or were perceived to be, in jeopardy by opponents to the Park.

The National Park Service had many options for meeting those needs. It could affirm the continuation of the policy that it would not seek condemnation power to acquire additional lands, thus addressing issues of security. It could begin to hire local employees and feature displays and presentations of local history from the perspective of those who were displaced or their families, thus affirming needs for recognition and for identity. And I suggested that the Park could put together an ongoing, multi-stakeholder advisory group that included opponents and supporters of the Park. Such a group could not only serve to offer ideas and advice; it would provide a forum for demonstrating the kind of respect for local identity that had been lacking for seven decades.

Such a multi-party group would also be able to foster the sense of relatedness that often serves as a vehicle for conflict transformation. Burton and others argue that emotions are the icebergs in a conflict that one needs to navigate through in order to reach the real goal, which is to begin the process of identifying solutions that might actually resolve the current conflict. I certainly spend a lot of my time with groups doing just that – helping them come up with solutions. But that view, I think, shortchanges that journey.

As I experience the processes of conflict transformation, it is in these encounters with one another, in which emotions play a driving role, that the hard work of conflict resolution is actually done. Yes, participants are sharing positions and yes, it is helpful to deconstruct those positions to understand the underlying interests (Fisher and Ury 1981) that provide the basis for bargaining and exchange.

But conflict transformation is more than that. Whether in a conflict or not, individuals are constantly constructing meaning out of their encounters with one another. That process is sharpened during a conflict of the sort involving the Park and its history and impacts on neighboring communities. Participants in these processes ask themselves at each moment, is this someone who understands what is most important to me? Is this a threat to my identity or a way of strengthening my identity if I continue this encounter? Will I be more or less secure if I continue?

My experience of long-term conflict transformation processes involving community and environment is that they typically follow the same path. There is an initial period of overt hostility and disruption, such as occurred during the public involvement phase of the Related Lands Study. There then can be a time and opportunity, however chaotic it may appear, during which the group is sorting out how participants will relate to one another, in which they begin to find that their engagement with one another becomes meaningful not because of their differences but because of their relatedness. For a situation involving issues such as those dramatized during the Shenandoah National Park conflict, where there was not an actual dispute over a particular demand or proposal (such as an expansion of the Park, or discontinuing access to the Park, or limiting a favorite use of the Park), this transition is common. In this phase, many participants – much to their surprise – often become invested in the meaning of their work, the protection of the resource and the relationship with one another.

The practitioner addressing deep-rooted conflict benefits from understanding how the need for relatedness – to place as well as to people – may find a venue for actualization in the continuing engagement with the same group with which one had originally found conflict. This indeed happened in a small way with the two most active opponents of the Park during my intervention, due to the relationship we developed. They did not act out any antagonism any more, and were in fact not only civil but forthcoming with their interests and concerns. I am convinced that they would have been willing to engage with Park issues had the Park Service undertaken the actions that I suggested to them. That Park personnel did not do so at the time meant a missed opportunity and an unnecessary continuation of the conflict.

Shenandoah National Park eventually made changes of the sort that I described, although this project had little if any direct influence on those changes. It took years of continued uneven relationships with surrounding communities and increasing interest by historians in the antecedents and formation of the Park to convince the Park Service of the value of that history. The stories of those who used to live in the area now contained by the Park are displayed throughout the Park, along with many books that explore this history. And my work continues to benefit from that initial class experiment, in which I tested the power of identity, recognition and security and relatedness.

Note

1 I wish to acknowledge the contributions of John Burton to my own thinking and practice. Burton was a challenging, caring, generous, perplexing, stimulating and enduring influence on my life and my work. He was responsible for one of the happiest moments of my life when he announced to me, barely half-way into my graduate study, that St. Martin's Press would be publishing a four-volume Conflict series and that I had earned co-authorship and co-editorship respectively of two of the books. For someone who only a few years earlier was running a small business restoring and tuning pianos, that was a transformational gift. Besides the recognition that such a publication would accrue, this validated to me that my thinking actually had a place in the conflict resolution arena.

References

Birkhoff, Juliana (2002) "Evaluation and Research," in S. Seneca (ed.) *Critical Issues Papers*, Washington, D.C.: Association for Conflict Resolution, pp. 48–69.

Burton, J.W. (1990) *Conflict: Human Needs Theory*. New York: St. Martin's Press.

Burton, J.W. (1969) *Conflict and Communication: The Use of Controlled Communication in International Relations.* London: MacMillan.

Fisher, R. and Ury, W. (1981) *Getting To Yes,* New York: Penguin Books.

Follett, M. Parker (1924 [1951]) *Creative Experience.* New York: Peter Smith; reprint with permission by Longmans, Green and Co.

Fromm, E. (1955) *The Sane Society.* New York: Holt, Rinehart and Winston.

Hirsch, S.F. and Dukes, E.F. (in press). *Divergent Views of Mountaintop Mining in Appalachia: Changing Stakeholders in Environmental Conflict.* Sterling, Virginia: Kumarian Press.

Jacobs, H.N. (1995) "The Anti-Environmental 'Wise Use' Movement in America." *Land Use Law and Zoning Digest,* 47(2): 3–8.

Kriesberg, L. (1982) "Social Conflict Theories and Conflict Resolution." *Peace and Change,* 8(2/3): 3–17.

Maslow, A. (1954) *Motivation and Personality.* New York: Harper and Row.

Perdue, C.L. Jr. and Martin-Perdue, N.J. (1979–1980) "Appalachian Fables and Facts: A Case Study of the Shenandoah National Park Removals." *Appalachian Journal,* 7(1/2): 84–104.

Sites, P. (1973) *Control: The Basis of Social Order.* New York: Dunellen Publishing.

Afterword

Kevin Avruch and Christopher Mitchell

Basic Human Needs: looking back

In our Introduction we noted that the "heyday" of theorizing in Basic Human Needs and conflict analysis and resolution, prevalent under John Burton's influence in the 1980s and 1990s, seems to have passed. Jamie Price's Insight theory for explaining conflict ends in doing away with the need for BHNs entirely. In his chapter, Solon Simmons remarks that, for "younger scholars today, the concept of human needs is largely displaced and relegated to little more than heuristic device." It was, in fact, especially after the heyday of functionalism in sociology and anthropology, never much of a conceptual force in those disciplines. Nevertheless – Avruch calls it "face validity" – the notion seems uniquely compelling, and every decade or so a new volume or a new collection strives to grapple with the idea. Burton pushed the idea in *Deviance, Terrorism and War* (1979). Katrin Lederer (1980) edited an influential collection that focused on basic human needs and development, partly in tandem with the UN's explicit but all-too-brief engagement with the "basic needs approach" to development in the 1970s; the book was produced as part of the United Nations' University's "Human and Social Development Programme." Many leading theorists of the time contributed to the volume and, perhaps not surprisingly, many did so critical of the idea. The bases of critique will not surprise: Are the needs universal? How many are there? What about cultural differences? Can we reliably separate needs from wants? What are the "political and practical" – we would say here, normative and ethical – implications of a basic needs approach? Interestingly, in her introduction to that volume Lederer deals with issues of methodology and positivism rather brusquely. She writes: "Is it possible to conduct research with conventional methods of empirical social investigation? After all that is now known about needs, the answer is, certainly not" (Lederer 1980: 11).

More volumes followed. Burton returned to the idea in his own edited collection, *Conflict: Human Needs Theory* (Burton 1990), hoping perhaps to consolidate its influence. Here, again, several of the chapters, by former students and then-current colleagues, adopted a critical perspective.

(Perhaps some of the needs are malign? How close are we flying to the old "natural law" debate?) At around the same time, the political scientists Roger Coate and Jerel Rosati, much influenced by Burton, achieved in some ways a stronger consolidation of the idea in *The Power of Human Needs in World Society* (Coate and Rosati 1988). Among other things, they succeeded in connecting the BHN part of Burton's thinking with his earlier contribution to the World Society debate in Britain (as elucidated in Dennis Sandole's chapter) and, as Avruch pointed out in his chapter, they recognized the virtual absence in Burton's thinking of a coherent linkage between the level of the individual's frustrated BHN, and the macro-level sociological and political functioning of identity and other struggle groups in social movements around conflict. This linkage, Avruch argued, came only with Burton's collaboration with Edward Azar, and his notion of *protracted social conflicts*. Meanwhile, Coate and Rosati hewed very close to the rational choice model of accurate "costing" by the parties of the consequences of continuing the conflict.

Lederer, Burton, Coate and Rosati, and now the present volume, offer proof, at least, that the idea of Basic Human Needs remains a perennially unresolved yet engaging problem for conflict resolution. We do maintain that the present volume has furthered the discussion, broadening it beyond International Relations (as in Coate and Rosati) or development (Lederer). This broadening, a reflection of the varied social science disciplinary backgrounds of our contributors, as well as the range of their practice and experience, meant that themes that were earlier overlooked or downplayed – the role of affect, for example; the unresolved dilemma of how BHN addresses asymmetries of power; bringing gender considerations into the discussion; the limitations of a rigid "costing" approach and over-reliance on rationality; and the sometimes fraught moral or ethical implications of adapting a BHN approach in practice (as Abu-Nimer argued), are now made explicit. Most of all, the majority of the contributors are no longer much detained by establishing the objective, genetic or evolutionary reality of BHN: Sandole excepted, and Price excepted insofar as the scientific ("Galilean") goal of *explaining* conflict is preserved – and this mainly by abandoning the ("Aristotelian") need for assuming the existence of BHNs in the first place. In this way most of the chapters sidestep the methodological conundrums that bedeviled Burton, and that Lederer simply dismissed by fiat: her view that research into BHNs escaped entirely (if regrettably, she implied) the received methodological requirements of "empirical investigation." BHNs are in this volume mainly parsed in narrative, rhetorical or normative terms. We think this is to their advantage.

Those among our contributors who write primarily from their practice present a sort of puzzle in our view. On the one hand, in striking contrast to the Burton rules-handbook approach (much altered and "softened" by various practitioners in any case, as Mitchell makes clear), BHNs seem loosely or at best "eclectically" tied to their conduct of their practice (see Fisher 1990, who uses the notion of "the eclectic" explicitly in his earlier discussion of needs and interactive problem-solving). On the other hand, acknowledging such needs, particularly identity, recognition or security, appears for some practitioners central to their craft (as Dukes makes abundantly clear in his chapter, where BHN functions as one of several "lenses" through which he seeks to understand the roots of the conflict). Herbert Kelman, in an early discussion of his use of the idea of BHN in his practice (unequivocally influenced by Burton's thinking), makes this apparent puzzle more understandable. Once again the term "eclectic" comes to mind:

> My concept of human needs is very broad and is not anchored in any particular needs theory. For my purposes, I find it best not to circumscribe the concept with too many specific assumptions. Thus, I do not assume that needs are necessarily organized in hierarchies.... I do not assume that all needs will somehow be satisfied ... although I view the large-scale frustration of basic human needs as a threat to peace and social order. I do not assume that the lists of human needs identified by various needs theorists are necessarily universal, although I do believe that certain needs are widely shared across culture and societies.
>
> (Kelman 1990: 283)

Kelman goes on to connect the satisfaction of basic human needs by social and political institutions as the ultimate, "empirical," test of their "perceived legitimacy and thus, in the long run, of their stability and effectiveness" (1990: 284). This is, in fact, Kelman's version of Azar's theory of protracted social conflicts, which highlights the frustration of basic humans needs due the persistent and pernicious disconnect between state and society. Put another way, this is how Kelman solves the puzzle of connecting the individual-micro to the macro levels in the context of his practice, invoking the key idea of legitimacy, an idea at once "psychological" and sociopolitical. Here theory and practice come together, and we can see one of the advantages in rethinking BHN in "theory" terms of discourse and normative categories. This means that the practitioner, unwedded to deadweight requirements of scientism, can now see basic human needs as fundamental to understanding the subjectivities of parties in deep conflict – and to recognizing and respecting the ethical responsibilities thus incurred by intervention.

Looking back, this is where the chapters in this volume have taken us. The old and telling critiques of Basic Human Needs mostly remain, and their place in conflict resolution practice while central is also eclectic – non-doctrinaire to be sure. But if the heyday of BHN theory in conflict analysis and resolution is past, at least in the sense that John Burton hoped, the core idea lives on powerfully in other discourses, as Simmons argued and as alluded to by Avruch at the end of his chapter.

Basic Human Needs: looking ahead

The core idea of Basic Human Needs can be found today strongly reflected in discourses of human rights and human security, particularly around "the need to protect" (R2P; see ICSS 2001). Even in Burton's 1990 collection relating BHN to conflict theory and conflict resolution practice, a chapter by Christian Bay, looking as it were ahead, linked the universality of BHN, so strongly featured in Burton's work, to the existence of universal human rights. Basic human needs were thus conjoined to needs-based rights: both universal, demanding of recognition and satisfaction, and morally inextinguishable (Bay 1990). Since then the human rights movement has taken the existence of basic human needs, particularly needs conceived as *freedom from* certain abuses, violence and limitations on individual or collective (identity group) freedom, as given. (This negative discernment of basic human needs is in contrast to the more familiar understanding of the idea, which sees satisfaction in term of their positive "fulfillment" rather the need to avoid or escape harm or abuse.) These are the rights, as Jack Donnelly, echoing Kant, put it, that humans have simply by virtue of being human (Donnelly 2003; and see Avruch 2012: Ch. 3).

Developing somewhat after, but today very much in tandem with the human rights movement, has been the move to supplement (if not, for some activists, actually supplant) the widely understood, conceptually and politically dominant idea of national security with the idea of human security. As one reads through this literature, the notion of inalienable basic human needs is at once pervasive and foundational (e.g. Kaldor 2007; Tadjbakhsh and Chenoy 2007). One can trace the rise of human security to, as Mary Kaldor put it, the post-Cold War prevalence of "new wars" that target especially civilian non-combatants, and to new regimes of "humanitarian interventions" that erode (friends and critics both agree) the shibboleth of state sovereignty. More directly, the notion of human security and the related ideas of R2P can be traced to a UNDP *Human Development Report* in 1994 that "synthesized threats to human security in seven components: food, health, environmental, personal, community and political security" (Tadjbakhsh and Chenoy 2007: 14). In fact, this United Nations' involvement in human security is in some sense the return of its earlier, aborted, engagement with human-focused development in the 1970s, done in then by the era of Thatcherism, Reaganism and the wide-scale imposition of neoliberal "structural adjustments" and monetarist policies (Jolly *et al.* 2009). Anti-globalization activism notwithstanding, such economic policies are still the dominant norm. Human security thus arises partly as a way to sidestep economics, where a "human-centered" approach is likely to fail, and instead engage in favor of Basic Human Needs at the level of politics and morality, where the game is more open and, given public opinion and perhaps emerging communitarian or cosmopolitan impulses, the outcome more hopeful (Ramsbotham *et al.* 2011).

This, it seems to us, is where the "theory" of Basic Human Needs – very much a matter of political and normative rhetoric and narrative – resides today, and powerfully so. Avruch closed his chapter by declaring "human needs are dead, long live human needs!" Human rights and human security is where, mostly, they now live.

We close by quoting another (often critical) champion of the idea, Johan Galtung, who wrote the Preface to Lederer's influential 1980 volume on human needs. Here, in concert with the times, the focus was on human needs and development, but Galtung's words can hold as true for conflict resolution or the notion of human security. Galtung (1980: ix) wrote: "That the concept of 'needs' is problematic this book will amply demonstrate. But some such concept is indispensable to give dignity to human beings." Like culture, like power, like so many other core and crucial ideas, Basic Human Needs is an *essentially contested* concept. It is perennially contested. It remains essential.

Problem solving in the future

If the theory of Basic Human Needs retains its essential, if pragmatic, utility, what can be said about the use of various problem-solving processes such as workshops, dialogues, trainings and the other examples of "Track Two" activity? Clearly, using this broad approach to seeking some resolution of the most intractable conflicts is going to continue, although it seems unlikely that all – or even many – initiatives are going to resemble the "classical" model developed in the 1960s and 1970s and described in Christopher Mitchell's chapter. As we noted above, just as there is a revival of academic interest in the theory of Basic Human Needs among academics, there is an increasing tendency to try to use some type of informal problem-solving process to get round the obstacles posed in the current plethora of asymmetric conflicts involving incumbents, unwilling to confer any level of legitimacy on their opponents on the one hand and, on the other, insurgents, unwilling to admit to the existence of much general support for their distrusted adversary. In spite of the regrettable recent history of unofficial consultants and facilitators over-claiming about the effectiveness of their methods and then failing to produce very much, plus the tendency to commercialize the whole Track Two endeavor and turn it into a profitable business, there is an increasing recognition of the usefulness of having alternative processes to official negotiations, which often deadlock over issues of status, recognition, entrapment and a continuing search for "victory."

That said, it seems likely that the use of the current variety of Track Two processes is going to become even more varied over time, as different organizations take up the core ideas of a basic, problem-solving approach – small groups close to decision-makers, informal, off-the-record discussions, the use of relatively impartial facilitators – and shape them to the needs of particular conflicts and conflict systems. A good example of the range of such recent workshops, parsed as "dialogue" as well as "problem solving," with attention paid to assessing success or failure, can be found in Ross and Rothman (1999). Likewise, all nine tracks of what Diamond and McDonald (1996) have described as "multi-track diplomacy" are likely to be used in different cases. There will be opportunities to involve participants from all three socio-political levels – elite, opinion leaders, grass roots – outlined by John Paul Lederach in his elicitive version of problem solving that leads – hopefully – towards conflict transformation (Lederach 1995).

Now that practitioners are more likely to have a realistic sense of what their approach might be able to achieve, it seems to us that we are likely to see an equally varied set of results from the use of problem-solving processes in efforts to mitigate and find solutions to contemporary conflicts. Some processes will contribute ideas to formal negotiations that have struck an impasse. Others are likely to be able to devise acceptable confidence building measures where no confidence exists. Yet others will help to set up cross-party networks or organizations that can form cooperative bridges between suspicious and hostile communities. At the very least, some initiatives will be able to pass on facilitative and analytical problem-solving skills to participants from rival parties so that these can form a resource to be used when occasions arise.

The success of any problem-solving process used in the future will inevitably depend on the relevance of the theories that underlie the analysis presented to participants, and it is often the case that, at least when the process seeks to suggest alternative means of achieving underlying interests for the parties, Basic Human Needs theory will be of assistance. However, one should never forget that problem-solving approaches developed well before BHN became incorporated into much of the basic analysis carried on in a workshop or a dialogue setting. Equally important have been some of the theories of cognitive consistency developed in social psychology, or ideas about action-reaction processes from political science, or findings about the nature of entrapment from organization development theory. There are many more useful analytical tools that can be used to make problem-solving processes an effective way of analyzing the trajectory of a conflict and of suggesting ways in which that trajectory can be altered in the future. Problem solving and BHN theory are mutually supportive but ultimately independent of one another, and as they are taken into the future it will be interesting to take note of how both of them develop, together or separately.

References

Avruch, K. (2012) *Context and Pretext in Conflict Resolution: Culture, Identity, Power and Practice*, Boulder, CO: Paradigm.

Bay, C. (1990) "Taking the universality of needs seriously," in J.W. Burton (ed.) *Conflict: Human Needs Theory*, New York: St. Martin's.

Burton, J.W. (1979) *Deviance, Terrorism and War*, New York: St. Martin's.

Burton, J.W. (1990) *Conflict: Human Needs Theory*, New York: St. Martin's.

Coate, R. and Rosati, J. (eds) (1988) *The Power of Human Needs in World Society*, Boulder, CO: Lynne Rienner.

Diamond, L. and McDonald, J. (1996) *Multi-Track Diplomacy: A Systems Approach to Peace*, West Hartford, CT: Kumarian Press.

Donnelly, J. (2003) *Universal Human Rights in Theory and Practice*, 2nd edn, Ithaca: Cornell University Press.

Fisher, R.J. (1990) "Needs theory, social identity and an eclectic model of conflict," in J.W. Burton (ed.) *Conflict: Human Needs Theory*, New York: St. Martin's.

Galtung, J. (1980) "Preface," in K. Lederer (ed.) *Human Needs: A Contribution to the Current Debate*, Cambridge, MA: Oelgeschlager, Gunn & Hain.

ICISS (International Commission on Intervention and State Sovereignty) (2001) *The Responsibility to Protect*, Ottowa: International Development Research Centre.

Jolly, R., Emmerji, L. and Weiss, T.G. (2009), "The UN and human development," *UN Intellectual History Project*, Briefing Note Number 8. Online. Available: www.unhistory.org/briefing/8HumDev.pdf (accessed August 16, 2012).

Kaldor, M. (2007) *Human Security: Reflections on Globalization and Intervention*, Cambridge, UK: Polity Press.

Kelman, H. (1990) "Applying a human needs perspective to the practice of conflict resolution: the Israeli-Palestinian case," in J.W. Burton (ed.) *Conflict: Human Needs Theory*, New York: St. Martin's.

Lederach, J.P. (1995) *Preparing for Peace: Conflict Transformation across Cultures*, Syracuse: Syracuse University Press.

Lederer, K. (ed.) (1980) *Human Needs: A Contribution to the Current Debate*, Cambridge MA: Oelgeschlager, Gunn & Hain.

Ramsbotham, O., Woodhouse, T. and Miall, H. (2011) *Contemporary Conflict Resolution*, 3rd edn, Cambridge, UK: Polity Press.

Ross, M.H. and Rothman J. (1999) *Theory and Practice in Ethnic Conflict Management: Theorizing Success and Failure*, New York: St. Martin's.

Tadjbakhsh, S. and Chenoy, A. (eds) (2007) *Human Security: Concepts and Implications*, London: Routledge.

Index